The Earth Is Our Mother

Jim Pepper (Karok), his two wives, neighbors, children, baskets of acorns and weapons (*St. Pk.*, 1894)

The Earth Is Our Mother

A Guide to the Indians of California, Their Locales and Historic Sites

Dolan H. Eargle, Jr.

Published by

Trees Company Press
49 Van Buren Way
San Francisco, CA 94131

Printed in the United States of America

Library of Congress Catalog Card: 86-50411
ISBN: 0-937401-04-8 (softcover)

Book design: Polly Christensen
Illustrations: Nancy Record
Maps: Julie Nunes
Editing: JoAnn E. Hendrickson

Grateful acknowledgment is made to the California State Parks and Recreation Department Archives and to the Lowie Museum of Anthropology, University of California, Berkeley, for permission to print photographs from their collections. All other photographs are by the author.

Photo credit abbreviations:

St. Pk. California State Parks and Recreation Department Archives, Sacramento
Lowie University of California, Berkeley, Lowie Museum of Anthropology
dhe Dolan Hoye Eargle, Jr.

Acknowledgments

Morris Babby
Steve Baldy
Lowell Bean
Lionel Carrol
David Chavez
Mr. and Mrs. Robert Craig
Rookie Davis
Lawrence Dawson
Claude Devers
Harvy Duro
Steven Elliott
Fred Emerson
Carmen Facio
Jack Forbes
William Frank
King Freeman
Mary Frost
Luch Parker Furr
Richard Gamer
Betty Gayer
Nadyne Gray
Edna Guerrero
Gladys Guy
Jim Helmer
James Henry
Robert F. Heizer
Oliver Hillman
Karen Hogan
Delvin Holder
Valentino Ibamez
John Johnson
Charles Lamb
Winnifred Lean
Raymond Lego
Josephine Leo
Kevin Mann
Malcolm Margolin
Jenny Maruffo
Henry Mauldin
Charlie McKean
Tommy Merino
Doreen Mitchell
Ed Montez
Sharkey Moore
Harry Morse
Byron Nelson
Ella Noris
Astrid Ortega
Julia Parker
Ray Patencio
Jane Pablo Penn
Carmelita Perry
Gilda Poliakin
Marian Ramirez
Eletha Rea
Elizabeth Rhoads
Manual Rocha
Furman Salas
Mr. Santana
Shirley Swearington
Robely Swank
Banning Taylor
Valacia Thacker
Wendy Thieler
Richard Tom
Frank Treppa
Frank Truvido
Eddie Vedolla
Bonnie Wall
Ron Wermuth
Sarah Worth

. . . and a great multitude of others whose names I don't know, but whose aid has made this book possible.

No man is an Island, entire of itself; every man is a piece of the Continent, a part of the main. If a clod be washed away by the sea, Europe is the less, as well as if a promontory were. As well as if a manor of thy friends or of thy own were. Any man's death diminishes me, because I am involved in Mankind.

John Donne, *Devotions,* 1624

Preface

THE NATIVE AMERICAN population of California in 1985 has been estimated to be more than one million persons, possibly half of whom are direct descendants of native California peoples. These native descendants live on some 541,000 acres of "trust" land, administered by the Bureau of Indian Affairs (BIA), and on several thousand acres of privately owned or rented land. This book is a guide to those California peoples and their institutions.

Slightly over 200 years ago, at the time of the first Spanish incursions into Alta California, as many as a million natives lived here in some 60 linguistic groups or "tribes," mostly small, autonomous units. Over the years, these peoples have been so decimated and dispersed that today it is extraordinarily difficult to locate the surviving remnants of their societies.

Some years ago, as a fond admirer of the harmonious relationship of Native American peoples toward Earth, and as a new Californian wishing to know more of my environs and its people, I attempted to find a general, overall guide to the present-day Indian peoples of California, and found none. An abundance of other people also expressed their need for such a reference guide. Thus, I went out over the state to learn, explore, experience, interview, read, listen, and learn much more of the California Indian peoples.

To know is to appreciate. And to know, it is imperative to experience a place and its people. This book offers my searches and inquiries to those who would also experience.

Many reservations have much to offer; their people welcome visitors with campgrounds, ancient sites, reconstructions of older structures, and museums for prompting the imagining of simpler, easier times. Others offer an opportunity to know the life of a contemporary group of people whose roots have grasped this land for thousands of years.

I have never found resentment or hostility, although in some of the smaller, more private places I felt a coolness, until the people realized I was there to learn and not to take. It is my hope that those who would discover the contemporary world of the California Indian peoples may be aided in their searches by my encounters.

The reader will find here personal observations of the more than 115 active reservations, communities, and Indian educational institutions. Locations and mailing addresses are provided for these, where appropriate. For each location I have described the environmental setting, occasional anecdotes or recent important incidents, the physical facilities, acreage, activities, sites to be visited (including dancehouses, museums, historical buildings, and nearby archaeological sites), and sometimes sketches on the people themselves. For each region I have also written a personal narrative.

The most extensive use of this book will be by those who have a limited general knowledge of the numerous California Indian people, and who wish to learn more through personal experience. For these persons I have arranged the locales in the text and maps in an order that will encourage a visit to experience the world of modern native peoples and sites of a particular region. In addition, these readers will find a comprehensive listing in Appendix D, of local, regional, and state museums which display Indian-related artifacts or historical material.

Students of California history will find this guide to be a reference not elsewhere encountered. I see a tendency to segment Native American studies into archaeology, anthropology, and sociology. Though brief and concise, the history I have presented here is an attempt to reverse this trend and to retain continuity and unity of these studies from the old times to the present. Thus, in addition to the general regional history, I have included Appendices A, B, and C which serve as a directory to the missions, ranchos, and military posts – places that once were producers of the storms and turbulence that raged in the lives of the Indians.

The researcher seeking a comprehensive listing or knowledge of what fragments of tribal societies remain and where to find them will find this book a first place of reference. Robert Heizer's superb Volume 8: *California,* of the Smithsonian's *Handbook of North American Indians*[18] is unsurpassed in its treatment of peoples before the 20th century, but it admits both to a paucity of present-day coverage and to the exclusion of tribes on California's eastern borders. This present guide does discuss, though briefly, the Great Basin and Colorado River peoples whose ancient and modern homelands straddle two or three modern states.

Of interest to many will be the listing (many entries with tribal source and translation) of California place names of Indian origin.

Listed also are the population estimates of the original tribal or linguistic groups.* Modern estimates are impossible to determine, largely because of intertribal marriages and loss of identification of tribal affiliation (off-reservation residence or personal preference for non-Indian identity). The BIA does maintain tribal rolls of reservation residents and reservation adherents, but many thousands of California Indian descendants are not on these rosters.

Because this is a guidebook to the Native Americans of California and their cultural institutions, it is not possible to treat in a meaningful way the majority of Native Americans who live in the larger urban areas or whose roots are from out of the state. The urban mix blots out many distinctions among the tribal origins. Moreover, a large proportion of Native American city dwellers tend to be temporary or transient, frequently returning to their reservation or tribe. Consequently, the urban Indian is discussed only in a short section dealing mainly with services and educational opportunities offered through the various American Indian Centers.

*Estimates from mission rolls, old Indian Service records, village sizes, historical accounts, ecological subsistence limits, *et al.* Today these early estimates are considered quite low.

Finally, a series of problems seems to run as a common thread through the lives and existence of the Indian today. The problems of land, health, education, employment, and religion–these are summarized in a short chapter, but are approached to varying degrees throughout the book.

Dolan Eargle
San Francisco, 1985

Contents

Northeast Peoples 52

West Central Peoples 65

Southern Central Valley and Central Coastal Peoples, West of the Sierra Crest 87

Introduction

REMOTE, BUT NOT CONCEALED; unseen, but not disguised. To discover, to encounter, to learn the native cultures of California can be intricate and perplexing. There are at least two reasons for this circumstance: one is the very nature of the California Indian people, the other is the historical treatment concerning them.

The California Indian peoples were and still are highly diffuse and dispersed. Their cultures are not spectacular, concentrated, or as well-known as that, say, of the Iroquois, the Sioux, or the Navajo. Yet there is probably not a flat, a marsh, or a valley in the state that did not once support a native village.

The observer can be easily deceived when most of the histories of California begin with the romanticized mission, then skip to the roaring forty-niners as the "settlers" of the state. Few people seem to have any realization of the genocide perpetrated upon the Indian population in the last century. Few accounts emphasize that those pretty, touristy missions were founded at a time when the spirit of the Spanish Inquisition was still alive. The policy of "heathen conversion," even at the cost of life, remained until 1820.

Few accounts reveal that the majority of the forty-niners were rather destitute types from slave states, where the lives of non-whites were cheap. Few accounts tell of the California Indians' retreat to the hiding places, the obscure seclusion where the hunted might go for refuge.

They left behind them no imperial cities, no great stone temples, not even apartmental pueblos. They left no monuments whatever to slavery, class oppression, or defensive necessity. They were self-governing and free.

What happened to these people, what survives of their culture, and what can be learned from those who survived are questions of genuine concern. Is there something left today that can be seen, can be felt, can be experienced?

I can tell of the history and present condition of some things, I can show where to go, but the *reader* must feel, must experience. I, too, was curious–I went to see, ask, listen, to find the Indian of California and to be taught.

What is the value of knowing any history or any culture? It is through that knowledge that we realize our connectedness to all humanity and perhaps learn of concepts superior to those we have been practicing. As I mentioned, the California Indian peoples are spread lightly over the whole state. Their culture is quiet and almost hidden in the rush of modernity around it. Within it, there is little entertainment value, as in the pueblos or large public dances; little architecture, except in the primitive structures. There are few opportunities to collect pottery or jewelry.

Nevertheless, there *is* an opportunity to learn of a part of our own history, a chance to see what life is like among the descendants of those who once made that history. Even at archaeological sites, the artistry and handiwork of persons long gone excites the imagination. There is a chance to catch a glimpse of an ancient philosophy that we are becoming increasingly aware must become part of our own, if we would survive.

A rock, a bush, a deer, a basket, a fisherman–they are all related. Indian societies knew this well. Plants and animals, landscapes and the elements demand a respect that springs from the recognition of equivalent human qualities in them. If we perceive that close link, then we treat respectfully all aspects of our universe.

The Indian societies perceived in all Nature attributes of humanness. *Things*, as modern societies conceive of them, are distant from us, being only objects which further our ends. Thus, the great gap between modern and traditional Indian societies.

Those Indian cultures with which we will come into contact today possess some aspects of both these attitudes. Dilution of the early cultures is inevitable, but there are some which have maintained an emphasis on the interrelationship of all things. These are the ones which strive to keep what I will call the *old ways*, and are the ones which will teach us the dependency of ourselves to our environment.

In my descriptions of these Indian locales, the reader will find that I have not approached several topics which may be found in more complete accounts of the cultural anthropology of the California native peoples–such social customs as puberty, marriage, and mortuary customs and rites, political organization, or intertribal conflict. I have barely mentioned many of the lingering traditions, except the dance.

Within the many Indian families, both rural and urban, numerous traditions continue–traditions not obvious to the outside or casual observer–things you cannot *see* on a visit: medicine, attitudes toward others, property, political organization, sexual roles (changing), food, games, language at home (or a trace of an accent); in short, the multitude of personal habits and attitudes which make up that which we call a *culture.* These are things I cannot tote up on a list, or direct someone to.

I have not discussed those outward social aspects of the people which have too often been stereotyped. Yes, alcoholism is a problem, but that is not what this book is about, unless you can draw from my accounts a reason why alcoholism exists. Yes, some places tend to be cluttered–are the reasons historical, a reluctance to part with things once used, economic, psychological, spiritual? Once again, this is not a sociology book.

My feeling for the people is a positive one–a sense of wonder in their survival and admiration for it–a sense of striving for oneness with other persons whose history has been different from my own, but whose historical identification with the land has been nearly that of my own. I want my readers to *go* to the land, maybe camp nearby, as I have done. Learn from the native how to relate to the land in an unhurtful way.

Walk by a stream, or spend a quiet moment at a burial ground. Hear the spirits. Know the people. Know the land. Know Mother Earth.

The Arrangement of the Book

This book is divided into three parts. Part One opens with a brief presentation of the early history of Indian California; it is an orientation. I refer you to the bibliography, to broaden and deepen your knowledge.

Part Two is divided into five regional chapters. Read the first section for each region to give you some feeling for the environs and societies of peoples (in other states called tribes) who originally dwelt in that region, as well as sketches of current life there. The latter part of each chapter is a guide to each group of today's people–if they have survived the holocaust and have reservation lands or a local community.

The listings of the reservations and rancherias have been grouped by geographical region. Within each region are descriptions of the reservation lands listed first by *people*, that is, by traditional linguistic relationships; secondly, by local tribal affiliation.

The numbering sequence on Map II is in the approximate order of a possible visit or trip to these places, such that, in making a visit to each point of interest, you may do so conveniently.

You will also notice that my descriptions are mostly physical–land type and ecology, home types, tribal facilities and extent of "modern" development–what there is to be seen or experienced. You may find occasional bits of history, and once in a while, attitudes. There are places marked PRIVATE where visits, other than observing from a distance, are not welcomed; heed my caution for the sake of politeness, propriety, or even self-preservation. The Native American peoples are proud and usually private, but you will find them like everyone else–not curiosities, but persons with a special heritage. Approach the people as you approach anyone, and you will find that most will share their experience with you. Be willing to be taught.

Part Three contains a section on contemporary problems, followed by six appendices:

A. The Missions, Presidios, and Pueblos
B. The Ranchos
C. The Military Posts
D. Museums with Indian Artifacts
E. Archaeological Sites and Dancehouses
F. A Calendar of Annual Indian Events

Included in Appendix A, along with the Missions, is a listing of the groups of indigenous peoples who were brought to them, and an indication whether the visitor might find a sense of the early Indian character there.

Appendix B, Ranchos, lists the principal spreads of the era 1820–50. Indian labor built these often impressive and opulent structures.

The list of Military Posts in Appendix C includes only those which either dealt with the natives directly or co-existed with them before 1900. Many more posts than these were thrown up, but I have given those for which some remnant exists, or which bear some landmark status–where there is something to see or where there are environs to experience. The vast majority of these forts and camps existed only one or two years, a few 10–15 years, and a very few to the present. Had the contest been between near-equals, I might be inclined to wonder whether these short times were indicative of Army efficiency or of Indian ineffectiveness. The true reasons however, were the really tragic Indian vulnerability to disease and their total lack of psychological preparation for organized conflict.

Appendix D, of Museums, is arranged by region, so that the reader might visit a regional museum before venturing forth into the field.

Appendix E is a summary of accessible and protected Archaeological Sites that the reader may wish to visit while traveling about the state.

Finally, Appendix F is an annual Calendar of Indian Festivals, Dances, Powwows, and Events open to the general public. These events are held within California or nearby; all serve California Indian peoples.

The Earth Is Our Mother

. . . it was reckless without hardihood, greedy without audacity, and cruel without courage; there was not an atom of foresight or of serious intention in the whole batch of them, and they did not seem aware those things are wanted for the work of the world. To tear treasure out of the bowels of the land was their desire, with no more moral pupose at the back of it than there is in burglars breaking into a safe.

Joseph Conrad, *Heart of Darkness*

We killed plenty of game and an occasional Indian. We made it a rule to spare none of the bucks.

Member of John C. Frémont's batallion, 1847

. . . the California valley cannot grace her annals with a single Indian war bordering on respectability. It can boast, however, a hundred or two of as brutal butcherings, on the part of our honest miners and brave pioneers, as any area of equal extent in our republic. Hubert Howe Bancroft, *Works*, 1880

The Indians know no restraint, save the fear of a superior power, and until they are made to feel the ability of the United States to punish the outrages, they will repeat them as often as the temptation to do so arises. An officer of Ft. Mojave

Some contemporary attitudes of the mid-19th Century:

I believe [the Government] was made by white men and their posterity forever, and I am in favor of conferring citizenship to white men, men of European birth and descent, instead of conferring it upon negroes, Indians, and other inferior races.

Stephen A. Douglas, Senator from Illinois, 1858, in debate with Abraham Lincoln

Then came the Black Hawk War, and I was elected a captain of volunteers—a success which gave me more pleasure than any I have had since . . . Abraham Lincoln, 1859, in a letter to a friend

If [Gen. Cass] saw any live, fighting Indians, it was more than I did, but I had a good many bloody struggles with the mosquitoes . . .

A. Lincoln, 1858

[Author's note: By a spurious "treaty," the Fox and Sac (Sauk) tribes of Illinois were forcibly removed west of the Mississippi in 1832. Black Hawk led a protest expedition with 500 braves and families. The group was attacked and, after peace emmisaries under the white flag were shot down, was nearly annihilated.]

Fourscore and seven years ago our fathers brought forth upon this continent a new nation, conceived in liberty, and dedicated to the proposition that all men are created equal . . .

A. Lincoln, 1863, Gettysburg, Pa.

I speak advisedly when I say that . . . killing a slave, or any colored person, was not treated as a crime, either by the courts or the community . . . Frederick Douglass, 1845, statesman, and ex-slave

Horses and men, cattle and women, pigs and children—all holding the same rank in the scale of social existence, and all subjected to the same narrow inspection, to ascertain their value in gold and silver—the only standard of worth applied by slaveholders to their slaves.

Frederick Douglass, 1945, in his autobiography

PART ONE

A Brief History of the Native Peoples of California

Map I:
Ancestral Homelands of the Early Peoples

The Earliest Times

THE OLD MAN'S practiced and sensitive hand feels the familiar tug on his fishing rod. With a sharp jerk he reels in his first salmon of the year. Like his Indian family, most of whom live more than a mile away, he wears a serious, but not stern, expression as he concentrates on his task.

The hook ready with fresh bait, he casts, then waits from his perch on the boulder by the rushing stream – a place his grandfather told him has always been the best spot, even for *his* grandfather. Somehow, the fish are always there.

Fishing alone triggers the part of his mind devoted to recollection. Many years ago his village had celebrations on the occasion of the salmon run. Today, some of the families who live along the river will get out their rods and reels, maybe a small boat. A few men who have a large family to provide for bring out nets and *their* boats, to a do a pleasant chore that has been done for as long back as anyone can remember. Swarming around the Indians like wasps, the white man comes, too; with fancy gear, campers, and boats. Hopefully, there will be enough for all. But village celebrations are fewer and different now.

The salmon run regularly every year – like a calendar. So regularly that the run became to his people a sort of New Year's event – an event that symbolized the renewal of the world every year.

The old man thought of how easy he had it today. In the old days they had to make their own nets from rushes or iris stalks – or even harder – chip obsidian spear points and shape wooden shafts for spear fishing.

Net fishing from the margins of a marsh. (From a WPA mural by R. V. Vallangca. *St. Pk.*)

That's what his grandfather had done, and what *his* grandfather had done before him.

His thoughts rambled to how many grandfathers had told how many grandchildren where to fish – maybe all the way back to when Coyote or one of the other Great Spirits created the world. So far as he knew, the people had *always* gone fishing here – for his people had no histories, tales, or myths of a wandering tribe who finally settled in this valley.

And his people are characteristic of most of the native peoples of California. There were no written calendars as such kept, just the yearly round. There were great traditions of ancient oral histories – as a matter of fact, when an outsider asked his grandfather when some great event took place (a flood, an earthquake, or even family births); he could recollect with some accuracy, dates up to five generations earlier.

The old man did not know that his distant ancestors had not always been fishing there and had migrated there many millenia earlier. He could not know that these ancestors might not have even *liked* fish. If the old man were living in northern California along the Klamath, his people might go back as far as 3000 years. If he were living along a fishing stream in southern California, his people might go back another thousand years. Either way, three or four millennia might as well be "since creation," as he knew it.

A Shasta "lifting net" used in Northern California rivers. (Drawing by S. A. Barrett, 1955. *Lowie*)

And who were these ancestors? Where did they come from? A few recent archaeological finds (not without considerable controversy and indefinite dating) put humans in such varied parts of California as Santa Rosa Island (off Santa Barbara) and the Calico Hills near Barstow (see p. 139) possibly as far back as 40,000 years ago.* Who these people were can only be guessed. At that time, great ice sheets probably covered the entire northern part of the continent, and anyone coming south must have done so by hop-skipping the coast by boat from Asia. At any rate, we know very little about them.

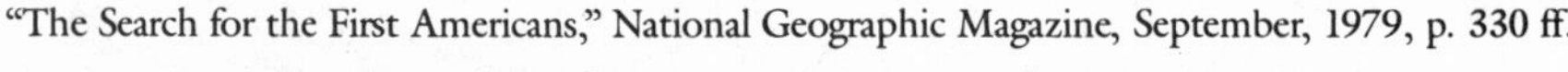

* "The Search for the First Americans," National Geographic Magazine, September, 1979, p. 330 ff.

California's earliest inhabitants preparing to replenish their larder. (From a WPA mural. *St. Pk.*)

12,000 B.C.

What is much more certain is that around 11–12,000 years ago, someone was here making elegant arrowheads.* The latest discoveries in Alaska and Canada indicate that an ice-free corridor opened up southward from Alaska through western Canada, which was wide enough for people to travel through *on land.*†

Apparently these people came directly to California for the same reason that people come here today–the weather and food supply were good. Things were still a bit chilly at the glaciers' edges, but California's great lakes were very attractive–lakes that today are either salt marshes or dry beds. Lake Mojave covered the Mojave Desert from Victorville east past Barstow; Lake Cahuilla (see p. 136) had shores near Calexico and Palm Springs (whose remnant today is the Salton Sea); China Lake covered the basin of that name; Owens Lake dried up only within this century; and Mono Lake, Searles Lake, and the salty sump of Death Valley were huge freshwater bodies.

Into this region came a people (called Folsom/Clovis, and sometimes called "Early Man")–the first settlers in California. Their deluxe arrow points have been found along the margins of Borax Lake (near Clear Lake in Lake County) and Tulare Lake (Kings County).

A Few Anthropological Definitions

"Archaeology" comprises studies of the records of human life and activities that go as far back as earliest man, and can take us up to even recent times (last century). But this term blends into another, favored by many Indians themselves–that is, "cultural anthropology," which might best be described as a study of the development of the cultural and social patterns and customs of the various peoples. A simpler term is "ethnography."

The persons who go into these studies have come up with a few terms which we should examine. First, the term "horizon" generally applies to the findings of artifacts deposited over a certain period of time. As we take the findings of the archaeologists to conjecture upon patterns of life that may have taken place, we separate (often arbitrarily) past time into periods with certain predominant characteristics. We'll see examples of this in the various horizons or phases of early life here in California.

A couple of other terms that anthropologists use are "prehistoric" and "protohistoric." The first simply means any time before written or recalled memory. There are few oral histories in California tribal life, and the first written or recalled stories are by the Spanish explorers.

Protohistoric means the time or events that were formative for the immediate historic period–a period usually just before contact with the

* A type of arrow point first found near Folsom and Clovis, N.M., with a "fluted" design, that is, a channelled center part for mounting on a wooden shaft.

† "The Search for the First Americans," National Geographic Magazine, September, 1979, p. 330 ff.

white man. Protohistoric information and facts can often be obtained from written accounts of people living in "historic" times or from relatively recent archaeological sources.

The more recent we get, however, the more touchy the subject of archaeology becomes. Many of our present Indian peoples and tribes are as understandably reluctant to have persons of *any* descent poking around their ancestors' graves as, say, whites would be to have "archaeologists" digging up Arlington Cemetery or Colma, California.

So our conjectures on early life of the first people of California must come from several sources: archaeology (diggings revealing tools, burials, etc.), from study of modes of life of other cultures living under similar circumstances, and, to some extent, from the historical knowledge of the ways of early Indian life, especially in language differences.

The archaeological record has given us indications of a few characteristics of the life of early peoples in the time periods before the present historical time. These are the archaeological horizons in California, but we must remember that, as the climates and ecologies and terrains of the state are varied, so were the developments of the peoples in those places.

The Earliest Period of Development–Early Man 9000–2000 B.C.

Before early man grouped into tribes, there were unsettled bands. As mentioned before, the earliest artifacts found in California are projectile points–probably for use with the *atlatl* (a sling-like stick for throwing arrows or spears), spears, and stone tools for scraping and working hides and wood. These have all come from sources in southern California and the Central Valley. The lack of seed-grinding tools seems to tell us that these peoples subsisted mostly by hunting.

These peoples hunted deer, birds, and fish, and also now-extinct early California animals like camel, bison, and horse. Some archaeologists think that the hunting techniques were so efficient that these animals were *made* extinct.

By 6000 B.C., milling stones for grinding seeds were being used, which means that more food was being collected from plants than before. People began to settle into more permanent communities, especially in southern California, as their garbage piles (*middens*) show.

Later, by 3000 B.C., the food sources were much more diversified, and included fishing on both land and sea, as well as hunting and plant gathering. Northern California had probably not yet been settled at all, but more distinctive cultures were developing in such widely varied places as the Cosumnes-Mokolumne River basin, coastal Santa Barbara-San Luis Obispo Counties, coastal Los Angeles County and San Diego County, and the desert (especially Owens Valley).

Burials became more elaborate, with offerings to the dead, indicating appreciation of beliefs in the after-life. Basketry became well-developed, and the household and village cache of utensils and implements was plenteous and varied–sharpening stones, cooking vessels, smoking pipes, fire drills, shell and bone ornaments, whistles.

Growth and Differentiation of the Early Cultures–2000 B.C.- ca. A.D.1500

The glaciers had retreated and melted, the climate was now warmer, and many of the larger lakes were evaporating and disappearing–in general, the ecology was becoming stable and more as we know it today.

Large numbers of peoples had settled into their valleys, mountain retreats, and coastal villages. Now was the time to improve on tools, to make more ornate and elegant baskets, woodwork, and regalia. Being more established allowed more time to differentiate, too. Languages became increasingly divergent, great religions arose and spread, art work increased in complexity and beauty, family relations and governance were more definite.

Along the Colorado River, groups adopted the techniques of pottery-making from nearby Hakataya peoples in Arizona.* They began to farm the land with beans, corn, and squash as major crops. They adopted other Hakataya strategies of living and religion.

Along the Santa Barbara coast, the peoples began to develop an extraordinarily complex culture. Everywhere, each group developed special characteristics–partly borrowed and adapted, partly invented for the ecology at hand.

Overall, two other important things happened. Someone, probably from the northeast, brought in bows and arrows, around 2000 years ago. Hunting was, of course, already well-developed, and the introduction of this new missile-launcher increased both the number and kinds of animals hunted.

At the same time, many more acorn-grinding tools were made, which tells us that acorn eating ("balanophagy" is the fancy word) had become a major dietary concern. Once the technique of leaching out the bitter tannin was discovered, acorns became popular and healthy, and have remained so until today.

To say that these bands became settled in doesn't mean that they necessarily were immobilized. In general, the peoples of the various cultures adapted well to their situations and surroundings, but from all evidence, some disruptions of populations took place from smaller bands wandering in. However, no large-scale "invasion" of hordes of tribes took place.

How do we know? From langauge and artifacts. Linguists have long known that early California was one of the richest language centers of the world. Map I shows the relation (or non-relation) of many of these. As a matter of fact, as we shall see, language is the most commonly used method of distinguishing the peoples of California.

* "Hakataya" is an archaeological name applied to the culture whose center lay mostly to the east, in Arizona.

One glance can show the reader that there was apparently a big penetration of the "newer" Penutian speakers into the center of the state, pushing the "older" Hokan speakers to either side and southward. Later, another penetration of Shoshonean (Uto-Aztecan) speakers came from the desert to the east, causing a great disruption of peoples.

Meanwhile, in the northwestern part of California, the visits from Athapascan speakers from further up the north coast became permanent.

This was the situation that the early explorers found – those who had any kind of ear for languages. Corroborating these suppositions of movements of people are secondary bits of evidence in the form of cultural paraphernalia: similarities or differences in beadwork, mortuary practices, arrowhead design, dietary preferences, value systems, and the like.

These are the things the anthropologists tell us. In the villages, though, there are other stories – dreamlike stories from great oral traditions of how their earth or their tribe was created. Sometimes the story tells that the first people emerged from under the earth; others say that they drifted in on a raft from the north; still others relate how man was sort of hatched from substances in the darkness. Perhaps the stories have something to tell *us*, if we listen.

The Protohistorical Time

It was this fabric of ecology, tribes, and people* and their customs that begins the era of contact with Ibero-Americans. Short sketches of these peoples, based on the various regions of the state, appear in this book just before the listings of the various reservations and rancherias of today.

California terrain is rather rugged in most parts, and where it isn't rough, it can be dry (at least before irrigation) and forbidding. For the early natives it was geographically divided in this way – once settled, the local tribes or peoples developed rather independently, and it seems obvious that the multilingual divergence only fed the continuing alienness and mild hostilities between groups. (Although it may be said that uniqueness and distinctiveness in peoples is a positive attribute.)

It is true, too, that in the absence of any large overall threat of invasion, war, or incursions (as in early Mexico or Peru), internal and external cohesiveness of groups simply isn't necessary. We will see how this separateness worked to disastrous consequences later. Nevertheless, there was much social intercourse between these many groups – in religion, trade, and military alliances.

A great trade network was set up around California, as was the case in Aztec Mexico, or even along the Mississippi River. Indeed, trading was, in some northwestern California areas, considered a dangerous oc-

* As described later (p. 34), a "tribe" refers to a small village community, while a "people" refers to the larger linguistic or cultural group.

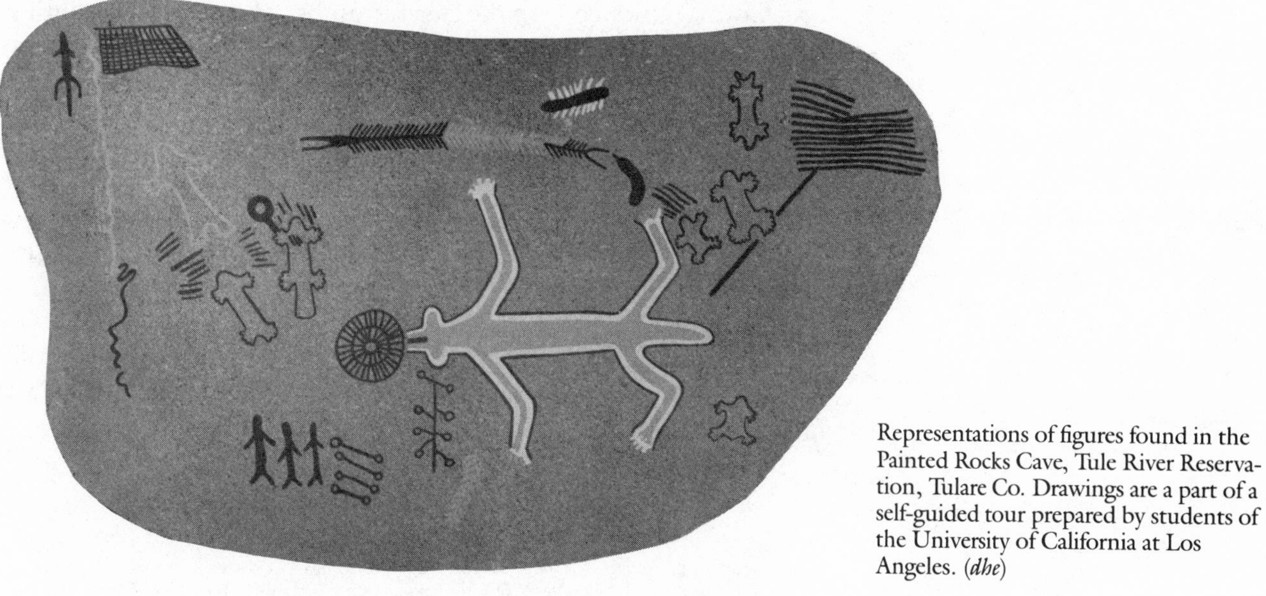

Representations of figures found in the Painted Rocks Cave, Tule River Reservation, Tulare Co. Drawings are a part of a self-guided tour prepared by students of the University of California at Los Angeles. (*dhe*)

cupation. Yet, there were literally dozens of trade routes and trails found in protohistorical California – in all parts of the state. There were traveling professional traders with diplomatic immunity who passed from territory to territory over well-known trade routes, using an elaborate money system.

How do we know? From first-hand historic accounts of routes – especially through the desert (some traces still exist), and from the simple fact that thousands of objects, mostly shell-bead money, hides, obsidian, and ornaments, ended up hundreds of miles from their procurement sites.

As the great religions of the various areas developed (see pages 39, 54, 66, 89, 90, 107) – the World Renewal, the Kuksu, the toloache – there was a tradition of each tribe or people to invite neighboring groups to its ceremonies. Obviously, this was a great chance to exchange goods, ideas, women (sorry, but it's true), and ornaments. The mutual feasting and dancing also served unconsciously as a means of minimizing rivalries and intergroup conflict.

Most of the rituals were supervised by a specially-chosen (by inheritance or spiritual inclination) member belonging to a secret society. These persons had considerable secular or "political" power within the community. In California, the dance leaders were either priests of a secret society or shamans (individuals with exceptional religious and medicine powers). In the south, leaders were often aided by ***toloache***.*

These shamans, as did those of the Great Basin, and those of the north, whether under the influence or not, did undertake extraordinary artistic activities in connection with their work – rock art.

* *Toloache* is the Spanish term for the datura plant, or jimsonweed, a common vine with white, trumpet-like flowers that flourishes over a large part of warmer California. Preparations made from almost any part of this plant are hallucinogenic, and fatally toxic if overdosed. Early California cultures used this plant, as their neighbors used peyote, to sharpen perceptions, to dream, to gain insights, and occasionally to find lost objects.

California is blessed with the largest number of examples of painting, carving, and chipping on rocks in all of the United States. Most of these works were done in the period from 500 B.C. to A.D. 1500.

In most cases, the art was undertaken for a purpose, that is, by the shamans to enhance success in the hunt, fertility, the magnificence of a ceremony, or, occasionally, the power of the rain spirit.

Several styles of rock art have been distinguished in California, and nearly all regions of the state possess examples, with the exception of the flat Central Valley, where later civilizations have obliterated them, or where rain or sand has etched them away.

Cambell Grant and others have prepared an extraordinarily beautiful book on rock art, which I recommend to anyone with interest in art, antiquity, or Indian culture.*

* Campbell Grant, *Rock Art of the American Indian*, Thomas Y. Crowell Company, New York, 1967 (ref. 8). A more detailed book of California rock art is that of Heizer and Clewlow, reference 12.

Part of the interior of the Chumash Painted Cave, Santa Barbara Co. (*dhe*)

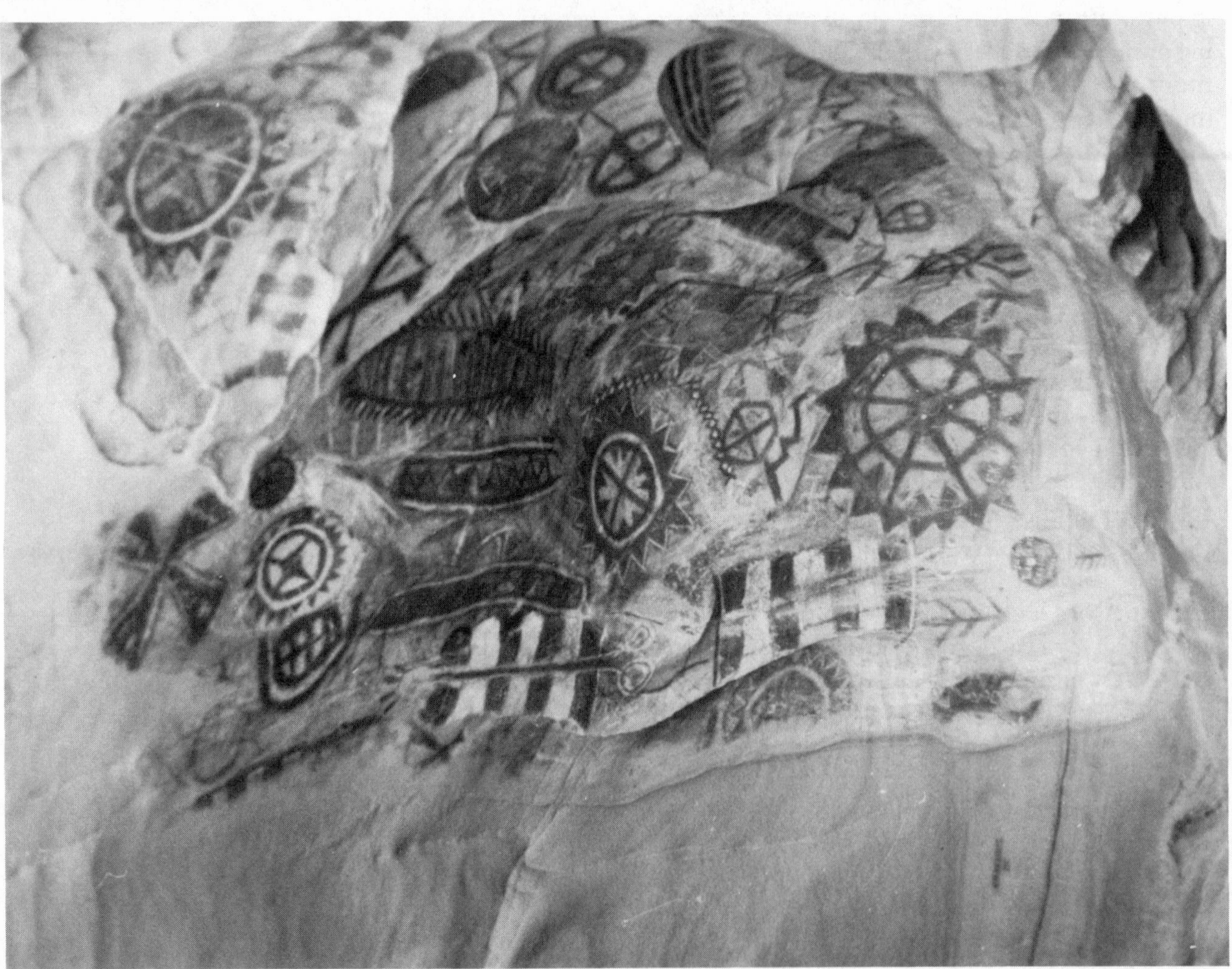

The Conflict Between the Indian and White Civilization*

AS THE OLD MAN SAT fishing from his rock, his thoughts were not only of fishing. His mind wandered back in time to the tales and stories told by his grandfather around the fire of their little assembly house in the woods, where all the men of the tribe gathered. And he had some tales of his own for his grandchildren – tales and stories that are remembered and told, but that some persons would rather forget – tales of the hard times.

And as stories are the stuff of history, we come upon the historical period of California Indian life – the slow incursions by the Spanish, English, Russian, Mexican, and Anglo-American.

Into a stable relationship of people in harmony with their environment, each other, and their spirits, came the first little needles of breach into their *land*, their rightful *place*.

It is still amazing to note the Spanish zeal to fan out over the continent, once they had made contact with the New World. Columbus sailed the ocean blue in fourteen hundred ninety-two; and it only took Spanish enterprise about twenty years to catch on. Then GOLD and LAND became the causes. For gold, Hernán Cortés took central Mexico in 1519, as Francisco Pizarro conquered Peru in 1532.

The First White Contacts

By 1529, Cortés and his contending successors had consolidated Spanish domination of Mexico. But, in spite of the incessant quarreling over spoils and territory that seems inherent in the Spanish style, several expeditions were organized to investigate lands to the north of Tenochtitlán (Mexico City) by 1540.

Imbued partly with a spirit of curiosity and exploration, but mostly with the lust for gold, Francisco Coronado headed north by land, and Hernando de Alarcón headed northwestward by ship, into the Gulf of California and up the Colorado River to the Yuma area. Thus, Alarcón was the first of the Spaniards to penetrate the Indian land of what is now California. Two years later Rodriguez de Cabrillo reported his visits to coastal villages. Sporadic visits by others over the next two hundred years only touched on the Indian civilization: Sir Francis Drake (1579), Sebastian Vizcaino (1602), Juan de Oñate (1604), and provisioning stops by occasional Spanish, English, Russian, and French ships.

In this two-century period of minimal contact, the Indian population was affected in varying degrees. During some ship layovers, crews

* This chapter title is borrowed from Sherburne Cook (ref. 4), because it best describes the actual situation.

had become violent with several natives, causing a bad reputation of the white to spread. Worse, the Colorado River peoples began to contract diseases. For example, the Quechans closest to the settled Spanish lost about one-fourth of their estimated 4,000 population between the 1740s and 1770s.

Other pressures were bearing down on the California natives. The Southern Paiutes were raided by Utes seeking slaves to sell to Spanish already in New Mexico (Santa Fe, 1609). Wheat came to the Colorado River as early as 1702 from Arizona missions of 1700, changing both diet and agricultural methods. In 1803, Lewis and Clark reported that the peoples to the north were well-versed in horsemanship; surely the horse was known to the Great Basin peoples before then.

Those earliest expeditions for gold were failures. It wasn't until 1769 that the Spanish viceroyalty in Mexico City mustered enough interest in California to send a colonizing expedition under Gaspar de Portolá. Russians and English were showing too much interest in the region to leave it alone.

Up to this time California had been benignly ignored–it had very little Indian gold and was too green. From what I have noticed of early Spanish settlement patterns, they tended to ignore the lush regions and settle first in places that looked more like home–the drier parts of Spain. But now, additional food was necessary for Mexico, and the international situation was slowly changing. The church would help. The prospect of thousands of new converts was not overlooked. This was the beginning of the end of native California.

"Settlement of Ross" (Fort Ross), Sonoma Co. An early Russian colony, established about 1812, with Pomo assistance, to provide staples for Russia's Alaskan colonies. (From an old Russian history book. *St. Pk.*)

The Missions, the Pueblos, and the Presidios–The Spanish Era

Numerous places (primarily mission bookshops) offer charming pieces on early life in the mission, usually justifying the "bringing a better way of life to the children of nature." Perhaps there is a certain sentimentality involved. To those convinced of the rightness of the padres' cause, I must say that there has been much successful propaganda. I myself once thought this way, considering only the undeniable beauty of the architecture and the nostalgia of an earlier–and totally unknown–way of life. My searches have led me into other paths of thought. Let me share.

As an arm of the Spanish government, their expeditions financed by the Empire, accompanied at all times by a squad of soldiers, the padres entered Alta California.*

Padre Fray Junípero Serra, a Majorcan Spaniard and Franciscan monk, had spent many years working in the Indian villages around Mexico City and had acquired a small group of sternly ascetic followers. It was he, with Gaspar de Portolá, who was sent to replace Jesuits in Baja California (as a result of church-state politics) and also to found new colonies in Alta California. Portolá initially headed for Monterey Bay, missed it, and subsequently left Serra to found San Diego instead; later, they went back together to Monterey.

Roughly, mission-founding technique was this: the well-protected padre (Serra at first, Lasuén later), after reconnaissance for an appropriate area, would proclaim a ceremony of dedication, then attempt to baptize some natives, who were seeking to obtain the great "power" of the whites. After spending a short time at the place, the padre-in-charge would depart to a new site, leaving supervision of the actual construction to deputies.

At the very first, it seems that those hard-labor construction tasks of adobe bricks, irrigation ditches, and the like, were accomplished by the "neophytes" (newly-converted) who were genuine proselytes. But it didn't take long for the ingrained traditions of the natives to grate against the intentions and behavioral notions of most of the padres.

Suddenly, these natives, who were accustomed to their own independent society, found themselves herded together, fed strange food, deprived of their religion, restrained from their own specific sexual customs, and then treated roughly by padre or soldier when they deviated from the Church's prescribed norm. They protested, became restless, even rebellious. More of this later.

Village life, work routines, family life, hunting, fishing–none can be carried on in the usual manner when disease strikes. Of all the agonizing alterations to Indian life in the New World, the introduction of European diseases was the most devastating. Europe, Asia, and the Middle East had undergone numerous epidemics, each wiping out as much as

* Alta California was that part of Spanish California above Baja California, and now mostly included in the present state of California.

An artist's rendition of Costanoans dancing in the plaza of Misión Dolores, about 1821. Usually, the natives managed to fuse some of their rituals with those of the Church–but always *outside* the edifice in the plaza. (*University of California* and *St. Pk.*)

three-quarters of the population. Europeans, consequently, emerged genetically somewhat more resistant to disease. But the American Indian had not yet received the sword of these virulent armies.

Whether endemic (in small areas) or epidemic–measles, smallpox, cholera, pneumonia, diphtheria, scarlet fever, syphilis, dysentery, tuberculosis, and typhoid–exacted an almost genocidal toll. Colds, fevers, and diarrhea affected nearly all the Indian populations at one time or another. The immunological susceptibility of the Indian made the spread of disease possible, but missionization made it worse.

Soon after the disillusionment of many of the "neophytes" with mission life, the padres found it necessary to maintain and expand the venture by exerting more than gentle persuasion. The army (two to twelve soldiers per mission) was dispatched to round up apostates and bring in even more natives, by force, if necessary. Punishment for escape resulted.

These natives whose rancherias (villages) sometimes numbered more than a thousand persons, were packed into the mission compound and segregated by sex. Occasionally, as many as a thousand were confined, making transmission of disease vastly easier. Even modern societal health would have had trouble coping with these crowded conditions. Stuffed into shuttered rooms with poor sanitation, in close physical contact with the Spaniards, often having to contend with a harsh climate for the first time (many were brought to the cold coast from a warm, dry interior), the native population succumbed by the thousands.

Reports by the padres and others on their inability to treat the illnesses and, in many cases, to adequately feed the mission population, were not lacking. Even though they were not versed in control of disease, it seems incredible that supposedly intelligent beings could not see what they were doing to the native population. Unless, of course, "saving" and "converting," (or, more cynically–running the mission) held higher priorities than protecting human life. Perhaps, all the padres could see was a bunch of naked savages running about with little to do, *obviously* in need of civilization and God. This notion has not yet died among us.

An early drawing of a Miwok or Wappo gathering at the Misión San Francisco Solano (Sonoma), about 1830. Thatched huts are visible in the field to the left. (*St. Pk.*)

An estimate of original native California population by Sherburne Cook[2] is about 112,000. Estimates using later data and educated opinions show that at least 300,000, and possibly as many as one million natives, were here in 1769. Estimates of the total in 1832 reduce it to less than 100,000, that is, less than *one-third* of the original population was alive after only 63 years! Since there was little warfare or outright killing during the mission period, most of this awesome decline must have been from death by disease and by a precipitous lowering of the birth rate.*

Life in the missions was hardly the idyll so often portrayed. Once things had settled down to a routine, and the raiding of distant tribes for new converts had tapered off, some of the romanticized accounts of "mission life" may have been possible, especially in southern California. Indeed, several peoples (such as the Luiseños), were allowed to retain village life outside the mission as long as they were thoroughly versed in the padres' expectations of family and public life.

Most of the time, the padres did seem to have the "best interests" of the "children" in mind. Although patronizing and dictatorial, they did teach agriculture, weaving, pottery, horticulture (olive and grape), and other useful arts. A good proportion of the produce, however, was usually sent back to interior Mexico in the form of wine, olive oil, tallow, hides, grain, etc.

Let us also consider the time span of the entire mission system, from the very first year in 1769, to the secularization (a process similar to nationalization) of the missions in 1834: *67 years*–only one lifetime. Not a single mission had time to become venerable. True, often 20 years would pass between epidemics; most missions experienced only one rebellious episode, if any. It was possible for life to be relatively settled and routine for a few years. Edward Castillo points out that of 56,000 bap-

*Many Indian women resorted to natural herbal abortive drugs, saying that they would not care to subject their children to the life which they themselves had lived.

tized Indians in this period, only 15,000 survived.[18] A "relatively settled" life, then, included the omnipresent spectre of death.

It was by no accident or whim of the architects that nearly all the missions were designed like forts or prisons–rectangular enclosures with thick walls, narrow, shuttered windows, towers, and heavy gates. They were designed to keep *in* and keep *out*. One natural and simple reaction of displeasure to captivity was to flee. This was rewarded by recapture and often severe punishment, such as lashing or even cutting off parts of the feet of repeated offenders.

Flight was difficult–there was the ever-present danger of being recaptured, but worse, where to flee? Traditionally, most Indians never ventured beyond tribal territory; to go further into alien tribal territory meant capture and sometimes death to the trespasser. To find the courage to flee, conditions must have been odious enough to leave family, risk recapture, and to brave the unknown.

Recapturing fugitive Indians must have been a popular sport, since so many prominent names were doing it: Luís Peralta (Santa Clara, 1805) killed ten and brought back twenty-five "head" on one expedition. Gervásio Argüello (Santa Clara, 1806) found 42 apostates and 47 unconverted out in the bush. Father L. A. Martinez (San Luis Obispo, 1816), with soldiers, brought back "only five persons."

Such tactics invited rebellion. Although California Indians had never mastered white military tactics–they had never known them–the Kameyaay in San Diego revolted and destroyed the mission after six years of repression. It was rebuilt anyway. In 1781, the Quechan, having had only one year of mistreatment, permanently destroyed both Spanish mission and army, and maintained their independence until the American invasion.

Other sites of revolt were at La Puríssima, where 400 Indians took over and held the mission for a month (1794), an incident at the San Gabriel Mission (1785), forays from both San Francisco and San José against apostates of these missions (1793 and 1797). During this time many missions incurred the wrath of the natives, but resistance was futile, owing to the superior force of the Spaniards.

As more and more immigrants from Spain trickled into California–rancheros, retired army, fortune seekers–the secular area was built up around the missions as *pueblos* (towns). Of course it was Indian labor which was recruited for work on the ranches and in the towns as laborers; yet the laborer was, at least in part, free. And the numbers employed were very small. Consequently, this aspect of Indian life is almost insignificant in relation to the mission.

A list of the missions, their asisténcias (outlying agricultural support parishes), the four presidios, and a few pueblos (1769–1834) is found in Appendix A. Also listed are the Indian peoples who were part of the missions.

• • •

The Mexican Period–The Ranchos

The move for Mexican independence of Spain, begun by Fray Hidalgo in 1811, was achieved in 1821, although few waves of change reached Alta California. Nevertheless, from all over Mexico came the cry of the captive Indian to be released from the bondage of the Church. The year 1834 brought the "secularization" of the missions, and their downfall as a power source. I have but one thing to say to the romaticizers of mission life: If the Indian so loved life in the mission, why was it that only two years after secularization (control by civilian authority), nearly the entire Indian population had fled? By 1848 the mission system no longer existed.

Since the early period of Mexican independence didn't change mission life much, Indian rebellion continued. In the San Francisco Bay area, three apostates made their names known by their rebellious exploits: Pompónio, Marín, and Quintín. The latter two are today immortalized with place names elevating them to a peculiar status–San Marin and San Quentin.

Even as late as 1837, José María Amador was out on a "recapturing" expedition. He found 200 Indians, half of them baptized. His party marched the Christians down a road, murdering each with four arrows. With the others, he poured a bottle of water on their heads in a mock baptism, then shot them in the back. Amador City and County are named after this man's family.

It was the intention, though weakly expressed, of the Mexican government to make the mission lands over into Indian pueblos, while retaining some land for the padres. What actually happened was the sacking of the establishments and seizure of the lands by greedy and powerful rancheros. In 1823, the year of the founding of the first Mexican republic, there were only 20 secular land grants in Alta California; by 1845 the number had increased to nearly 800; a few actually were Indian.

Thus, the Indian once again became the pawn in the land grab that solidly entrenched the *hacienda-peón* system. The Indian became the peón.

More names came to prominence: General Mariano Vallejo, whose rancho in Petaluma spread over nearly 100,000 acres, and whose luxurious life was supported by his Indian mercenaries. His troops raided nearby and distant tribes for laborers, and in one battle killed over 200 protesting Wappos.

José Andrés Sepúlveda managed to acquire a large rancho from former San Juan Capistrano (ex-Luiseño Indian) land. He used, of course, Indian *vaqueros* to maintain the life-style of the ranchero.

Outlanders moved in: John Temple into Los Cerritos (1844); Hugo Reid into Santa Anita Rancho (1839)–largely San Gabriel Mission (ex-Gabrielino) territory.

At the end of the first half of the 19th century, the big land-grab was getting more agitated as missions declined and immigrants arrived.

Eventually, the missions fell into disrepair as most were abandoned. Control of the churches proper was returned by the U.S. government in the 1860s, while most of the buildings remaining in the 20th century were restored by the State Parks Department, in cooperation with the local parishes.

Nearly all of former mission land in California from San Diego to Sonoma Counties was divided up–some into huge ranchos, others not so big. They, too, eventually disappeared, as did their labor force and their lifestyle.

A listing of the most notable California ranchos is found in Appendix B.

The Domain of the Non-Mission Indian

Elsewhere in California, outside the mission lands, reverberations were rippling. Those tribes and peoples farthest from the central and south coast were lucky–for a while. And the Colorado River peoples managed to stay autonomous. The tribes in the far north, in the mountains, and in the desert regions fared best–simply because they were more remote.

Because contact between tribes was frequent and often intimate, disease outran the white man. Peoples nearer the missions suffered raids for support of Church and rancho. Any groups along the Central Valley were vulnerable and fair game for kidnappers. More and more immigrants from all over the world were filtering in, especially Americans, and all "needed" laborers.

Small battles continued. One Estánislao (Stanislaus), apostate of the San José Mission, managed an attack on the San José and Santa Clara missions, fled to the Valley, and at least once (1829) defeated his Mexican army pursuers. Eventually, most of his band escaped a siege in the brush country, to fight again and again until 1838.

John Sutter came from Switzerland to set up his little empire in Sacramento County (see p. 164), and, after the pattern of Vallejo, utilized Indian to fight Indian.

The Indians were losing lives, land, and livelihood–the land upon which to feed themselves–but not yet in so rapid a way as the next decade would bring.

In fairness, it should be emphasized that in many ways the attitude of whites toward Indians in the Spanish/Mexican period was at least that of incorporation of the Indian into society. The padres looked upon their charges patronizingly, but as humans. Even in 1845, the Spanish population of Alta California was no more than 4,000–not a great number. As in the rest of Mexico, the Indian was looked upon as a part of the society–although not completely equal. This attitude of the white Californian was to change radically quite soon. I would like to quote Sherburne Cook in a singularly perceptive statement: "We find . . . a direct collision between two forces, each characteristic of,

WPA artist F. Petersen's depiction of a roundup of natives for labor on the rancho. (*St. Pk.*)

and inherent in, its own type of civilization: the [independent] predisposition of the Indian culture and the integrative or fusion tendency of the white mission-military culture. The two are mutually exclusive; no compromise is possible."[4] The last sentence becomes even more pertinent to the next phase of California Indian history.

The American Period

Nothing in California history is more painful, offensive, or unforgiveable than the invasion of California Indian lands and the slaughter of its inhabitants by the Anglos and other gold-greedy raiders.

The skirmishes for "independence," instigated in 1846 by John C. Frémont's U.S. Army batallion at the behest of Anglo settlers, were the first spasmodic stirrings of the impending invasion. But the subsequent Treaty of Guadalupe Hidalgo in 1848, by which Mexico relinquished Alta California to the United States, was decidedly more significant to the Indian culture. It is here that most "histories" of California begin.

That year was also the occasion of the finding of gold on John Sutter's rancho. The invasion and deluge of white barbarians that arrived with lust for gold were to the Indian as the Huns were to the Roman Empire. The attitude of these men toward everything was that *nothing* was more important than their pursuit of the metal. As Jack Forbes puts it: "The conquest was . . . a direct result of the westward movement of a vast horde of armed civilians [with a] warlike nature, and indifferent to the boundary claims and property rights of already established but alien peoples."[5]

The attitude, carried from East Coast to West, and echoing 1626, might be paraphrased–"Your land is my land, from California to the New York Island ($24)."

Let some figures speak: the white population of California in 1848 was 15,000; in 1850–93,000; in 1860–380,000. In ten years, more Anglos trekking to California overwhelmed the entire Indian population.

Hollywood has done a good job of presenting the miner/cowboy side. "Law" was only those limitations which the white immigrants (called "Argonauts") cared to set upon themselves for claim-staking. There was a sort of "gentlemen's agreement" order set up–but it didn't apply to Indians, blacks, Asians, or Latinos.

No doubt most of these seekers had some moral sense, but in the general melee, it was submerged to the outrageous behavior of the worst of the lot. Right behind them followed the pioneers–families who usually followed a moral inclination, but who picked up the anti-Indian sentiment quickly.

The natives, recoiling from the gold-seekers, reacted as best they could. It is likely that the first Argonauts were conditioned in their attitudes of the Indian as enemy by the very militant actions of the Plains Indians–peoples highly skilled in horsemanship and tactics and often skilled in arms. On the other hand, California Indians, though fine horsemen, had little experience with organized cavalry, as did the Plains and Great Basin peoples; and they were so poorly-oriented toward the threat that resistance was practically nil, or at best sporadic. The miners found it easy sport to pick off the native Californian.

Into the confusion trooped the U.S. Cavalry and slogged the U.S. Infantry. They were the *only* source of law and order, but they were also white–convinced of "manifest destiny" and the "right" of U.S. citizens to settle wherever they pleased.

When the first wagon trains penetrated eastern California, they were usually set upon by the natives, who saw their lands being invaded and their rare water sources being expropriated. The Army came to the rescue of the immigrants, establishing at the springs a series of protective forts and encampments along the desert trails into California (see pp. 167–169).

For the most part, the Army supported the whites–the rancheros, the miners, the pioneers–rather than mediating the conflict. The Army was called upon to perform the most unpleasant tasks, like removing the Indians from their villages to reservations, or giving a legal look to a revenge raid, or often to protect Indians from non-Indians.

As mentioned earlier, not a single tribe or people escaped the European diseases. However, one rather interesting situation was found in the first decade of Yankee invasion: very few of the formerly missionized peoples suffered from further ravages of disease, and few suffered from Army action because there was little gold in the southern Coast Range or San Diego Co. mountains. This doesn't mean that the southern valleys weren't attractive farm land. They were, and still are. Therefore the native peoples weren't as molested as in the north. They *were* pushed

A detachment of Troop "C", 4th Company, from Ft. Bidwell, on the march in the Warner Mountains to subdue local Paiutes. (*St. Pk.*, 1892)

In only six years, the Shastas were defeated by the Army and the flood of settlers that arrived at Ft. Jones, Siskiyou Co.; State Landmark Plaque **317**. (*dhe*)

into worse areas and much land was expropriated for the ranchos, but the expropriators still required a close source of cheap labor for their big spreads. This is not to say, either, that anti-Indian sentiment didn't infect the south. (It occasionally continues to the present; see p. 145.)

Yet, it was the Central Valley and northern California that received the brunt of the invasion. By 1850 disease had already begun to weaken and debilitate the people through pneumonia, influenza, tuberculosis, and venereal diseases. In addition to the murderous callousness of the miner/settler, the Indians found their food sources devastated–their staple of acorns, fish, game, seeds. Much of the countryside appeared as though a thousand tornadoes had passed–the after-effects of mining operations. Almost every fishing stream flowing from the Sierras was laden with silt and rubble; the foothill valleys were gouged out; settlers fenced off "their" land and turned cattle loose on the abundant grasses of formerly open fields.

What resistance the Indians could muster to the depletion of their food sources and the threat of starvation took the form of drawing upon the white man's larder. This, in turn, aroused reprisal and vengeance far in excess of the "injury" done. Occasionally, the Indian would react violently and the vicious cycle was on.

Here, as in all the West, the Army was called upon ostensibly to "protect and restrain" the Indians. "Protection" was minimal, and "restraint" was enthusiastic to the point of pursuit. From 1846 to the 1880s, more than a thousand U.S. Army forts and frontier posts were established in the West, and almost 200 in California. Although persisting elsewhere until 1900, Indian resistance in California culminated in the Modoc War of 1872–73, said to be the single most expensive campaign in the West.

Allow me to recount a few of the events of this period:*

Two settlers, Charles Stone and Andrew Kelsey, oppressed Clear Lake Pomos on their rancho, the ill-treatment included lashing, rape, slavery, and murder. Stone and Kelsey were executed by two irate natives. The other Indians, fearing reprisal, fled to an island at the north end of the lake. But the Army was called out, brought boats, and massacred 60 of the 400 on the island, now called "Bloody Island." Women and especially children were reported easy prey. Pursuit took another 75 Indian lives, including some "hanged and burnt." A Treaty of Peace and Friendship followed, in which the Pomo relinquished their lands for a gift of "10 head of beef cattle, three sacks of bread, and sundry clothing." 1850–51, Lake Co.

At a feast given by whites for 300 Wintu, all Indians present were ambushed one-by-one by soldiers and volunteers. 1850s, Shasta Co.

Nearly 100 Yuma and Mohaves were drowned in an alkali lake in retaliation for raids on cattle and immigrant trains. 1865, Inyo Co.

White settlers in the Sierra were kidnapping Maidu children ($50–60 for a cook or servant) and women ($100 for a "likely young girl"). 1861, Nevada Co.

Reports of slaves being bought and sold were common:

- kidnapping of children for Sacramento, 1854.
- kidnapping of children for southern ranchos, Chico, 1857.
- enslaving of children for San Francisco, 1858, 1863.
- enslaving children from Humboldt and Mendocino Counties following Army raids of villages, 1861.
- killing of adults to get the children, Round Valley, 1867.

(There were only three arrests and no convictions for these and other similar crimes.)

One hundred of nearly 500 villagers near Yuba City dead of cholera. 1849, Yuba Co.

At one of Sutter's farms, 40 of 48 dead of an epidemic. This tribe lost 500 from smallpox and typhoid the next year. 1852, Placer Co.

On the Trinity River, the Indians (Hupa) were displaced by whites. Upon returning to fish, they were shot. 1855, Humboldt Co.

One General Kibbe reported a policy to drive the Achumawi into the mountains to starve during food-gathering seasons. 1850, Siskiyou Co.

* My accounts are taken from Cook, Forbes, Gillis, Hart (1965), and Heizer (1978), in which are presented many more tragedies.

Anthony J. Bledsoe[4] reports on numerous events in Humboldt and Trinity Counties, where many of the worst depredations occurred–nearly 50 rancherias and encampments attacked, burned, ambushed, inhabitants slaughtered. 1855–63, Humboldt and Trinity Cos.

Survivors of three Eel River tribes were encamped on Indian Island in Humboldt Bay, Eureka. While the men were away fishing, the local whites descended upon the women, children, and elderly, butchering them all. (Author Bret Harte denounced the raid, and was relieved of his journalist job. The place was renamed Gunther's Island, obscuring its past.) 1860, Humboldt Co.

Juan Antonio Garrá, a Cupeño, organized a successful revolt of several southern California desert peoples. The Colorado River and parts of the Mojave came under Indian control, but the movement collapsed when Garrá was betrayed by pro-white Indians. The Army destroyed the food supplies of the involved peoples in retaliation. Garrá was executed, and the chief Cupeño village was burned. 1851–52, San Diego, Imperial, Riverside Cos.

In retaliation for attacking an immigrant train, a detail of 58 dragoons and infantry dropped 20 Indians near Ft. Mojave, but retreated to San Bernardino (1858). The Army returned and took the land, this time peacefully, though taking six chieftains hostage. Hostilites again erupted, with the Army killing 23 Mohaves and destroying their crops. 1859, San Bernardino Co.

Short-lived and sporadic resistance by Indians arose in several places:

Hamakhavas (Mohaves), 1850–1860s.
Owens Valley Paiutes and Shoshones, 1850s–1865.
Northern Paiutes, 1860s.
Klamath War, 1851–52.
Kern River War, 1856.
Pit River "Massacres," 1867.

No contest ended in Indian success. These examples are only a fraction of the horrors of the holocaust in which the California Indian was nearly exterminated–not in large wars and pitched battles as in the plains states; but in small groups, isolated raids and massacres by Army, state militia, vigilantes, yahoo gunmen, and by disease and starvation.

California, too, had its share of the tragic "trails of tears"–those long, forced marches of the weary and bedraggled remnants of once-happy peoples, being removed from their homes to reservations–reservations that were worthless spots of land bereft of any food or shelter. The establishment of every reservation entailed a forcible removal of natives to it.

The Achumawi and Maidu of the northeast were driven to Round Valley (Mendocino Co.), 1860.

Another roundup of the Central Valley drove peoples to the Nome Lackee Reservation (Tehama Co.), 1863.

Cupeños removed from Warner Springs to Pala (San Diego Co.), 1903.

Even as early as 1853, reservations were established. In 1851–52, U.S. treaty commissioners negotiated with various native peoples. The terms of "peace" included setting aside 7 million acres of California reservation lands and instruction in agriculture and reservation maintenance, in return for native cession of land rights, cessation of hostilities, and settling on the reservations.

Congress never was able to ratify the treaties, which the Indians had begun to accept–until the treachery was found out. The reservation lands were sliced down to less than 500,000 acres, in useless and unproductive places. Not only was the land incapable of supporting the people, the government failed miserably to supply food for the starving native populace.

The reservations turned out to be concentration camps of the worst sort–the inhabitants fell victim to fraud, appropriation of supplies, maltreatment, and gross neglect by the administrators. Furthermore, the Army lacked protective control–even *inside* the reservation. In 1862, 45 of Round Valley's inhabitants were murdered in camp. The following year, 20 more Wailaki were killed there. The only Indian defense was to flee, as they had the missions, although some reservations served as essential refuges from the more malignant civilians.

But this time there were precious few places to hide. Some took to the bush–as did the Yahi–who perished to the last person, Ishi. Others disappeared into remote areas. Others banded together in small gypsy-like colonies, living at the rural edge of the newly-established white society. Many took refuge with other Indian groups, others with friendly whites or ranchers. *Very* slowly, a number of rancherias were set aside for residential purposes.

Prominent Battles or Massacre Sites in which Indian and Settler or Army Forces Contended (1829–73)

1829 Vallejo *vs.* San Joaquin Valley Indians (San Joaquin Co. **214**)
1850 Bloody Island Massacre (Lake Co. **427**)
1850 Fandango Pass/Bloody Point (Modoc Co. **8**, **546**)
1850 James Savage Battalion in Yosemite Valley (Mariposa Co. **527**, **790**)
1855 Battle Rock (Castle Crags) (Shasta Co. **116**)
1862 Bishop Creek Battle (Imperial Co. **811**)
1862 Mayfield Canyon Battle (Inyo Co. **211**)
1867 Infernal Caverns Battleground (Modoc Co. **16**)
1867 Chimney Rock (San Bernardino Co. **737**)
1872 Land's Ranch Battle (Modoc Co. **108**)
1873 Captain Jack's Stronghold (Modoc Co. **9**)

[Throughout the book, the numbers in **boldface** refer to State Historical Landmark number.]

A Time of Survival, Withdrawal, Regeneration

Very slowly the enormity of the Indians' terrible condition made itself felt on the white consciousness. Little dabs of help began to be applied–a little food, a few white culture schools, a little agricultural assistance, medical assistance, and water supplies. Yet all the while, much of the residual intolerance and greed of the local settlers continued to make demands–on the soul of the Indian culture (schools and religion) and on the body of the Indian person (labor and land).

A few of the people of this time could lead a self-supported existence in remote areas or on the reservation. Others found menial labor under the white system as cheap labor in agriculture, ranching, mining, etc.–although the idea of working for another man as an employee for the white man's money caused great conflict. After all, the native had had less than ten years to adapt his entire lifestyle to the new system.

Most Indian families found it necessary, *wherever* they were, to erect their own dwellings. Consequently, in some places, the most primitive of dwellings were put up–after the manner which they knew best and for which materials were available. Many Colorado River people, for instance, lived in wattle huts until the 1950s. In places where lumbering was available, rude homes were constructed, often tiny one-room affairs no larger than their parents had known. In the south, adobe was easy to make and use.

Some of these original homes may still be seen–lived in, often expanded, and now equipped with some modern conveniences. Only in the last ten to fifteen years has the government seen fit to provide monies to improve the homes of the Indian.*

Very slowly, too, the native American has regained rights. Obviously, there were *no* rights in those first decades after the deluge. No private property was possible for individuals, though by 1881 the Yokayo Pomos were able to purchase, as a group, a rancheria, and some Luiseños settled on some poor land and sought to improve it. But then the Dawes Severalty Act of 1887 allowed allotment of parts of reservations to private families, in an effort to relieve the federal government of any and all responsibilities for Indians.

Still, within the contradictory policies of the federal government, new reservations and rancherias were established, even as late as 1930, and some up to the present day. (See p. 34 for a discussion of the word "termination.") There was, and still is, extant the thought that if *all* reservations were done away with and *all* the Indians forced to adopt white ways, then the "Indian problem" would go away. This idea has not prevailed. The reservation remains at least one place that some federal restitution of past failures may be made in the way of assistance–medical, housing, education.

* Speaking for myself, I would like to see a few of the century-old dwellings preserved–as a monument to ingenuity, history, and perserverence of a whole people.

Scraping and tanning hides was one task of the Indian for the white master. (An F. Petersen mural for the WPA. *St. Pk.*)

Schools for native Americans began to appear around 1880, but many eventually closed owing to lack of students. The California Indian census decreased to a low of only 15–16,000 persons in 1900, though thousands were quietly hiding in many locales. Some boarding schools were set up in the large reservations from 1881–1898; schools to which many students were taken from their distant homes and forced into deculturalization programs. Several times, the students in their wisdom actually burned their buildings in protest.

Very slowly, the native children were accepted into public schools, and today a few schools are located right on the reservations. Some now offer Indian cultural courses, and several reservations (with government funds) have recently opened Education Centers and Cultural Centers where young and adult alike can further their education and knowledge of their own people; places which you may find in the Reservations Guide in Part Two.

There is a long way to go. *All* schools should teach the native American cultural heritage as the beginnings of their own heritage, but even more important, the literacy rate among the Indians must be improved, so as to cope with the reality of the society around them. Very few Indians graduate from high school, even fewer ever see a college campus.

Today, there are two specifically Indian post-primary educational establishments: Sherman Indian High School in Riverside (a government boarding school established in 1901), and D-Q University in Davis (formerly including Latin American studies). A number of University of California and California State University campuses offer Native American Studies programs in varying strengths, depending on the continual pressure needed to perpetuate them.

Once defeated, grinding poverty was forced upon the Indian, and certain modes of life have not changed for 75 years. (*dhe,* 1979)

Typical of many new Indian health centers around the state is this one in Round Valley, offering medical care and counseling. (*dhe*)

Indian voting rights were validated only as late as 1924, and not without incredible struggle. For 70 years there was not even the right of free speech or assembly on most reservations–the Indian Service (later the Bureau of Indian Affairs) administrators saw to that. Justice and equality for downtrodden people were hardly recognized either.

Fortunately, in these areas there has been remarkable progress in just the last few years. The majority of BIA positions are now staffed by Indian people (although I've heard much grumbling that they are simply white Indians, and "Nobody leaves positions with less than a new car.").

Nevertheless, the reservation and rancheria elected leaders (today called chairpersons or spokespersons) along with the tribal councils, hold considerably increased autonomy over the functions of their respective reservations. Almost half of the chairs are held by women, and most are held by persons who are adamant in securing the financial benefits that are becoming available. It is *still* a struggle to understand the white man's bureaucracy (for all of us!) and to be able to extract from it what one is due. Today's leader is not just a leader of people, but a bureaucrat, alas.

I fear that budget cutting may be used as an excuse to cut back Indian benefits at the state and federal levels, though funds for housing and reservation improvement still seem to be forthcoming to those who have the knowledge of how to probe for them.

Health services to the reservations have *very* slowly grown. Although discontinued in 1955 by the BIA, health services have recently been reintroduced in many areas, usually in conjunction with servicing the needy of all races in the area. A few on-reservation clinics are serviced part-time by nurses or doctors; many communities have instituted nutritional programs–either by "meals on wheels" to invalids, or by busing needful persons to a central dining hall. Nevertheless, some communities refuse to recognize the necessity of aiding their citizens, and much is yet to be done. Of necessity, much Indian family self-help has been forthcoming.

Quite evidently, during the last century's traumatic events, then during the period of recovery in isolated remote places dominated by a white-run bureaucracy, Indian political organization was difficult. It was hard enough just to keep a family together. The great diversity of the California Indian peoples and the petty jealousies perpetuated by outside interests have so far prevented formation of a vigorous unified Indian voice.

At present, organization is numerous primarily in specific interest areas–such as the California Rural Indian Health Programs, Urban Indian Health Projects, numerous Native American Cultural and Indian History Studies groups, U.S. Department of Housing and Urban Development–Office of Indian Programs, the California Indian Education Association offices, Mission Indian Development Corporation, as well as the Inter-tribal Council of California (originally dictated to by the BIA, but today more independent). Such a diversity is confounding, but I have listed these to show that finally, considerable effort is underway (though belated and often wrapped in red tape) to redress the wrongs of two centuries and even more importantly, to restore to mankind an entire people, and much of this effort has been Indian initiated.

Through all of this incredible debasement of a race, somehow there was a will to survive, to perpetuate, even to grow. It seems phenomenal that the strength of these peoples maintained as much of the ancient customs and heritage as did survive. Probably the determined will or cultural remoteness of this civilization allowed it to persist, to regenerate, to exist even today amongst us, around us, without our knowledge.

Modern civilization is so caught up in itself that it pays little attention to the undercurrents in its midst–the minor cultures which continue to propagate in spite of our overall ignorance or uncaring nature. "What? Indians in California?"

If these last several pages seem to the reader to be a chronicle of unmitigated grief and struggle, I have but one thing to say: It is so.

Happy times for the Indian? Far back, maybe now for those not weary or spiritless, but even at the turn of the century, when it was possible to spend a night gaming with friends, simply to spend a few hours in a remote forest, listening and waiting–or to simply fish from a boulder over a rushing stream.

No fear can stand up to hunger, no patience can wear it out, disgust simply does not exist where hunger is; and as to superstition, beliefs, and what you may call principles, they are less than chaff in a breeze. Don't you know the devilry of lingering starvation, its exasperating torment, its black thoughts, its somber and brooding ferocity.

Joseph Conrad, *Heart of Darkness*

It was a wild and desolate canyon, barren and rocky, miles from every human habitation.

A visitor to Ft. Piute in 1866

PART TWO

A Guide to the Early Native Peoples of California and Their Present-day Reservations and Rancherias

(including Educational Institutions and some Archaeological Sites)

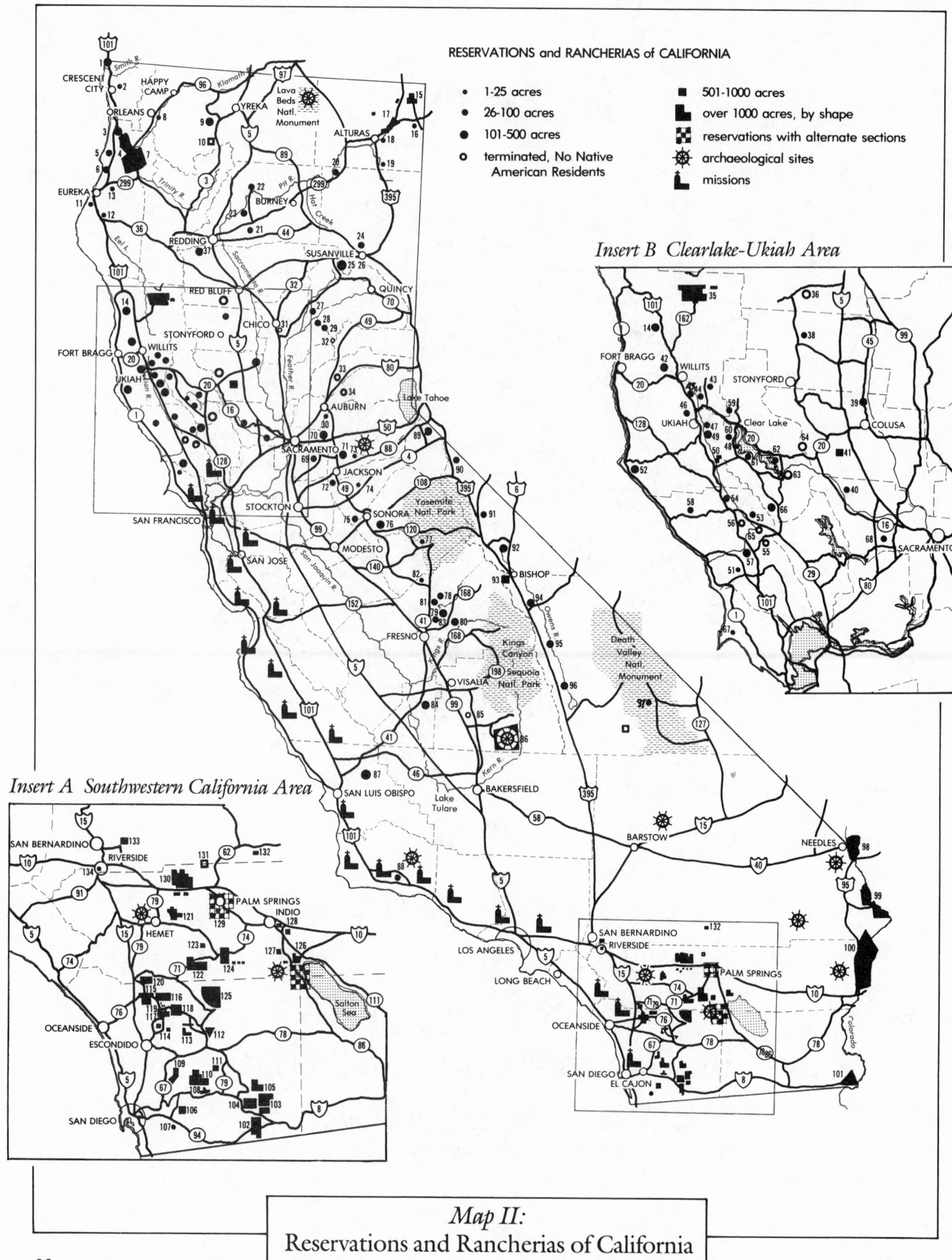

Map II:
Reservations and Rancherias of California

Introduction

ARCHAEOLOGIST, ANTHROPOLOGIST, demographer, sociologist, novelist—these are some of the people who study Native American culture and life. And most accounts by them tend to isolate eras: ancient (pre-1800), 19th century, early 20th century, or modern (but often with earlier settings).

Yet a continuity of time, ancestors, spirit, and customs exists within a people themselves and is not divided as perceived by outsiders. Life is not compartmentalized, separated, or disjointed. Life is continuous, with input from all the senses, as well as from undiscernable and unfelt origins. All of us, of any race, realize this in our own lives, that our own "history" is all that has influenced our lives, not least including our parents and antecedents. Life has a thread, woven into a fabric of other lives. We are not best seen as strings to be examined fiber by fiber.

It is this continuity of native life, though changed, modified, and adapted through the years, that I wish to emphasize in this guide. Here, today, are the descendants of the original native people of California, and here is where they had their origins and history. Here is a brief introduction for the reader of how and where they live.

"I know who I am. Why should I care about people wanting to classify me?" a Pomo elder once asked of me. I could only smile and shrug and wonder if he didn't have a point.

Nevertheless, the native peoples *do* have different origins, and with them a rich variety of customs and histories. To differentiate and sort them out requires some degree of classification.

How to classify is a large question, but fortunately a number of anthropologists and cultural historians have been confronted with the same problems, and a few have proven understanding and sensitive to the human issues involved.

There are several approaches to discussion of the native cultures of California: by language (but often very diverse groups claim a common language), by cultural customs (religion, burials, kinship, etc., but few groups share all customs alike), by organization (but most California groups had little or no "tribal" organization), by biological ancestry or physical characteristics (though adjacent, like-language groups may be quite different).

The discussions in the following pages will include something of all of these; but because this is a guidebook to the present-day Native Americans of California, it is arranged first by section of the state. Often, the environs of a particular region will determine most of the activities of the people there.

Second, you will find discussion of the people of a region, usually by similarity of their traditional *idiomality* (that is, by similar language, which usually indicates the closest kinship between peoples). Exceptions lie in cross-sectional relationships–people in various parts of the state who may be related in one way or another.

Third, the individual entries are arranged by local or tribal affiliation. Further, they are entered in the approximate sequence of a possible regional visit. Map numbers follow tribal affiliation first, then geographical proximity. You may wish to refer first to the maps and the "vocabulary" of denominating California Indian peoples.

To read this section of the book as narrative, simply pass over the reservation directories and proceed to the initial portions of each of the five regional divisions.

A Vocabulary of the Designations of Native Americans of California

People: A group of people speaking a similar language or dialect ("idiomality"). In an older and still popular usage, this is a "tribe."

Tribe or **Band** (sometimes **Colony** or **Community**): The group of people residing in a particular reservation, rancheria, or community. Early usage called this a "tribelet" or village community (up to several villages). Not to be confused with the older term used east of California of "tribe," a usually well-organized people [such as Sioux (Lakota) or Navajo (Diné)].

Chairperson or **Spokesperson** ("chief" or "chieftain" no longer used): Nearly all groups have tribal councils, presided over by a chairperson, spokesperson, or president, whether or not there is a reservation.

Ranchería: A small reservation, normally large enough only for residences and tiny farming plots.

Trust land: Indian land held by the Federal Government (BIA) in "trust," whose Indian residents are technically "wards" of the Government.

Allotted land: Land which is under direct control, often ownership, of an Indian person. It lies within the boundaries of a reservation.

Terminated land: Former trust land that has passed into private ownership. Most of this land has passed into the hands of non-Indian persons. When Indian land is terminated and deeds issued to the resident Indians, they generally lose certain rights normally afforded reservation residents, such as housing assistance, education, tax exemption, health services, utility connections, and certain kinds of welfare and unemployment benefits. Because of gross failure of government agencies to terminate properly and to explain these losses to potential "terminees," a large portion of formerly terminated land has been recently (1984) returned to trust status.

In all parts of this guide, the following system of evaluation is given:

***	Most desirable for a visit in experiencing the "Indianness" of a place. A visitor will gain both historical and present-day knowledge of the site.
**	A place of interest: For a reservation, no museum or public facilities. For an historical site or mission, much Indian character evident.
*	A site of lesser interest: a smaller reservation, a mission with much Indian character gone.
(no symbol)	General access to public visits, but of little interest to the visitor: includes minor rancherias with a character indistinct from that of the locale, historic sites with little Indian character left. Includes terminated lands with nothing of Indian interest, save one's knowledge that once, Indian people lived there. Look around you; blot out the present: imagine, if you can, being there 100 years ago. Terminated lands, whether or not there is an extant native population, are so designated in the text.
PRIVATE	These are very private lands. Respect the privacy of the residents, and do not trespass.

Note: Fifteen of the rancherias terminated and removed from federal control during 1961–70 were totally abandoned and sold. These sites are included for completeness, and for the person who might wish to sense the environment of the Native Californian of earlier decades. They are listed on p. 141 and may be found on Map II: Reservations and Rancherias.

[Throughout the book, numbers in **boldface** type, for instance–**388**, refer to State Historical Landmarks number.]

Northwest

Athapaskan Speakers*
Tolowa
Hupa/Chilula/Whilkut
Mattole
Wailaki/Nongatl/Lassik/Sinkyone/Cahto

Hokan Speakers†
Shasta
Karok
Chimariko

Algic Languages‡
Wiyot
Yurok

FROM THE DAMP Pacific seacoast of dunes and lagoons, through thick redwood forests, up the steep-banked, densely-forested rivers to the 7000-foot Siskiyous and 14,000-foot Mt. Shasta in the east, we pass through the most varied ecological assortment in California.

This ample variety provided a magnanamous bazaar of growing things for food and living–salmon and eels, sea lions (food and pelts), shellfish, shorebirds, seaweed, shore grasses, deer and elk, smelt, redwood and fir (homes and boats), oaks (acorns), marsh waterfowl, and tule rushes.

In the northwest corner of California (mostly in what is now Del Norte County) the Tolowa built huge seagoing, fishing, and trading dugout canoes–30 to 40-footers up to 10 feet wide. Of other California Indians, only the Chumash of the Santa Barbara region had such craft. Here, too, Yurok of the lower Klamath River built river-worthy canoes, so popular that they sold many to the Hupa people upriver.

With the primeval forest at hand, it was only natural that wooden family homes were built by nearly all the peoples of this region. Imagine yourself an explorer of the early 1800s coming upon a northwestern California Indian village. The homes are rectangular, built of well-trimmed planks, with low-pitched gabled roofs, and feature flagstone patios out front. You might guess that this design must have been borrowed from European houses. But no, this design has been with the Tolowa, the Yurok, the Hupa, the Shasta, and others for many hundreds of

* A linguistic stock remotely related to such diverse peoples as the Tlingit (of southeastern Alaska), the Navajo, and the Apache.

† An ancient linguistic stock related to peoples in many parts of the state, possibly even distantly related to groups as far as Sonora and Oaxaca, Mexico. (See also, footnote *, p. 52.)

‡ Sometimes called Ritwan-Algonkian–distantly related to the language of some central and eastern U.S. peoples.

years. The structures are unusual in that they were set below ground level, like a roofed-over basement, but with an odd round hole for the entrance-way. Several homes of this design may be seen today on the Hupa Reservation (see page 49). (Athapaskans to the south didn't construct such elaborate homes: they preferred a plank-covered "tipi"-like structure.)

In the villages over nearly all of northern California could be found a sweathouse. The Indian sweathouse is not a sauna. Made as a separate structure, it is an institution. Smaller than a village dwelling, it has been a male-dominated place that serves many functions. In some ways it is like the *kiva* of the Pueblo peoples, whose central fire is the eye to the earth.

The California sweathouse gives heat for a wholesome sweating, but, far more than that, it is the nerve center–the temple, the meditation room; the seat of inspiration, purification, and resolve for the individual. It is the meeting-house for the decisions of the tribe, the relaxation center for gambling and chatting, a workshop for crafts.

The sweathouse is found not just in California, but earth-oriented California natives made of it more of a tribal institution than other North American peoples. The sweathouse of today is yet such an institution, sometimes liberalized to include women, although even in the earlier years women might be included on certain special or urgent occasions.

At this point I must be careful not to generalize. *Most* villages of the northwest had many features in common, so my descriptions will be of "typical" villages, but bearing in mind that not all peoples or even villages possessed these characteristics.

Around an encampment or village we certainly would have found basketweaving, net-making, and woodworking–the chief vehicles for fine geometric artistry and ornamentation.

Nearly every native culture has a means of expressing art–Eskimos (Inuit) with stone carving, Northwest peoples in woodcarving, Southwest peoples in pottery and sand painting, Plains peoples in beadwork and tent painting. Here, in California's north, the artistic specialty was basketry.

Baskets were, of course, a necessity for holding goods, but here the art was developed in a way that substituted even for pottery! A fine, tight weave was developed that would swell with moisture and create watertight buckets and water bottles. Since pottery or stoneware was not known much north of the Big Sur area, liquids and mush were cooked by dropping hot stones into the basket contents. Other baskets were fashioned to carry everything from seeds to fish. Even woven hats were popular.

The basketmakers didn't stop with technology, which utilized a wide variety of both coiling and twining techniques–their designs are generally conceded as North America's finest. Countless roots and stems and grasses provided an assortment of basic colors and materials, while decoration of beads, bright bird feathers, or shell were inlaid. California Indian baskets have become valuable collectors' items, occasionally to the chagrin of some tribal groups, who find another piece of their heritage dispersed. Nevertheless, even today, the few who practice the art of basketweaving can command high prices for their beautiful art.

Other artists were makers of beadwork, a form of decoration and money. Beads were obtained from a variety of materials: olivella, clam, dentalium, or abalone shells, magnesite (an iron rock), bone, antler, and obsidian. Also the Indian artists designed their finely-colored, feathered headdresses. In California they were generally like wide, flat belts, rather than the eagle feather war bonnets of Plains peoples.

Bandied about the villages were many tales of the unseen spirits. Especially popular were tales of clever Coyote, who mangaged to get himself and humans into much mischief.* Of all the animals of the wild, the coyote became a folk hero. Possibly because of observations on the dual personalities of the canines–at once cautiously friendly and cleverly sneaky. Then he, or his character, the trickster, grew to include those parts of our nature that seem to be forever contradictory or incompatible.

The favorite place for the telling of tales was in the quiet of night by the fire of the roundhouse. Darkness masks distractions and allows the mind to better fashion a reality for phantoms. The roundhouse or dancehouse is the community center–for dancing, storytelling, almost any village meeting. These are the largest structures built by the California Indians and were built according to strict specifications.

The ceremonial dancehouse, with the sweathouse, are the most obvious symbols of the earth-orientation of the California natives. The dancehouse

* Tales of Coyote may be found in the recent book, *The Way We Lived* (ref. 16.).

A Yurok village, Wahsekeo, in 1890, with typical 3-pitched roofs and paved patios. (*St. Pk.*) *above*

An early drawing of hand games, an Indian pastime from ancient times that survives vigorously today. (*St. Pk.*) *top right*

The magnificent artistry and design of California Indian basketry can be seen in this selection. (*St. Pk.*) *middle right*

WPA artist M. Lee here imagines the *Procuring of Fire from the Valley People*, a legend not unlike that of Prometheus of ancient Greece. (*St. Pk*) *lower right*

is sunken into the earth, covered with long beams and branches. In the center is the fire, the opening to the earth's center. Once inside, you are in the womb of the Earth Mother. We can experience this return, since occasional ceremonies are open to the public.*

Another pastime that would sharpen the wits was to haggle. Some northern groups got quite a reputation for this. One topic of great concern would be over the prices for brides – the negotiations being between the prospective husband and the father-in-law-to-be. Such an "arranged" marriage might actually be a result of mutual attraction, although such arrangements may have been rather calculated – for wealth, family or tribal alliances, or some other object of clan advancement.

Violence within a tribe was certainly not productive, and in the California societies intertribal strife was minimal. Territorial disputes were not frequent, since natural boundaries delineated lands very well. Personal confrontations, however, were bound to arise, and resolution could take many forms – bewitching was popular, as was personal revenge. Personal conflict was known to expand into clan feuds, but open warfare was expensive: the winner was expected to pay reparations for dead and injured. Haggling over redress and fines for misdeeds could take years, a shrewd substitute for continued warfare.

When the people weren't fishing or hunting or preparing food or repairing shelter, someone would be playing games of archery, dice, a hand-guessing gambling game (a sort of "which hand?"), or a stick game something like shinny or hockey.

The favorite recreation was, and still is, the deeply psychic hand-guessing games. At almost any Indian gathering, except the most serious, one may expect the drums and chants to begin in the afternoon and not end until late at night, when the best team wins. It goes something like this (with local variations):

Two teams sit facing each other. Their equipment consists of either a log beaten with sticks or a (more modern) skin drum, four short "bones"– two marked with dark rings and the others plain, and ten or twelve playing sticks. The ultimate object is to obtain all the playing sticks, but only through an involved guessing of which hand has the marked bones.

Bets are placed by supporters and members of each team, and each bet from one team must be covered by one from the other side. A bundle containing the bets is tossed into the center. In the old days, beads and other items were bet. Lately, I have seem some "pots" containing $3–4,000; it's pretty obvious people are convinced of their side's powers or chances.

Two persons are chosen to hide the bones, one in each hand, sometimes under a small bundle of grass straws (hence, "grass game"). It is hoped that the hider will have psychic powers strong enough to deflect or confound the powers of the opposite team's guesser. Drumming and chanting begins by the side doing the hiding – their chanting of ancient tunes and songs will help prevent the guessing powers from penetrating the mind of the hider. The chants (always in the old language) are frequently amusing in their insults: "You old bat. You couldn't guess your way – out of a hat."

Later – never sooner, as a single game may last for hours if both teams are evenly matched – one team wins the "pot." I never get tired of watching or betting. Neither do the participants, until their psyches or finances are worn down – usually about dawn.

Each village would require the services of a shaman – the Indian equivalent of doctor, priest, and pharmacist. Often there were two types of curers: an herbalist and a "sucking" doctor, who could suck the "pains" or ills from ailing persons. Various peoples ascribed different functions to their "medicine" persons – but pains or diseases were withdrawn by sucking in highly specialized rituals by specially-inspired shamans. In this region the shaman was usually a woman; but if a male wished shaman powers, he could become a transvestite or "wergern," a socially acceptable role.

Among the Yurok, it is said that young women wished to become doctors in order to become rich. Some shamans could work evil as well, and were often held to account for it. Some things don't change.

Other shamans possessed poisoning or bewitching powers and offered services for a good price. Their services were for revenge of offenses, real or imagined. They were feared, but they were deemed necessary, however unsavory.

Nearly every village held dances. Some were performed in dancehouses, others out-of-doors. Some of the dances were "pleasure" or secular dances; others were highly religious, such as the World-Renewal dances (something like a New Year's Day-Easter ceremony). As do all cultures, the earliest Californians

* See page 98.

Hupa participants in the Jumping Dance, given at a Yurok village in 1893. This dance, and the White Deerskin dance are occasionally performed today, but are never photographed. (Photo by A. W. Erickson, 1893. *St. Pk.*)

The Hupa White Deerskin Dance, one of the most important ceremonies of the Klamath River peoples. (Photo by A. W. Erickson, 1897. *St. Pk.*)

developed religions. Not elaborate, but embodying respect for the life-force, the natural world, and human needs. Even though cultures and tribes were separated by language and geographic divisions, with only slight variations, religious thought and practice was somehow common to very large areas of California and the Northwest. And everywhere the shaman commanded respect as the holder of the supernatural power, the one whose altered state of consciousness could influence the nature of all things.

Dance was a ceremonial method of expressing respect toward nature. Dance was a ritual, a rite. Dance honored the coming of the salmon, it honored the deer, its rites assured the renewal of life. In many places the spirits became personified in the dancers, much as do the Kachinas of the Pueblo and Zuñi peoples. Most prominent of these dances were the Brush Dance, the Jumping Dance, and the White Deerskin Dance, some of which are performed with exquisite care today.

These little villages, seldom of more than 200 persons, were never part of any big "tribal" organizations. There were more like little village-states, and groups held themselves together through kinship ties, common language, and customs.

The countryside is rugged, but the meandering rivers have shaved off numerous flats–places where oaks grow and where a village might sit. They were independent and in harmony with nature and the land; there were no big overlords or threats by powerful peoples, or conquering by power-mad bands–until the white man. Most things have changed now, but a remarkable store of cultural traits remain.

The short stretch of asphalt ended with a bump. Bushy alders of the Klamath River floodplain began to crowd onto and over the black, muddy ruts. Ominous threats to trespassers appeared at the front of little wooden homes dotting the riverbank.

At last I found a long driveway without the now-usual cautions and at the end of the road, a small knot of men were chopping wood and fixing cars. Approaching people like this in their backyards always takes a little boldness, but this time I was apprehensive, considering the events of recent months.

I had arrived on the Resighini Rancheria, the tidewater end of the Hoopa Valley Extension Reservation of the Yurok people. I left my car and hailed the woodcutter, who was splitting logs for smoking his salmon catch. The things he told me left me without questions.

The lower Klamath River, of which Resighini is a part, has frequently been the site of various controversies: over land, fishing, and timber rights, and flood protection. In 1891, an Executive Order supposedly gave Yuroks all the rights to the lower Klamath from the Hoopa Reservation (Trinity River confluence) to the Pacific, with a one-mile jurisdiction on both sides of the river. A glance at any highway map shows this extension,* which is ignored for several miles upstream of the mouth. A glance at the countryside near the mouth shows the beautiful evergreen mountainsides logged, *not* with Indian authorization.

A glance at the rapids east of the mouth shows a large flood diversion levee which protects the white homes on the north shore, but its position endangers by floods the Indian homes on the south bank. A glance at the map *or* highway on the south bank at the mouth shows a state park–land removed from Indian control without authorization from the residents.

Fishing rights are under Indian control? Recently, very small group (two) of local Indians thought they might snatch the entire salmon catch for themselves (without, of course, tribal approval). Federal Fish and Game folks, along with Coast Guard and local lawmen moved in with a large CG cutter, slicing the large nets of the offenders, along with the small ones of the many regular fishers. Small boats were purposely overturned by the wake of the cutter, motors were lost, and when the Indians swam ashore, they were clubbed, along with the cameras of

* See page 47.

The interior of a fisher's home was always more functional than decorative. Here, salmon is smoke-dried over the hearth. Today, salmon is smoked in special enclosed out-houses. (*St. Pk.*)

The Hupa people have meticulously restored several ancient homes in their valley reservation. These cedar slab homes feature a paved patio outside, and a split-level indoors. A carved ladder is used to ascend from the lower fire pit and living space to the upper sleeping deck. The entrance is a round hole, and the cracks serve as chimney. (*dhe,* 1980)

newspeople on hand to film this safeguarding of the white man's fishing privilege. Eventually the Feds apologized. This happened in *nineteen* seventy-eight. Finally, in 1984, federal courts restored Yurok control of fishing rights on the Klamath.

So, indeed, two greedy adventurers sullied the sport and livelihood of some whites *and* Indians, including Yuroks, Hupas, Karoks, and even the Achúmawis far upstream (who were properly incensed). But it was the Feds who assumed control over an Indian problem. Let me repeat what one of the Resighini fishermen, friendly though adamant, told me: Non-Indian tourists are not welcome at Resighini itself.

East of the docks and lumberyards of Crescent City, I searched for the terminated Elk Valley Rancheria and found the few homes that are its remnants. Knocking at random upon a door, I asked the older gentleman who answered for a little information about the place. The hesitancy and suspicion in his face and voice told me that he thought I was a government man. Suddenly his mood changed, "Come on in, I've got something to say to you." And I received an outpouring of emotion – warm, touching, yet stirred by anger. He and his wife told me of his being removed from his grandfather's land so that a state park might "preserve" it; they told me of a string of lawyers who came bearing tales of how no Indian rights would be lost on termination* – but they lost medical, educational, welfare rights, and, most importantly, land tenure; they told me of little or no help from federal or state agencies for improving their sewer connections (without which the county could take their land from them). He is disabled, having worked all his life in lumbering. I was told by an agency in Sacramento that some help (determination and allied benefits) is coming. When?

The Trinity River Valley is a secluded one, and was undisturbed by outsiders until 1850, with gold discovery. Nevertheless, I was amazed to find many of the village and settlement sites within the 12-mile square of the Hoopa Valley Reservation to have been in continuous habitation for up to seven thousand years – not in the fashion of the permanent pueblos of the Southwest, but in the manner of the semi-subterranean wooden homes and dancehouses of northern and central California.

The people of the reservation have kept or restored a number of original homesites along the Trinity River: among them Ta'kimildin, a religious center, a mile north of the town of Hoopa; Medildin, a residential and now, ceremonial site; and Djistanadin, a residential site [spellings variable]. There were twelve of these villages. Vestiges of eleven remain. At the restored sites there are four or five structures typical of this region. Unlike the rounder homes further east and south, the Hupa and their neighbors built rectangular homes of hand-hewn planks, covered with sloping planks, much like the standard clapboard home of modernity. Outside the front entrance we find a stone terrace, and paving stones are also used in other places likely to become muddy.

* See page 34.

Inside, however, I lost the feeling of being in a "modern" home. The entrance is a small round hole to afford easy entrance to the almost-basement room inside. The room itself is a sort of cellar for living area and hearth, with an earthen deck around all four sides for sleeping.

At the Medildin site are two types of homes: those for women and girls, while the others are sweathouses for men only. Outside are several work tables for the daily chores and an open dance pit for ceremonies.

Exploring the villages gave me a profound feeling of "being there," though without people about, I had to synthesize my visions of old photographs with the reality at hand. The whoosh of the wind from the sharp evergreen tips on the mountainsides with the quiet gurgle of the river easily draws one back in time.

In a most unusual move, the members of the Karok people living in the rugged mountains of the middle Klamath River Valley have bought seven acres of land for a reservation for themselves. Their thin, wiry chairman shared with me some of their enthusiasm for the new projects: not only have the people themselves provided their reservation, they have also built a spacious community center with a grant from the Presbyterian Church. The center is shared with non-Indian groups from the town of Orleans.

Homes are being provided on this small, new reservation for some of the 450 Karoks of the region who have never had a reservation, or even a center of their own until now.

In Happy Camp, some 45 miles upriver, the Karok Tribe, Inc., has been organized to provide a center for the nearly 700 native people of that portion of the river. I found here a most unusual spirit of industriousness among the leaders of the center. I learned there are both basket weaving and Indian dance classes (public) as part of a wide-ranging Karok cultural program. Here, too, it is planned that deeds to ten acres will be secured for homesites and a cultural center to house a million-dollar Karok collection being kept at the Smithsonian Institution in Washington, D.C. Happy Camp is earning its name with the Karok people.

Traveling along the river highway near Soames Bar, I found that several sacred Indian sites have been marked—an ancient ceremonial area and spiritual trails among them.

The middle Klamath is a truly spiritual region—it is isolated, with few roads, many forests, and much solitude. (Along the river's edge is one of the few places in California where it is nearly impossible to pick up even a radio signal in the daytime.) The isolation seems to have been a benign protection for this people.

Although not greatly upset by gold miners of the last century, the people have had some trouble preserving their sacred sites (such as Titus Ridge and the Clear Creek dance area) from desecration by lumbering.

Many persons of the modern world have lost touch with the sanctity of natural places, having acquired some sort of edifice complex. A sacred site is not recognizable as such unless it has had some "constructive improvement" made upon it.

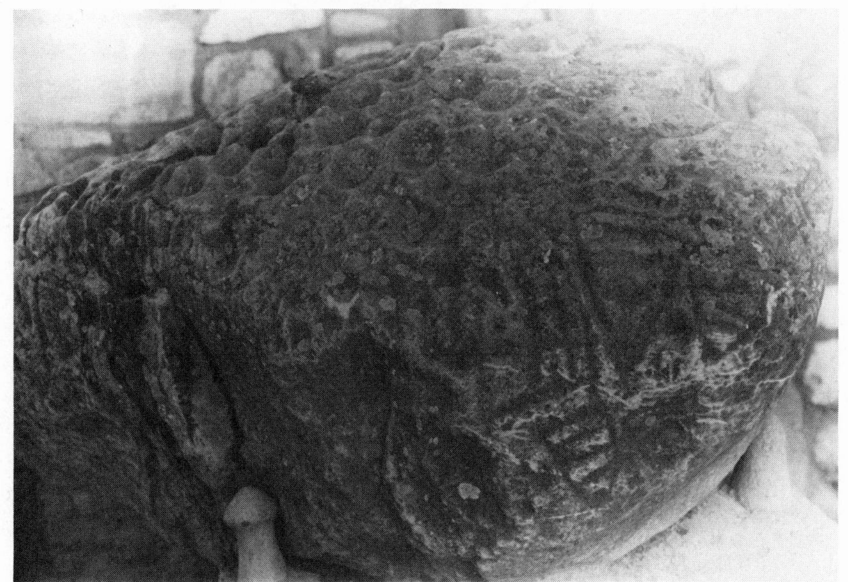

This large, pitted stone in Ft. Jones is called variously a "rain rock" or a "baby rock." As a rain rock, it was recently covered by a local Indian shaman, who was hoping to stem the torrents of rain then falling. In times of drought, the holes are filled with water. As a baby rock, the cavities are intended as a sort of multiple female symbol, to be used in fertility ceremonials. Supporting the rock are phallic "charmstones," also used in fertility rites. (*dhe,* 1978)

Yreka is a three-county (Siskiyou, Humboldt, Del Norte) center for the Indian Youth Guidance group, as well as for other cultural activities of the Shasta and other peoples living in the Yreka area. Though this is traditional Shasta country, the people have had only one tiny reservation, Quartz Valley, and that now is essentially Karok. The remnants of this people reside in private homes scattered about Siskiyou Co.; their dispersion and near-extinction as a culture is almost complete.

A visitor may inquire of local Shasta activities at the Native American Center in the town. Here an Indian counselor looked at me and said, "The white man brought alcohol, guns, and the wheel . . . None have been much good to Indians *or* the white man."

Several Indian peoples of this immediate region have never had a reservation "home." For some, their people were nearly annihilated before reservations were set up; with others, the few survivors were gathered in and intermixed with other peoples on reservations. Finally, a number of families remain to this day on private holdings scattered about the small towns and dense forests, especially along the Mattole, Eel, and Van Dusen Rivers.

Only loose family ties, rather than Indian or tribal affairs, hold these people together. And owing to the scatter, most of the old ways are fast-disappearing. As one elder of Rohnerville told me, his mother was the last of his family to have medicine powers, and she knew of the hour of her death days earlier.

The peoples of this region, the Athapaskan "Eel River tribes" and others, include the *Mattole* [Mä-tōl'], *Sinkyone, Lassik, Nongatl,* and *Chimariko.* The *Wailaki* survive in a few families at Round Valley Reservation, some miles east.

In the remote forest along the Eel River east of Garberville, you can find an unusual intertribal group. It meets nearly every month in the local Grange Hall for dances, bingo, food, and local concerns. This group is the X-IT [Crossing of Indian Tribes] Indian Organization, c/o Mr. Wayne Stillwell, P.O. Box 197, Alderpoint, CA 95411. (707) 926-5272.

Northwest California place names derived from Indian sources (translations may be only approximate):

Wiyot Talawa (a Wiyot name for the Tolowa people), Weott (the Wiyot name for the Eel River delta), Mattole ("clear water")

Yurok Klamath, Orick (place names), Weitchpec (from *wé-itspūs*, "meeting of the waters," i.e., the Trinity and Klamath Rivers), Requa (*rék-woi*, "creek mouth"), Hoopa (a Yurok name for the Hupa people)

Wintu Wailaki (a Wintu name for their western neighbors)

Karok Pick-aw-ish (the sacred place of Clear Creek)

Shasta Shasta (from *chasta*, a name of unknown origin)

Pomo Cahto ("swampy lake")

Estimated populations of the Northwest California peoples before 1830:*

Mattole 1,200 / Wailaki 2,800 / Nongatl 2,300 / Lassik 1,400 / Sinkyone 4,200 / Bear River 1,300

Hupa *ca.* 1,000 / Chilula 500–600 / Whilkut *ca.* 500

Tolowa 1,000
Cahto 1,100
Shastan (4 groups) *ca.* 3,000
Karok 2,700
Chimariko *ca.* 250
Wiyot 1,000–3,000
Yurok 2,500–3,000

Northwest Reservations and Rancherias

This Shaker Church on the Smith River Rancheria (Tolowa) is one of the few left in the Western United States. Shaker worship, with a strong Pentecostal and spiritual flavor, was often attractive to the California Indian religious temperment. (*dhe,* 1979)

* **Smith River Rancheria** *Tól-o-wa* and *Yúrok.* (1908) Del Norte Co.

In the far northwestern corner of California, the salmon run twice a year. In the old, old days, the rivers were fished only by the Indian; today there are others who fish also, but the salmon are still caught by the descendants of the early Tolowa and Yurok natives. The homes, at the edge of the sea, look out upon the windswept, offshore, rocky islands of the Pacific.

On the 160-acre rancheria are a 1929 Shaker church and a well-kept burial ground, where the sounds of surf and wind in the pine and fir quiet the soul. The Tolowas here are the remnants of a coastal people whose original lands included the extreme of northwestern California as far south as Crescent City and north to southwestern Oregon.

In the town is Guscha Hall, a community center serving both the local Indians and non-Indians as a nutrition center. There are daily van pickups for several older persons of the area, as far as 10 miles off.

1 *In Smith River, Mouth of Smith River Rd., to South Indian Rd., right in a loop via North Smith River.*
Smith River Rancheria
Box 82
Smith River, CA 95567

* The numbers given here and in other sections are early estimates, and they are doubtless low. They are presented to show the relative populations of various groups.

Elk Valley (Crescent City) Rancheria *Tolowa* and *Yurok*. (1909) Del Norte Co.

The rancheria is a small, mostly wooded plot with three Indian families living on five or six parcels. Its inhabitants have not been spared great problems (see p. 43).

2 *From Crescent City, take Elk Valley Rd., about 2 mi. to Norris Ave. east to its end.*
Elk Valley Rancheria
260 Norris Ave.
Crescent City, CA 95531

Resighini Rancheria *Yurok*. (1938) Del Norte Co. PRIVATE

The Yuroks have always been fishers. They still are. The salmon on the Klamath run two or three times a year, but the fishers are out year-round–the Yuroks have nominal control over the lower Klamath fishing. Much of the Yurok catch is dried in little smoke sheds for their own consumption, but some salmon "jerky" is sold in shops along Highway 101 at the rancheria.

Resighini [its 228 acres named for an early French settler] smoulders over white interventions in its lower Klamath homelands. Consequently, non-Indian visitors are not welcome on the reservation lands proper. However, in the exceptionally beautiful and historic Indian village of Requa, an entrance to Redwoods National Park and the north-shore river mouth, there are several tourist facilities, including a boat launching ramp.

3 *South shore of the mouth of the Klamath where U.S. 101 crosses it. Better to visit Requa on the north shore road and view the entire Klamath mouth from the Park road.*
Resighini Rancheria
P..O. Box 212
Klamath, CA 95548
(707) 482-3371

Hoopa Extension Reservation *Yurok*. (1891) Humboldt Co. *

Although the large Hoopa Reservation (see p. 49) was established for the Hupa, Chilula, and Whilkut peoples of the Trinity/Klamath region in 1864, the Yuroks were generally not included because of the traditional antipathy between Hupa and Yurok, and because that region was originally not Yurok. Yuroks won recognition of much of their ancestral land in 1891 (see also Resighini Rancheria, above), but it perversely bears the name of their southerly neighbors and is administered from the town of Hoopa.

The reservation is rather large (7,028 acres), rich in timber and a scenery of forest and rivers. Originally, it occupied a mile either side of the Klamath, from its confluence with the Trinity to the Pacific, but that has been whittled away to a fraction of that portion of the river. The whole stretch is dotted with small settlements, some in continuous habitation for more than a thousand years. A ceremonial center is near Weitchpec, where an outdoor arena on a beautiful riverbank setting is used on special occasions such as the famous Brush Dance in mid-October. The other Yurok center of activity is around Requa and the Resighini Rancheria.

4 *Tribal offices in Hoopa, but the reservation extends for some 20 miles down the north-flowing Klamath to Johnson's on a local paved road off State Rt. 96 from Weitchpec. Or, approach via Redwood National Park from Orick over a dirt road.*
Hoopa Extension Reservation
P.O. Box 1348
Hoopa, CA 95546
(916) 625-4691

PRIVATE **Big Lagoon Rancheria** *Yurok.* (1918) Humboldt Co.

The ocean, in its ceaseless effort to sculpt the shore, many centuries ago formed the sand bar creating Big Lagoon. The still, brackish, black water is a perfect place for settlement–an abundance of fish and shellfish, birds, tule, evergreen forest, and fresh water.

Apparently, a band of early coastal Yuroks found this perfect also, because for several centuries the village of 'Oketey has been here. A couple of families reside there now, maintaining privacy on their 9 acres. The north shore of this lagoon is spoiled by a lumber company presence, but the side seaward of U.S. 101 is idyllic.

To visit the lagoon is to experience the ambience of an ancient coastal village, an example of a type that once dotted this entire coast. (Tsurai and Smith River remain, but are greatly changed.)

5 *Roundhouse Creek Rd. from U.S. 101 to Lynda Lane will pass near the rancheria, but do not take the roads beyond. The setting of the quiet rancheria may be viewed from a short distance from U.S. 101, on the south shore of the lagoon.*
Big Lagoon Rancheria
Orick, CA 95555

Old Tsurai, a Yurok fishing village nestled under the town of Trinidad, is today marked by a brass plaque. The new rancheria with a well-equipped new health center, is located on a high cliff just left of this 1900 photo. (*St. Pk.*)

* **Tsurai (Trinidad) Rancheria** *Yurok.* (1917) Humboldt Co.

Trinidad Head is a "natural" place for settlement–it has a well-protected harbor, numerous fishing sites, fresh water, and plenteous forests, supporting both game and plants. The original site of Tsurai (Churey) in the town of Trinidad is even commemorated by State Landmarks plaque **838**, which mentions the first contact with whites here in 1775, by Spanish Captains Bodega and Heceta.

Today the 44-acre rancheria is a tidy seacliffside community, with a beautiful new health center and tribal offices building. Health centers such as this provide health care not only to residents of the rancheria, but to other off-reservation Indian families in the area, and often to needy non-Indians as well.

6 *From U.S. 101, west at Trinidad exit, and then first major road (the coast road) south about 1 mile to a road (opposite a rocky island) leading up the slope to the new building of offices and health center.*
Trinidad Rancheria
P.O. Box AA
Trinidad, CA 95570
(707) 677-0211

Hoopa Valley Reservation *Hupa, Whilkŭt, Chilula, Yurok.* (1864) Humboldt Co. ∗∗∗

The Hoopa Valley Reservation, at 86,728 acres, is the largest reservation in California, both in size and population. It is also the only one that can come anywhere near adequately supporting its people with its resources, which consist mainly of timber, some fishing, and some farming.

The people residing here are not just Hupa from the Trinity River Valley, but also peoples of the Klamath River, Redwood Creek, and other tributaries of the region–brought here in the 1860s from Whilkut, Chilula, Chimariko, and Yurok territories. It is said that there probably are few purely Hupa people left, because the amalgamation with the other area peoples has been so complete.

Numerous ancient village sites may be visited (see p. 43), and I unhesitatingly recommend this reservation as one of the valuable places to gain a feel for native living today and yesterday. On the reservation are a fine rodeo grounds, campgrounds for visitors, a very informative Indian museum, a complete health care center, schools, and a new tribal office center, whose low, wide, brown architecture is in harmony with the early structures of the region.

Here also are some of the buildings of old Fort Gaston (see also p. 163)–some now occupied by the BIA, others by various governmental agencies. An old adobe fort building of 1853 is preserved–and even General Ulysses S. Grant was reportedly stationed here in the 1850s, before establishment of the reservation. The fort was built because of frequent hostilities between the Army and the natives which lasted until 1892.

7 *From Willow Creek on State Rte. 299, take State Rte. 96 twelve miles through the spectacular Trinity River gorge into Hupa Valley.*
Hoopa Valley Reservation
P.O. Box 1348
Hoopa, CA 95546
(916) 625-4691

Orleans Karok Reservation *Karok* [Kā́-räk or Kā́-rook]. (1977) Orleans, Humboldt Co. ∗

Karok Tribe, Inc. Happy Camp, Siskiyou Co. ∗

The Orleans Reservation is a small, 7-acre space, bought by the Karok people and given over as trust land. A community center and several homes are also results of the people's efforts to raise their own well-being and preserve their culture (see p. 44).

The other center of Karok activity is presently centered in Happy Camp (10½ acres), where enthusiastic persons are building a new future for their people by administering funds for education, housing, and cultural activities. As of this writing, other tribal areas are in litigation.

8 *In Orleans, the reservation is just east of the Klamath River bridge on State Rte. 96. In Happy Camp, the Karok center is in a downtown area.*

Orleans Karok Council
P.O. Box 265
Orleans, CA 95556

Happy Camp Karok Council
P.O. Box 1098
Happy Camp, CA 96039
(916) 493-5305

Quartz Valley Reservation. *Karok* and *Shasta.* (1937) Siskiyou Co.

A few Karok and Shasta people live on this de-terminated land, which was originally designated for Shastan people. The reservation is located in a rather dry, remote valley of the Scott River, adjacent to the Marble Mountain Wilderness (near Fort Jones). The Karoks here are active in the Happy Camp Karok councils.

9 *From Fort Jones, take the road toward Hamburg. About 8 miles out, go toward Mugginsville. The site is about 2 miles further, just before the second crossing of Shackleford Creek. There is very little to see, but I recommend camping in the neighboring Marble Mountain Wilderness Area to give one a feel for the nature of the Shastas' ancestral lands.*

* **Table Bluff Rancheria.** *Wiyot* [Wē-ott]. (1908) Humboldt Co.

The embers of Wiyot culture glow in these tiny acres, set on an open, foggy, and windswept terrace above the Pacific Ocean. It is amazing that they do at all, for it was the Wiyots, with two other groups, who were nearly wiped out by the 1860 massacre on Indian [Gunther] Island in Eureka.

The homes on this isolated, grassy plain are small, old, and rather austere, occasionally protected by windrows of low trees. I saw no evidence of governmental housing help. Plans are alive for a regional Indian museum on Indian Island.

11 *South of Eureka about 10 miles, take Hookton Rd. exit off U.S. 101 (in the direction of Humboldt Co. Beach Park) to Indian Reservation Rd.*

Table Bluff Rancheria
P.O. Box 519,
Loleta, CA *95551*
(707) 733-5537

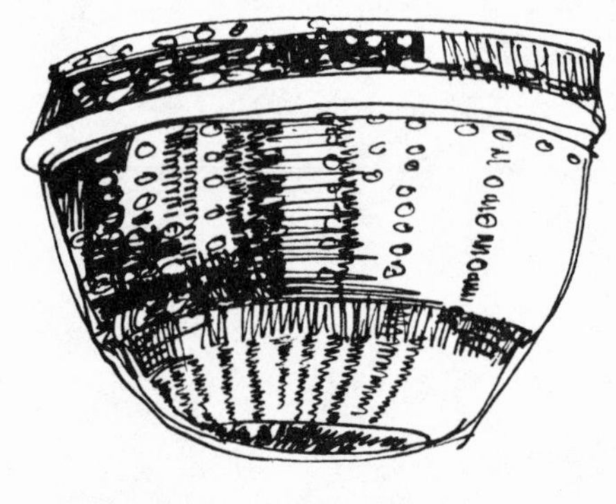

Rohnerville Rancheria [originally] *Wiyot.* (1910) Humboldt Co.

Although terminated in 1958, three families still reside here. According to one resident, he prefers to be called a member of the Eel River tribes–a term which would include a number of the Athapaskan peoples to the south (upriver).

The homes of the rancheria are very tidy, with gardens and orchards, and sit on a bluff in the shade of tall redwoods.

12 *From Fortuna, access is from Rohnerville Rd. to the south entrance of Loop Rd. Go east ¼ mile up a zig-zag road to the top of the bluff.*

Blue Lake Rancheria *Wiyot.* (1908) Humboldt Co.

I found only one family living here now–the original 26 acres have been bought out almost entirely by non-Indians. The residential area is rather chaotic-looking, with many mobile homes and small houses, although this countryside along the Mad River is attractive in its tree-covered low-mountain greenery. Nevertheless, a dozen lumber mills don't improve the scenery. Blue Lake was terminated in 1958, but is once again in federal trust.

13 *From the center of Blue Lake, take Chartin Rd. southwest several blocks to Rancheria Rd.*

Laytonville Rancheria *Cahto* [Käto] and *Pomo.* (1908) Mendocino Co.

This little enclave of 200 acres holds the remnants of a small band of people of the Coast Range, linguistically related to the Eel River tribes. It is located in their original territory of lightly-forested interior mountains and valleys.

On the rancheria, a quiet hillside cemetery overlooks the Cahto Creek valley community of some remodeled homes, wide yards and trees, but most interesting of all, a new dancehouse of slab bark on wood stands in the center of the village. I believe this signifies a definite rekindling of interest in the old ways, in a cultural revival and renewed sense of being Indian.

14 *From U.S. 101 in Laytonville, take Branscomb Rd. west through a left "S" turn, then a slow westward turn, about 2 miles. The rancheria is on the south, as the road straightens.*

Laytonville Rancheria
P.O. Box 1239
Laytonville, CA 95454
(707) 984-6197.

A Wiyot woman, basket weaving in the dunes near Eureka. (Photo by A. W. Erickson, 1900. *St. Pk.*)

Northeast

Hokan Speakers*
Pit River Bands
including Atsugewi (Hat Creek)
Yana-Yahi

Penutian-Speaking Groups†
Maidu
Konkow (Northwestern Maidu)
Nisenan (Southern Maidu)

Lutuamian Language Family‡
Modoc

Shoshonean Speakers§
Northern Paiute (Paviotso)
Bannock

THE MODOC PLATEAU covers a large part of northeastern California. It is a high, relatively flat expanse, ranging around 3,000–5,000 feet in altitude, but sharply sculpted by a few rivers, lava beds, long spines of mountains that form the lower Cascades and the northern Sierra Nevada. Occasional spectacular volcanic cones such as Crater Peak, Crater Mountain, and Lassen Peak rise like pencil points held under a black sheet.

For the most part it is cold in winter and cool in summer. Pines and fir cover the loose soil where they can find a foothold. The meandering rivers are frequently arrested by natural dams, forming swamps and marshes that support waterfowl, fish, and grasses. Not many oaks, that staple source of so many other California peoples, are found in these upland meadows—the territory of the Modoc (of the lava beds), the eleven Pit River bands (often called Achúmawi), the Atsugewi (of Hat Creek and Dixie Valley), and the Maidu (of the upper Feather River).

Along the western edges of the Plateau lie the down-slopes toward the Central Valley—a region of fairly dry, rugged foothills, scratched by creeks flow-

* See footnote †, Northwest, p. 36.

† Penutian language stock comprises a large group of central and northern California languages. It is likely that its origin was in California.

‡ A group of languages spoken by people to the north—Modoc, Klamath, and eastern Washington peoples.

§ Part of a large family of Uto-Aztecan languages used by peoples of southern California, the Great Basin, the Comanches, and even the Aztecs of Mexico. (See footnote †, So. Cal., p. 105.)

ing down to the flat floor of the Sacramento River Valley. The groups seeking the water of the streams and the oaks of the flats along them were the Yana, the Konkow, the Nisenan, and the Yahi (Ishi's tribe).

Over the Warner Mountains and the northern Sierra peaks on the far eastern border lies the country of the Northern Paiute (or Paviotso). That desiccated terrain called the Great Basin was their land. The Paiute, although not part of what the anthropologists like to call "California culture," were (and are) to be found all up and down that imaginary line that separates California from Nevada. The Paiute, like their Shoshone cousins, were nomadic, as one must be when food supplies are sparse.

It was necessary to spend much time in the daily tasks of preparing for winter. Dwellings, then, were only the most temporary wickiup of arched branches covered with brush. Dancing and dances were seldom. There was kinship with sky and father, unlike the "Californians," whose more sedentary spirits felt more directed toward earth and mother.

Up on the high plateau where the forests and marshes provided sustenance and the life was tranquil (except for occasional outbreaks of intertribal hostilities), the people wove nets for fishing, but made few canoes, because the water is usually quite rapid. As almost everywhere in California, the people demonstrated their artistic powers in arrow points, woven baskets, and feathered ornaments.

In this cold climate, however, they differed from others in collecting root and tuber species (from the marshes) for winter storage and in fashioning articles of fur and skins. In fact, the Pit River got its name from the local Indians' method of trapping deer–digging a pitfall.

Over all this land Lassen Peak stands sentinel–it is at the "corner" of several peoples' territories–the Atsugewi, the Yana, the Maidu. In its active days it must have been truly a religion-inspiring phenomenon.

Dwellings on the plateau needed to be strong against the cold winds, but not so elaborate against the rain as in the northwest. For this, it was convenient to make an insulated house of cedar bark or slab strips, laid in a conical "tipi" shape. However, other less substantial structures might be built of brush, tule, or thatch for a temporary summer shelter, a fishing blind, or a hot weather sun-shelter. A few Yana and most Maidu and Konkow people preferred an earth-covered semi-subterranean home, especially for those who dwelt down at lower elevations.

The other peoples in geographically northeastern California dwelt at or near the alluvial fans of the eastern Sacramento River valley–the places where Sierra streams began levelling out onto the plain. These consisted of some bands of Yana and Yahi, some of the Konkow people, and the Nisenan, leading lives somewhat different from their more mountainous kin.

The climate here is warmer, the ecology different, as were the foodstuffs; moreover, food was available year-round. Seasonal harvesting obviously was necessary, especially for the acorn, grass, and herb crops that came from the summer-dry lower plains, and the salmon that ran in the spring.

In this region of the margins of the plains and mountains, game was abundant–deer, antelope, elk, even an occasional black bear. Grizzlies, however, were respected through fear of their size and ferocity. Many tribes paid their deference to this largest of native California mammals in their Bear Dance.

One other common practice of valley and plains peoples (common, because of abundance) was to have grasshopper and cricket roundups. Dried, these insects (and many others) made a healthy, tasty (?), and easily available food source that can be stored for long periods. Modern man might consider taking advantage of this potential food source. After all, the not unsimilar shrimp and lobster are delicacies.*

The peoples of northeastern California were not too different from those of the northwesterners in their abilities and desires to exhibit their artistry in handiwork. Their legends, myths, tales, and medicinal practices, likewise were similar, but seldom identical, to other central and northern California peoples. Those who heard the tales say that Coyote, for instance, was downright lewd, and the myths were more storylike and less tied to ethics.*

It is said that the people of this region respected ability and personal attainment, and paid much less obeisance to wealth and position than some northwesterners, for example, the Yurok. Perhaps this is because these bands were required to move about more for their subsistence, so accumulating things would have become a burden.

It was *via* the Paiute people that an unusual religous

* A number of Central Valley peoples were also accustomed to dig for several varieties of grubs, roots, and insects. For this reason, an early term "Digger" was applied to them by squeamish whites. This term carries the same derogatory effect that its rhyme does when applied to blacks.

movement came to the California peoples–the Ghost Dance. Ghost Dance began as a dream by a Nevada Paiute, Wovoka, in which ancient Indian spirits would return to earth, the whites would disappear, and Indians with Ghost shirts would be effectively protected from bullets.

The illusions were a last hope. As the Ghost Dance idea moved through the rapidly declining and discouraged California peoples, it picked up characteristics of Kuksu (see p. 9), infusing it with an almost Pentecostal character. It was a lost hope. It died when the dreamt-of salvation of the natives failed to occur.

A Pomo woman and her children of Ukiah Valley holding their meal of roasted caterpillars, a high-protein delicacy. (Photo by S. A. Barrett, 1904. *Lowie*) *top left*

Mrs. Lizzie Enos (right), and friends (Maidus) preparing acorn mush in the old way, 1958. The acorns are ground, the tannin leached out, then the mush cooked with preheated rocks placed inside the basket. (*St. Pk.*) *right*

Women of Great Basin tribes digging for roots or grubs. Pioneers considered this practice "nasty," and called the foothills tribes "Diggers." It isn't difficult to perceive their analogy. (Early 20th cent. photo. *St. Pk.*) *lower right*

Once upon a time, the beautiful, mountain-locked meadow-valley named "Indian" was a Maidu valley. After the whites came, there were two rancherias of about 375 acres—Greenville and Taylorsville. Since 1966, one of the reservation lands has disappeared, but not the Maidu. The valley is mostly farmland and ranches, with a sawmill of the Louisiana-Pacific Lumber Co. furnishing most of the local employment to white and Indian alike.

One evening I met Tommy Merino, organizer for Plumas Co. Indian Association. He told me some of the problems of his people, many of which stem from the difficulty of getting recognition, not as Indians, not as needy persons, but as a tribe. His dislike for the bureaucracy of BIA and Indian Health Service (IHS) isn't unique, but it sure is there. Case-in-point: At an IHS conference, it was claimed that some 18,000 California Indians were "officially" recognized. At the same time, then-Governor Jerry Brown recognized approximately 212,000! Case-in point: Special educational efforts are provided for about 100 Indian children of Plumas Co. In reality, about 200 need it and should qualify.

Mr. Merino knows that when Gen. Custer was leaving the fort for Little Big Horn, he gave himself a grand parade, lining up officials from the BIA on one side of the parade ground, the other side with IHS bureaucrats. Rearing back on his horse, just as he departed, he roared, "Now remember, don't do *anything* until I get back!" His instructions are still being followed.

The center of Maidu activity in Indian Valley is on Old Taylorsville Rd., four miles east of Greenville, at a place called the "Indian Mission," on the land of an old boarding school, now church-owned and Indian-occupied.

At a modern, new building housing the tribal offices, I found that I was with a group of people raising themselves from a century of neglect. Not only are the administrative offices here, but also a large dining room and nutrition center, and Indian education classrooms. During my visit, a door was opened for me—inside was a blackboard with strange phonetic characters on it, a nearly bare table, and at the table, an elderly lady, writing down as many words in Maidu (the blackboard characters) as she could remember. It's a part of a broad project of the Maidu people to

A Maidu camp at Indian Valley, Plumas Co., about 1900. The dancehouse and home are their adaptation to a new life using the available materials, shakes and shingles. (*St. Pk.*)

recover and sustain as much of their cultural heritage as possible. Even the once-terminated Greenville Rancheria has been brought back into trust status.

In a light December snowfall, I wandered among the wood slab-marked graves of the ancient hillside burial ground, listening to the spirits, watching the flakes fill the sky above the flat valley floor, as though it were the smoke of a hundred village fires of 150 years ago.

A few miles away in the shade, in an enveloping and protecting pine forest, the Forest Service says it "protects" the decaying slabs of the fallen roof of Satkimi Watum Kūmhu, an ancient Maidu dancehouse and an adjacent sweathouse. These sites were once the center of life for the band who dwelt on the wide, green meadow that is now Quincy.

Further to the north, Pit River country is among the most varied of any in California–from Mt. Shasta to desert, with forest, lava beds, and swamps in between. Present-day Achumawi land is, of course, only a fraction of that, but much of it is picturesque. No amount of picturesqueness, however, can support life without good land and water. For example, the X-L Ranch Reservation doesn't have much of either, except in the upper headwaters of the Pit River.

Here the high, dry hills are covered with scrub oak and pine, capped with lava flows like the spines of huge, fossil dinosaurs spread over 8,000 acres. Six separate parcels are highly dispersed about the countryside north of Alturas. The homes are likewise dispersed, and they belong to no less than eleven bands [tribelets] of the Pit River [Achumawi] people.

Actually, the name "Achúmawi" derives from only one of these bands, but the entire people have been so designated. This is analogous to the fact that Holland is really only one province of The Netherlands.

It is unfortunate, but one finds some divisiveness among the Pit River people–at least in their organizing. I heard descriptions of "legitimate" Pit River people, "usurping" Hat Creeks, "illegal" Wintus, etc. The kinship of being Indian hasn't yet caught on. Old tribal rivalries and regional antagonisms remain. Or, perhaps, when a people are so beaten down, there are few alternatives to hitting on one another.

Deep in a Shasta County pine forest, by a turbulent tributary of the Pit River called Roaring Creek, lives one family on a self-sufficient rancheria farm–with pond, geese, cows, pigs. Some income is derived from repairing cars. Once overseeing all this was Mr. Raymond Lego, a fiercely independent man, uncommonly knowledgeable about legal and tribal history. To ask him "how things are" was to trigger a flood of tales of bureaucratic cajoling for him to terminate the family rancheria. All efforts were unsuccessful. Mr. Lego died recently, but passed his spirit on to his family.

Unless you are Native American or your car needs fixing, I wouldn't advise dropping in for a visit. Much bitterness endures against acquisitive whites.

However, not far up the road is the site of the Pit River Indian land claims movement, where concerned visitors are welcome. In 1938 some 9,000 acres of these forested lands were set aside for Indian lands, but the Pacific Gas & Electric Co. has been attempting to grab it for timber. PG & E already has control of the local water for hydroelectric purposes. The organizers of the movement to reclaim the land appreciate help. If any readers wish to assist the movement, write the Rancheria (p. 61). The local trailer headquarters, located in a clearing near the road, has sometimes been removed by PG & E, as this is land in active conflict.

Burney, a little mountain town, is the center of Indian administrative activity for most of the local Pit River peoples' tribal offices on an 80-acre plot. Several of the neighboring rancherias are officially (BIA) designated Pit River land, but to the BIA, "Pit River" includes the northern "Achúmawi" bands and the southern Atsúgewi (Hat Creek) groups. In reality, though, these are two somewhat different groups with markedly individualistic attitudes.

The Atsugewi have never had a real reservation for themselves. They live on their own land parcels alongside Hat Creek, three to four miles south of the town of Hat Creek, on the east side of State Rte. 44. One place for gatherings is a Protestant church camp in that area, lodged amongst huge piles of crumpled lava.

Hat Creek itself meanders through open meadows of dairy pastures, flowing northward from the black slopes of Lassen volcano, an Indian sacred place, shared by Atsugewi, Maidu, Pit River, and Yana.

The Yana, a people just to the south of the Pit River and west of Mt. Lassen, have ceased to exist as a culture. The last of the independent-minded Yana, a band of Yahi, fled to the bush in 1865. Hounded by whites, they were killed or captured, one by one, until the last of their band, Ishi, surrendered to the Butte County sherrif in 1911.

Ishi was taken to San Francisco, where, at the University of California, he taught whites his Hokan language and his ways of survival in the

In 1914, Ishi was taken from San Francisco back to Deer Creek in Tehama Co. by anthropologist A. L. Kroeber to demonstrate his skills in the wild. Here he shows his method of harpoon fishing. (Photo by A. L. Kroeber. *Lowie*) *left*

Official Army photograph of Modoc Chief Kintpuash, called Captain Jack, on his capture in 1893. For having held off hundreds of U.S. Army troops with less than 60 men for 5 months, he was hanged–shortly after this photograph was made. (*St. Pk.*) *right*

wild. He died of tuberculosis in 1916. His story *must* be read by everyone.[15]

The Modocs of northeastern California and southern Oregon were a feared and often hated people. The Pit River peoples feared Modoc slave raids. The Warm Springs tribe to the north to this day boasts that a tribal member led the U.S. Cavalry to the capture of the most famous Modoc, named Kintpuash and also called Captain Jack.

It was in 1864 that the Modocs were herded onto the Klamath Reservation* with other enemies, the Klamath tribe. Intertribal friction rose to such a level that Kintpuash, with his people, decamped to their former homelands. The struggle of the U.S. Army to return them to the reservation resulted in the Modoc War (1872–73). In the rough, black, jagged lava beds of Tulelake,† Kintpuash and 60 Modocs heroically defended themselves under the siege by 600 Army troops for *four months*.

Eventually, the band was forced to surrender; Kintpuash and five other colleagues were hanged. Much of the Modoc tribe was shipped to a tiny enclave in northeastern Oklahoma.

Indian-source place names in northeastern California: Although nearly every river flat, every mountain, and every river had its local Indian name, hardly a single original place name remains–possibly a few do in translation, as in Goose, Eagle, Coyote, Sage, or Willow.

Modoc (*Móatokni*, "southerners," i.e., S. of the Klamath people); Modoc County (for the people, of course), and Yuba City (from the Nisenan village name Yupu) are about the only prominent names left. The obliteration of the culture by denying its historical reality was nearly total.

Estimated original populations of northeastern California peoples before 1830:‡

Achumawi (all Pit River bands): *ca.* 3,000

Atsugewi: 850

Yana/Yahi: 1,500–1,900

Maidu/Konkow/Nisenan: 9,000

Modoc: *ca.* 3,000 (California and Oregon)

Northern Paiute: majority in NW Nevada and SE Oregon, California figures not available

* The Klamath Reservation was in a large flat by Upper Klamath Lake, OR. Its prior existence is marked today only by a highway plaque and a resort (!) called Klamath Agency.

† The battle site, "Captain Jack's Stronghold," is a part of *Lava Beds National Monument*, and his story is told with sympathy and admiration toward the Modoc people. Within the Monument are also two examples of ancient Modoc abstract paintings, and Northern California's most extensive example of petroglyphs, carved on a cliffside of an ancient lakeside.

‡ The numbers given here and in other sections are early estimates, and they are doubtless low. They are presented to show the relative populations of various groups.

Northeast Reservations and Rancherias

Fort Bidwell Reservation *Northern Paiute (Paviotso).* (1897) Modoc Co. **

The piney eastern slopes of the Warner Mountains don't attract a lot of water from the passing clouds, but enough to keep green a 5,000-foot-high desert valley. About 175 Paiute people reside on the 3,335-acre reservation and several others in private homes of the vicinity. The Paviotso are a people of the desert–with a plains history rather different from that of the secluded Coast Range peoples.

Their life now is sedentary–residing on ranches and small farms at the edges of the desert along the California-Nevada state line. In various patches on the panorama of desert and mountain we find an ancient cemetery, an old town center ghosting away, new HUD homes grouped around cul-de-sacs, and green to gold alfalfa pastures surrounding the wooden barns of ranches. Horses and cattle give the place an old-West atmosphere.

The ruins of the Army-built hospital at Ft. Bidwell, Modoc Co., overlooking the Nevada salt flats and hills. (*dhe,* 1979)

The fort itself (**430**) was established in 1866, to subdue the Modocs, the Paiutes, and the Pit River peoples. The fort was made over into an Indian school and the lands given reservation status in 1897, after subjugation. All that is left of the fort now is the ruins of the hospital. An old school building has been converted into residences.

Schooling is no longer offered on the reservation–the Indians must use local white facilities in Cedarville, but there is a plain, newish community services and tribal office structure and a new (1984) health clinic. There is little employment in the local Forest Service office, because, as one ranger told me, the Indians don't trust anyone in a federal agency.

15 *From State Rte. 299 at Cedarville, take the county road north 20 miles (good road) to Fort Bidwell community.*
Fort Bidwell Reservation
P.O. Box 127
Ft. Bidwell, CA 96112
(916) 279-6310

Cedarville Rancheria *Northern Paiute.* (1915) Modoc Co.

In the little historic town of Cedarville at the edge of the Nevada desert, with its infinite vistas, about fifteen Indian people dwell on a little rectangle of 17 acres. As on a number of other rancherias, the residents are people who have married into the Paiute group from other places–Montana to Arizona. What employment exists is mostly in ranching.

16 *Behind the county fairgrounds and up against the water tank foothill in Cedarville.*
Cedarville Rancheria
P.O. Box 142
Cedarville, CA 96104

X-L Ranch Reservation *Pit River.* (1938) Modoc Co.

The Pit River peoples consist of some 11 traditional bands, numbering nearly 1,000 persons (see p. 56). The X-L Ranch Reservation, some 8,700 acres in six parcels, is divided up among the bands: Achomawi, Hammawi, Atwamsini, Astarwawi, Madesi, Ilmawi, Atsuge, and Aporige.

A portrait of a Pit River family, taken in 1890. Dress at that time, fostered by missionary and social pressure, was adopted pioneer style. (*St. Pk.*)

A few facilities exist to improve life, such as a small health clinic and tribal office.

17 *Both sides of U.S. 395 for about a mile either side of the State Rte. 299 junction. Local tribal office is by* BIA *Road 76, N of the State Quarantine Station on U.S. 395. Other portions of the reservation are near Goose Lake, Big Sage Reservoir, and Fairchild Swamp.*
X-L Ranch Reservation Pit River Tribe
P.O. Drawer 1570
Burney, CA 96013
(916) 335-5421

Alturas Rancheria *Pit River (Achúmawi* and *Atsúgewi).* (1924) Modoc Co.

This rancheria of 20 acres consists of four or five deserted, ancient dwellings and a mobile home in a dry little rectangle at the edge of the high, northeastern desert (4,400 ft.).

18 *About ¾ mi. E of Alturas on the south side of County Rd. 56.*
P.O. Box 1035
Alturas, CA 96101

Alturas is also the 14-acre home of the **Pit River Home and Agricultural Cooperative Association**, the organization that coordinates some local activities of the Pit River peoples.
P.O. Box 1035
Alturas, CA 96101

Likely Rancheria *Pit River (Achumawi* and *Atsugewi).* (1922) Modoc Co.

Of the original 40 acres, only about 1 acre remains—a burial ground.

19 *About ½ mile S of Likely, from U.S. 395, a dirt road east crosses the Southern Pacific tracks—go about ¾ mile to the lonely place marked only by old trees.*

Lookout Rancheria *Pit River (Achumawi* and *Atsugewi).* (1913) Modoc Co.

For sixty years, this 40-acre plot was primitive residence and tiny ranch for a few persons, barely maintaining their culture. Lately, however, the residents, infused with progressive ideas on Indian well-being, have been constructing a couple of new homes. The site, looking out over pastures and fields up the low mountains of Modoc National Forest, has recently had electricity brought in and its one road paved. (And you thought electricity had been everywhere for decades? . . . not on Indian lands.)

20 *Two miles E of Lookout on State Hwy. 87, N of the road.*
Lookout Rancheria
P.O. Box 87
Lookout, CA 96054

Montgomery Creek Rancheria *Pit River (Achumawi).* (1913) Shasta Co.

The countryside is dry, forested foothills. The access is 5 miles north of Fender Ferry Rd. on State Hwy. 299 onto the worst road in California. Strewn about the forest are twenty-odd junked cars, trash, two lean-tos, and a seldom-used ancient trailer. It's too bad that the natural beauty of this site has been so mistreated.

21 Montgomery Creek Rancheria
P.O. Box 282
Montgomery Creek, CA 96065

Big Bend Rancheria *Achumawi, Atsugewi, Wintu.* (1916) Shasta Co.

The town of Big Bend is remote–at the end of the main road. In the summer, a few people come here to fish and hunt and to be in the wilderness. At other times, loggers are here. It's hot in summer, cold in winter; but the 75 rancheria residents don't complain much. They live in the 40 acres of Pit River bottomland and find some work in the area's lumbering.

Though the area is pretty, and the surrounding wilderness large, upkeep on the rancheria is poor.

Once in a while, I'm told, the people dance–when it is propitious. I believe a dancehouse or arena is here, but I didn't see it. Some fine basketweavers also live in the area.

22 *Through the town of Big Bend (access via Big Bend Rd. from State Rte. 299, about 20 miles), across the Pit River bridge to the river flats on the north side.*
Big Bend Rancheria
P.O. Box 255
Big Bend, CA 96001

Roaring Creek Rancheria *Achumawi.* (1915) Shasta Co. PRIVATE

(For a description of the 80-acre rancheria, see p. 56.)

23 *From State Hwy. 299, take Big Bend Rd. about 10 miles, turn left (W) on Cove Rd. and go about 4 dusty miles to a Pit River Indian claims trailer site on the right. The Rancheria (private) is nearby.*
Roaring Creek Rancheria
P.O. Box 52
Montgomery Creek, CA 96065

Susanville Rancheria *Northern Paiute* and others. (1923) Lassen Co.

The rancheria is five blocks long and two wide, in typical fashion. Just off the west side of the rancheria lies a shady, old burial ground surrounded by a white picket fence.

The hub is a new tribal office-community center building, gym, and some playground equipment for kids. Here, too, are 15 or 20 new homes, unexpectedly better than most of the surrounding community, with a good feel of unconfined space.

The original land was 45 acres. Later diminished in size, it has recently been expanded to 150 acres.

Although this is historic Maidu country, few, if any, Maidu live here, preferring to reside out of town in nearby Greenville and Janesville.

24 *North side of Susanville on Chestnut St.*
Susanville Rancheria
Drawer U
Susanville, CA 96130
(916) 257-6264

Greenville Rancheria *Maidu.* (1897) Plumas Co.

The more than 700 Maidu of Plumas Co. celebrate the Bear Dance in the spring, either at Greenville or at the Janesville dancehouse located across a low mountain range to the east. Since 1966, the Greenville Rancheria has been totally in private (partially Indian) hands; the old Taylorsville Rancheria is today the valley rodeo grounds. (See also p. 55.)

25 *Tribal offices of the local Maidu are on Old Taylorsville Rd., 4 mi. E of town.*
Plumas Co. Indians, Inc.
P.O. Box 833
Greenville, CA 95947

Berry Creek Rancheria *Maidu.* (1916) Butte Co.

Tucked away in a corner of a dark, remote forest, watered by a little stream channeled into an aqueduct, with no electricity for miles, hides this 33-acre tract, once property of the Central Pacific Railroad. It must be close to the ultimate solitude, because not even their nearest neighbors know that Indians live here–it took me two tries to find it. These people obviously appreciate their seclusion.

The homes are three trailers, in front of one is an acorn grinding rock, possibly still used.

27 *Near Berry Creek on Bean Creek Rd., off State Rte. 162, up against Plumas National Forest.*
Berry Creek Rancheria
1779 Mitchell Ave.
Oroville, CA 95965
(916) 534-3859

Enterprise Rancheria *Maidu.* (1915) Butte Co.

The Enterprise perches on a hillside, in a foothill region of small oaks and pines, laced with a labyrinth of little roads, serving a growing number of folks fleeing the urbs. It has been called home by a few Maidu for many decades; today its 40 acres are occupied by three residences.

28 *From the Oroville-Feather Falls Rd., one mile NE from the Feather River bridge, take Oregon Creek Rd. (dirt) 1½ mile in the direction of Toyon Hills, past a tire repair depot and several old buildings. Left, uphill to 3 homes.*

Enterprise Rancheria
P.O. Box 7470
Feather Falls Star Rte.
Oroville, CA 95965

Mooretown Rancheria *Konkow* [formerly called *Northwestern Maidu*]. (1894) Butte Co.

Some years ago the grandfather of the four present residents divided up the 80 acres of the rancheria, according to terms of its termination. Consequently, most of the former Konkow lands are still in Indian hands. The ranch-style homes here are very fine, with accompanying farmland, resting under the pines of the high foothills.

There is no formal tribal organization—all functions are strictly family, with reunions here or in Taylorsville, where grass games and other specifically Indian sports are played.

Incidentally, the Konkow are culturally and linguistically closely related to the Maidu; they maintain close familial ties as well.

29 *One mile S of Feather Falls, on ½ mile N of Island Bar Rd., off the main road from Oroville to Feather Falls, on a dirt road going east. (Nothing to see but some nice homes.)*
Mooretown Rancheria
P.O. Box 7630
Feather Falls Star Rte.
Oroville, CA 95965

Auburn Rancheria *Nisenan* [formerly called *Southern Maidu*]. (1916) Placer Co. *

On a high Sierra foothill covered with oaks and grass, squeezed between the Southern Pacific tracks and the old Auburn-Folsom highway, is the little 20-acre rectangle of the rancheria. It is one of the last refuges of the people known as Nisenan, the people who once occupied the area from Sacramento to the Placer Co. foothills.

Succumbing to the coaxing and blandishments of the bureaucrats, Auburn residents forced their own termination in 1958, but at least six or seven families have held on to this land until now. Termination has prevented the people from being able to receive many benefits otherwise available to other Indian groups; consequently, most of the homes here are aged, much cooking and heating is with that ecologically-touted fuel, wood. A visit here puts one back in time. Except for autos, it seems life has not changed much in 50 years.

But termination or not, people here are active in several ways—the Placer Co. Indian Association (young dancers), the Equal Rights Indian Council, the Auburn Nutrition Center.

An historic old Protestant church mission serves some residents. Associated with, and near the rancheria is an ancient Maidu Burial Ground, once used as an all-Indian burning [cremation] ground.

30 *About 2 miles S of Auburn, at Indian Rancheria Rd., on the old Auburn-Folsom Highway. Burial Ground about 1 mile N of rancheria, same highway.*
Auburn Rancheria
P.O. Box 3035
Route 3
Auburn, CA 95603

* **Chico Rancheria** *Maidu, Wailaki.* (1939) Butte Co.
[Terminated Rancheria with no Indian activity]

All that's left of the 25 acres of the Chico Rancheria is a cemetery, shaded by tall old trees, well-kept, squeezed in between the buildings of Chico State University student housing.

31 *It can be found on W. Sacramento, ½ block E of railroad tracks, N side of the street; the oldest stones date back to 1895, and strangely include some Hawaiian names. It is maintained by a local Indian family.*

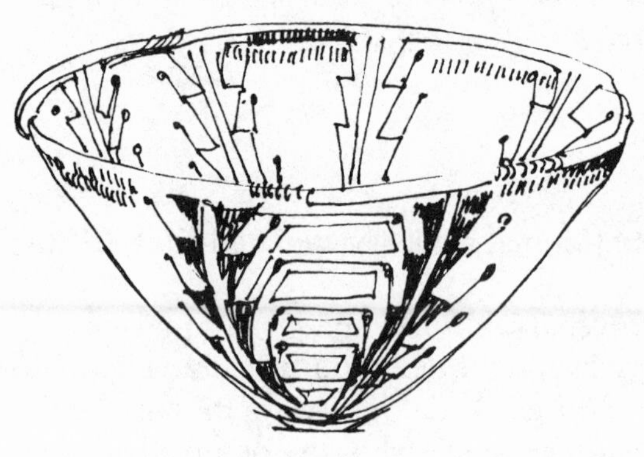

West Central

Hokan Speakers*
Pomo family (7 groups – *Northern, Northeastern, Eastern, Central, Southwestern, Southern, Kashaya)*

Penutian-Speaking Groups†
Wintun family – *Wintu, Nomlaki, Patwin*
Miwok Language – *Coast and Lake Miwok*

Yukian Speakers‡
Yuki
Coast Yuki
Huchnom
Wappo

THE WESTERN CENTRAL portion of California, north and west of the Sacramento River is one of relatively similar geography; that is, Coast Range mountains, their valleys, the coast on the west, and the Central Valley on the east.

Within this area were the territories of the Wintu, Nomlaki, and Patwin – extending from north of Redding to Suisun Bay, along the eastern slope of the mountains.

A rather surprising number of broad, somewhat protected valleys are found between the main mountain ridges. The Pomo, Yuki, Wappo, and Coast and Lake Miwok peoples settled into these valleys. Clear Lake, a huge fresh water feature in one such valley, was particularly attractive to a large group of tribes, because the lake was considered an incomparable source of sustenance.

Of all these peoples, the Yuki possessed at least two unusual characteristics – a most unusual language, and physical features more slender than any of their neighbors. The Coast Miwok and Pomo groups living along the coast spent more time in littoral (shoreside) occupations than their inland kin.

Nevertheless, the people of this region followed similar customs, often called the Central California culture. The "culture" is not confined to this area, though, and is found generally in the Central Valley and its margins.

The countryside was provident year-round, and the topography between valleys rough enough that bands tended to be fixed in their locations – both influences making residences and territories fairly rigidly defined.

The dwellings of the people varied a little, but would consist of, for temporary habitations, a few slab or bark tipis. In more permanent villages, the

* See footnote †, Northwest, p. 36.
† See footnote †, Northeast, p. 52.
‡ A small family of languages found only in this region, possibly distantly related to Sioux.

The Pomo village of El-em in its early location on Rattlesnake Island in Clear Lake, Lake Co., 1870. Homes are made of thatched tule reeds. Though presently occupied by a developer, the Pomo lay claim to this island. (*St. Pk.*)

A Northern California sweathouse, about 1900. This one, from Chilula country, is notably smaller than either dancehouses or homes, but resembles them. (*St. Pk.*)

usual lodging might be accompanied by a circular dancehouse, excavated two or three feet down, with a bark roof set on long logs and supported by heavy vertical beams. These might also serve as sweathouses. Village sites would be moved within the valley when food sources became scarce in an area.

In most of central California the sweathouse was an institution (see p. 37), for social, community, and probable health purposes. As we have seen in the north, the dancehouse, or roundhouse, was the community center. Dances in this region tended to be more complex and numerous than other parts of the state, although much knowledge of dance in southern California has been lost, owing to the Church's eradications of "pagan" customs.

As in northwestern California, many of the dances were, and in some places still are, related to the religious concept of existence called World Renewal, mentioned earlier (p. 9 and p. 39). In central California these dance rituals evolved into what was then called the Kuksu belief system, in which the dancers represent, and may embody, the spirits of deities whom they impersonate in exotic feathered regalia. Their vision of transformation is akin to that of the Kachinas of Pueblo and Zuñi peoples.

The dance also maintains the world renewal purpose. Most religions incorporate the idea of yearly renewal into their system–spring, regeneration, Easter, etc. The dancers and, indeed, many of the participants in the ceremonies, were required to be members of various secret societies. Anyone with any aspirations of leadership, be it tribal or medicinal, found it indispensable to be a member. Such societies not only passed down many of the secrets of powers, they also held ties with their counterparts in other tribes in one of the rare, true intertribal connections.

Many dances are held in the fall season (acorn festivals), in which a sort of thanks is given for the harvest past, and the expectation of the fall rains is conveyed. This is high contrast to the ceremonies of cold-climate religions, where fall brings a symbolic dying with the winter snows–in central California the fall rains bring *life* and *green*. The reader may sense the depth of these perceptions in the ceremonies at Chaw-Se (see p. 98).

Had we been in the villages of earlier times, we might have heard tales of Coyote and a whole society of animal spirits, each having rather human characteristics. In such places where wealth was less important than clever and wise leadership qualities, the legends of Coyote also changed their emphasis. Here, tales dwelt less on tricks and chicanery, and Coyote became more lusty and even lecherous. Stories and tales were more for pure entertainment than for teaching principles. But who would say that any tale doesn't include some kind of ethic?

Although everyone made functional utensils and tools, it was in the Pomo villages, more than in any others in California, that the artistry of basketry was demonstrated. Not only were the two major techniques of coiling and twining used, but also exquisitely fine designs were incorporated, and baskets of rare shapes and functions were fashioned.

These weavings were so well made and are of such intrinsic artistic value that even fragments of old ones have become expensive collectors' items. A few examples: finely woven caps with multi-colored designs, a funnel-like bowl with a round hole in the bottom for preventing spillage from a mortar, an incidental container laced with bluebird feathers, a headdress with crimson woodpecker feathers, a coarsely-woven cone some two feet across for carrying wood and heavy objects (a "burden basket"), an open-weave cradle with hood, a seed beater, a woven watertight bottle sealed with pine pitch.

You may see many of these marvelous art objects at the City Museum in Lakeport, the Indian Museum in Sacramento, or in North Fork at the Sierra Mono Museum. Probably the best collection is in the Lowie Museum of the University of California, Berkeley, but they are mostly squirreled away from public view.

Such a variety in design could only be matched in the United States by the pottery of the Pueblos. Many baskets of all Indians of California had to be woven to a watertight fineness, since much cooking was done by placing hot stones directly into a liquid mush contained in the basket.

All peoples of Clear Lake fashioned a sturdy reed boat, amazingly like those of the Indians of Lake Titicaca in the Peruvian-Bolivian Andes. Of course, fish nets were woven to accompany these fine fishing craft, as well as nets for fishing in the local streams. The tules* gave them their raw materials, and the tules gave them shelter material, clothing, and even tule shoots that supplemented their food supply.

All over the state, there are peoples whose cultural history was not protected with reservation status (no guarantee, at that). This includes most of the Athapaskan peoples (see p. 36) – the Mattole, Lassik, Sinkyone, Nongatl – and in central California, the Coast Miwok; elsewhere, the Esselen, the Yahi. In some places, tiny remnants of these peoples live on in small family groupings, but as speakers of a language and practitioners of a set of customs and beliefs, the culture is no more.

* Tules are a round, common marsh reed, with a cluster of small seed pods, something like cattails. Their shoots taste like asparagus.

Woven seed beaters, resembling jai-alai baskets, were used in the early times to gather the many natural grass seeds prevalent in Central California. (WPA sketch by R. V. Vallangca. *St. Pk.*)

A Pomo fisher with a fish basket in his tule reed boat on Clear Lake, 1880. Tule boats like this one were used also in the San Francisco Bay and Central Valley marshlands. A number of local museums hold replicas of these boats. (*Southwest Museum*)

Other peoples had no reservation (or have none now), yet vestiges of the culture survive – like the Wappo organization of the Healdsburg (Sonoma Co.) area, the Karoks of the Klamath River, a few Athapaskans of the north coast forests, some Salinans of Monterey Co., the 215 members of the Ohlone Tribes, Inc. of San Francisco Bay Area, the Gabrielinos of the Los Angeles area, and the Coast Miwoks of Marin Co.

The Nomlaki dancehouse at Grindstone Creek Rancheria in Glenn Co. is probably the oldest in use in California. (*dhe,* 1979)

The Indians began to arrive by the thousands at the powwow, riding in Colts and Broncos, Mustangs and Pintos, Chargers and Pacers. The site was an encampment near the ancient Nisenan tribal village called Momol. They came for three days of dancing to the drums, storytelling by the elders, crafts markets, displays of art, demonstrations of agility in handgames and boat handling.

One hundred and fifty years ago it would have been unlikely for their ancestors to have held a meet this large, though they walked to smaller trading markets, having no horses. This, however, was the Annual California Indian Days Intertribal Powwow, held every September near Sacramento. And the place is now called the California Indian Museum in the "village" of Sacramento.*

They say that in the old days dancing went on into the night. It does here, too. And the chants and drums of the handgame participants may be heard long after midnight. Sometimes venison and plank-roasted salmon send their odors from a nearby cooksite.

Vast intertribal gatherings from all the Indian nations of North America are relatively new to California. After centuries of victimization of the Native American, the glimmerings of a renewal of Indian pride and consciousness are being seen. And dances and ceremonies of centuries-old traditions are offered to spirits that refused to disappear.

The eastern slopes of the Coast Range are on the leeward side of the mountains; thus, the heavy rainfall of the Pacific coast doesn't reach these rocky hills. Even so, the mountains slowly release their water even in summer, so that, in earlier days, there was plenty for sedentary bands of Indians camped in the occasional broad, sheltered valleys. There was water, there were fish, there were oaks and grasses and game.

The whites now have most of those flats, the Indians relegated to the drier places and small plots where roaming was not possible. One such

* The location of this gathering may vary, but is usually at the Sutter's Fort site on the third weekend of September.

place is Grindstone Creek Rancheria, small (80 acres), on a good-sized, reservoir-fed creek. But like most rancherias, it is strictly a residential place with no arable land. Like others, it is a place of high contrasts—there is a new water supply, but the roads and yards are all dry and dusty; one finds a fine new tribal hall, but most homes, even new ones, are unkempt; in the center is a well-kept historic dancehouse, but the surroundings are cluttered.

Some psychologists say that clutter indicates a lack of pride, but how to explain the roundhouse, tribal hall, and intense cultural interest? How, then, to explain the great interest in the local softball league, in large part Indian? An old wooden Protestant church survives. A fair number of residents were employed at the Louisiana- Pacific lumber mill in nearby Elk Creek, when it was operating. Perhaps this community is an instance of the persistence of cultural traits, mixed with economic necessities. I'm not sure about the clutter, but I did find the rancheria of interest; and the people not unfriendly, in spite of all their evident economic problems.

One day in 1978, a particularly enthusiastic baseball game caught my attention in Elk Creek on my first visit there. As it turned out, about half the local team was Indian, a healthy sign, I thought. The ballpark was unusually well outfitted; I learned later that land, light, and bleachers had been furnished for the town by Louisiana-Pacific.

Suddenly, all changed. The California Water Project (known then as the Peripheral Canal Project) wanted Elk Creek for a lake and the Grindstone Rancheria as a dam site. All persons involved would be paid well for their land, said the commission in charge. Then L.-P. closed their mill permanently, throwing Indians and whites alike out of work and the town into financial chaos. L.-P. even dismantled the ballpark.

Few communities are ever threatened with this kind of annihilation. But the final destiny rides on the tribal decision of Grindstone, since theirs is federal land guaranteed to them.

The irony—many of the local whites remember their grandparents having taken possession of this land from the Nomlaki, who now have the final say-so. The Grindstone Nomlaki aren't overly concerned with the whites' distress, since it was, in 1863, *their* immediate grandparents whose children were dashed against stones and whose parents were shot by the U.S. Calvary for lagging behind in the forced march across the mountains (see p. 23).

Nevertheless, the Grindstone people aren't jumping at the chance to become economically comfortable. They and their forefathers were born here, their roundhouse is sacred ground, their roots are finally here. To be uprooted and move would likely disperse the tribe and its culture forever. They are quite aware of this risk.

Yes, the roundhouse could be moved, but only by water, say the elders. Too, the people might be allowed to prosper elsewhere. The final decision has not been made, and the Peripheral Canal fever is dormant, though menacingly unforgotten.*

* For a moving and emotional documentary film on this place see "The Probable Passing of Elk Creek," by Rob Wilson (1983).

Seventeen miles of dirt road and several gates (one locked, at the entrance to an intervening private ranch), will get one to Cortina. The Wright brothers, Edward and Amos, along with a few farm animals, lived here alone for decades.

This dry and inhospitable place was once home for many more. It has had one salty well, no electricity, two tiny clapboard houses, a tiny sweathouse, and, a long time ago, a dancehouse. Recently, in possible preparations for more new residents, a new well has been dug and a "meeting house," a new $40,000 prefab, had been brought in. There is no way for food to be grown here–it must be brought in, except for the chickens and lots of squirrels. It's too dry even for deer. Nevertheless, Amos Wright wasn't happy to have his many years of solitude disturbed.

Cortina left me with confused feelings. The good part is that it is old, traditional land where near-total isolation can keep a culture alive. But, how is a culture to survive if only old men practice it and no families can share it? Continual isolation is death on tradition.

Halfway between the two summer-arid spots of Grindstone Creek and Cortina lies the community of Stonyford.

PRIVATE **Stonyford** (Community) *Northeastern Pomo.*

All year long Stony Creek flows its life-giving waters onto the flats below the mountains. This makes Stonyford a perfect site for a village–as the Northeastern Pomo people found long ago. The flats are best for oaks, homesites, and grasslands, while the mountains furnish habitats for other flora and fauna. The stream is good for water and the fish which once ran every year.

Just west of town, on the property of Mr. Arthur Moody, are the sites of two ancient roundhouses. Today they appear to be sinkholes, with trash someone dumped there decades ago. While we sat in his jeep, Mr. Moody described to me some later history of Stonyford.

The area was "settled" by a group of Mormons fleeing justice–perpetrators of the Mountain Meadows Massacre in Utah, 1857. Attempting to discourage other immigrants from passing through Utah, they had dressed as Indians and slain nearly an entire wagon train. When they arrived here, I doubt that the native Pomos were treated with utmost respect.

At any rate, the Pomo people had erected an unusual dance or sweathouse. There are a large number of baked stone fragments around the site; the stones were heated and water thrown upon them for making steam–an Indian Turkish bath.

Mr. Moody showed me some early trenches dug by the Mormons for irrigation, and a smaller trench dug by himself, with a large loop bypassing a shady flat. The flat is a former Pomo burial ground–still respected but totally unmarked, characteristic of most California Indian peoples' burial customs. Known to the natives, but who else needs to know? Today the whole field of cemetery and roundhouse is barren of all but stones and star thistle. (Caution: Mr. Moody is unhappy about trespassing.)

Some of the Indian people who remain live in a cluster of a few primitive cabins, the size of garages, on the opposite bank of the creek, in the open chaparral, with a vista of St. John's Mountain. There is electricity and water from an irrigation ditch; and prosperous non-Indian farms are all around. The place is in actuality a rancheria, in the early sense of the word, but its 80 acres are privately owned, with a big NO TRESPASSING sign on the main gate over the dirt road access. The Northeastern Pomo were never given government reservation land. Some local employment is with the U.S. Forest Service and lumbering outfits. If you really want to, you may *see* the rancheria from a campground of Mendocino National Forest on Fouts Spring Rd., just west of Stonyford.

Out on the main road about the Glenn-Colusa county line is Sharkey Moore's fine ranch. His grandmother is buried in the cemetery mentioned above. Sharkey was born at the old Stony Creek rancheria, an Indian settlement long gone. He spared me a few moments from his busy ranching day to tell me of one of the Salt Springs battles of the early 1800s.

A few miles up the road trickles a famous salt spring in Northeast Pomo territory that furnished salt for most of the neighboring peoples. Salt, then as now, is very important for food preservation and health, and it was considered by the local people their most available trading commodity.

It seems, however, that the spring was coveted as well by their neighbors–the Wintu, the Yuki, Miwok, and other Pomo tribes. One day some outsiders (not named) sneaked in from the south, and while making off with a load of unpaid-for salt, they were slain for their insult. Some nights later, avengers from the outsiders' camp were spotted coming through a pass by a Stonyford sentry, who warned his villagers. The villagers hid nearby, the avengers burned the village before dawn; and while boasting of the "victory," were ambushed. Further troubles from the south aren't recorded.

The salt springs are part of the Garlin Ranch, from whom permission to visit *must* be secured. (All around this region, watch out for "buzz tails"–rattlers.)

In 1958, the Paskenta Rancheria in the same locality was terminated. It lay not far from the desiccated and desolate Nome Lackee Reservation (1854–63) **357**, the destination of an infamous Central Valley Indian roundup. Many persons starved to death here. Across the road from the rancheria site, two Nomlaki families choose to remain, but they participate in tribal and family affairs in Grindstone. A local lumber company occupies the 260 acres now.

In town, I encountered some envious bitterness from local whites who resented that the Indians should even possess a trailer to live in. Such is the fate of another rancheria.

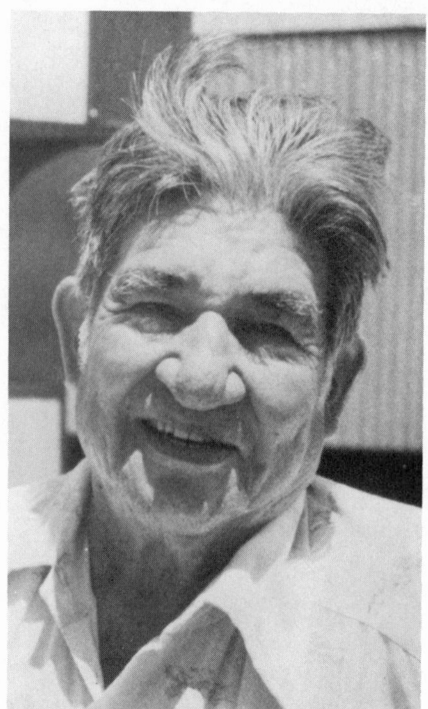

William Frank, Yuki, tribal historian for the Round Valley Reservation, Mendocino Co. (*dhe,* 1978)

A Pomo warrior in his "flak jacket" of willow and tightly-woven fabric, about 1900. Armor was rather uncommon among Indian peoples of California, but so was intertribal strife. (*St. Pk.*)

Even reservation status did not guarantee that land designated for native occupation would remain so. Consider the case of Round Valley Reservation. Some of its fortunes were told me by a Yuki, William Frank, an outstanding historian of august and commanding bearing.

Round Valley is a particularly inviting, fertile valley which became the Army's repository for tribes removed from several counties (see p. 23). Once hesitantly and reluctantly settled in Round Valley, the people found whites moving in to grab land. Though the valley is good farmland, the bands brought here had never been farmers. One group, while on a foraging party on a nearby mountain, sighted Mt. Shasta, a sacred landmark near their old home. The next morning, the entire band had vanished into the forest.

To survive, most of these deported peoples filtered away, back to their own traditional areas, with or without reservation land. Eventually, owing to white settlers, Round Valley was divided in half–the northern half Indian and the southern half to one "Farmer White."

Even then, the Indians lost more land. Apportioned parcels were sold or lost as late as 1920–often through gambling, a venerable native custom, thoroughly exploited by the whites.

In spite of the diversity of peoples living here (five bands with very different backgrounds), inter-tribal strife is extremely rare. The people have an understanding of their differences, but have a common cause. Unfortunately, cultural events specific for any one group are no longer held. The last roundhouse disappeared in the 1930s, but the construction of a new one heralds a resurgence of at least some common cultural interest. The one unifying all-Indian celebration is held at Christmas.

Sprinkled over the map around Ukiah and Clear Lake are nearly twenty rancherias, mostly Pomo bands. The Pomo never were a consolidated "tribe," as were the Mohaves, for instance. Language and customs among the groups were similar, but not their governance. Some of this autonomy is reflected in the large number of rancherias of the region, and has led anthropologists to name most groups by a simple geographic designation.

The fortunes of these rancherias vary from progressive (an intense interest in cultural preservation) to extinct. Some were swallowed by engineering projects–Lower Lake is an airport, old Coyote Valley lies under Lake Mendocino; some were overrun by urban sprawl as were Redding and Pinoleville. The latter are, in reality, urban subdivisions–the towns have grown to meet them.

Their acreage, all laid off in square streets, looks like any other group of houses at the edge of town. The rancherias are mostly non-Indian, since they were once terminated and most plots of the dry, flat land sold off. Though distant hills and some open fields lie nearby, neither is one of the more scenic attractions, nor did they have anything environmentally special to offer. But they *were* Indian centers of culture, and are no more.

In this vicinity, much former rancheria land has been totally lost through the ugly termination process (Alexander Valley, Mark West, Lytton, Cache Creek) or has been severely diminished.

Potter Valley is one of those flat, oval valleys tucked away between Coast Range mountains. It extends some eight by four miles on the uppermost reaches of the Russian River, and formerly was home for three villages of Pomo people, including the village of "Pomo," whose name has been given to the entire Pomo people.

The rancheria, two parcels once totalling 96 acres, now consists of only two small farms owned by elderly persons. The older people have died out, the younger people have gone to the cities or to more prosperous or active Indian communities. What has happened here is typical of a number, but not by any means all, of the rancherias. When the population aged, the rancheria was terminated, divided up among the residents or families, and sold piecemeal–usually for subsistence, welfare being unavailable or grossly inadequate.

Redwood Valley, Guidiville, and Big Valley have been more fortunate through great efforts to keep their native life alive. Big Valley, however, has suffered much land loss.

Two other bands took land matters into their own hands–at Yo-Ka-Yo and Upper Lake. It's not hard to notice that most of the Mendocino county rancherias came into official existence around the early 1900s. However, one group of Pomo people took matters into their own hands very early and bought their own land in 1881, calling their place Yo-Kā-Yo [from which *Ukiah*]. They suffered numerous legal battles to retain their land–remember, Indians had almost no legal rights at that time.

Finally, in 1904, in a "land" mark decision, the State Supreme Court ruled that the people could maintain it "in perpetuity." Today, it flourishes on 170 acres of rich valley land and scenic hillside, with more than 20 homes. You can read a pamphlet on the history of this unique place at the Ukiah City Hall.

Clear Lake once had an "upper" northern portion, before the lake bed was reclaimed for farmland. The once-large (1000-acre) Upper Lake Rancheria, lying along a hillside above and partly among neat orchards near this land, now is smaller, much of the former land in the hands of non-Indians. However, an original 90 acres of this land was purchased and settled as early as 1878 by the people themselves, as at Yo-Ka-Yo.

I have seen the people remaining trying hard to make a better life for themselves–installing water systems and rebuilding homes. The elderly are being served by community health and nutrition centers. Though with few resources, the strength of this band of people is great.

A few of these rancherias have held on by maintaining a remote privacy, such as Middletown (Lake Miwok and Pomo people), Hopland (Central Pomo), and Sherwood Valley (Northern Pomo). Native culture remains in their homelife, in family connections, and often in dances and get-togethers at more active centers.

Although the newest of the rancherias in this region, El-ém is the site of an ancient village, inhabited for many years. Tule reeds sway in the gentle waves of Clear Lake; fishers daily embark in their small boats. Even the ugly scar of the now-silent mine beside the rancheria is slowly growing green. A well-appointed dancehouse is used almost weekly, and the personnel of the tribal offices are active, new, and eager.

The dancehouse of El-em (Sulphur Bank Rancheria) in Lake Co., 1930, when the community was quite small. (*St. Pk.*) *left*

The El-em dancehouse 50 years later, expanded for a much greater capacity. Since this photo was taken in 1978, a new roof has been constructed. (*dhe,* 1978) *right*

If this sounds idyllic, some of the older residents are concerned about what else in happening on their 50 acres. A whole group of comfortable new homes are being constructed–drawing formerly non-reservation and city people to the quiet of the lakeside.

But the culture perseveres, and culturally, El-ém is probably the most animated center in the renewal of Pomo history in Clear Lake, Lake County, and even Mendocino County. The dance house functions also as a local weekend center for young people, many of whom are coming back to the rancheria from the cities and towns. Some dances are even open to the public.

Place names with Indian sources in West Central California (translations may be only approximate):

Nomlaki Paskenta (from *paskenti*, "under the bank")

Wintu Yolla Bolly (*yola boli*, "high, snow-covered peak"), Yreka (name for Mt. Shasta)

Wintun Tehama (a place name), Sonoma (*sonom*, "nose")

Patwin Solano (Spanish name for a Suisun chief, Sem-yeto), Napa (*napato*, "bear shaman", or *napo* "house"), Suisun (a place or local tribal name), Putah (*putato*, a place name), Capay (*co-péh*, "stream"), Colusa (*coru*, a place name)

Pomo Calpella (from a chief, "shell bearer"), Ukiah (*yo-kā*-ya, probably "deep valley"), Pomo ("at red earth hole", a mine for red clay, for coloring and flavoring bread), Gualala (*wa-la-li*, "meeting place of waters")

Miwok Bolinas (*baulines*, a place name), Tomales (*tamals*, "westerners"), Tamalpais (probably "Tamals of the mountain"), Olema (*olemaloke*, "coyote valley"), Petaluma ("flat place"), Hookooeko (local tribal name)

Original populations of West Central peoples before 1830:*

Pomo: *ca.* 8,000
Wintu/Nomlaki/Patwin 12,000–14,000
Wappo: 1,000
Coast Miwok: *ca.* 2,000
Lake Miwok: 500
Yuki/Coast Yuki/Huchnom: 2,000

* The numbers given here and in other sections are early estimates, and they are doubtless low. They are presented to show the relative populations of various groups.

West Central Reservations and Rancherias

Round Valley Reservation *Nomlaki, Yuki, Wailaki, Konkow, Achumawi*. (1856) Mendocino Co. *

Beside an overlook on the snaking canyon road leading into the quiet secluded Round Valley, there is an Historical Landmark plaque stating, "This valley was discovered . . . in 1854." This presumptuous sign was news to the Yuki people, who had lived there undisturbed for several thousand years. As a reservation, it is one of the oldest in California, established in 1856 as the Nome Cult Indian Farm.

Events in its history have been those of tragedy and misery–Round Valley was the regional "depository" for those bits and pieces of tribes unfortunate enough to have been rounded up by the U.S. Army in sweeps of this part of the state in the decade of 1855–65.

A large sign at the edge of the reservation states that persons from "Pit River, Waylackie, Concow [Konkow/Maidu], Little Lake [a Pomo band], Nomlaki, and Yuki" peoples live here. This is really only part of the story. At times, many other peoples were brought here–Cahto (from west), Modoc (from northeast), Yana and Atsugewi (from east), Huchnom and Pomo (from south), and the Wailaki's Athapaskan relatives, Mattole, Nongatl, Sinkyone, and Lassik (from northwest).

In such a melange of peoples, several cultures have disappeared or become totally merged with others. In 1854, on the eastern foothills of the Coast Range, the large Nome Lackee [Nomlaki] Reservation had been established, and a good many remnants of peoples bordering on the Central Valley removed to it. However, no provision whatsoever had been made for support of these persons, and greedy whites immediately claimed the land; consequently in 1863, these people were herded over the mountains to Round Valley, with considerable loss of life, during a two-week "trail of tears."

Ownership of the 18,700 acres is a mosaic divided between tribal lands and trust lands (deeded to individuals and families–often subdivided). There are a number of Indian ranches, and dozens of new homes, many on one- to two-acre plots, only lately furnished with electricity and water. The reservation is generally very neat, with a new (1977) clinic, a county school in Covelo (no Indian culture courses offered), a new tribal center (where there are cultural programs for children).

Employment here is largely with the Louisiana-Pacific Lumber Co, with the Forest Service, and in some dairying.

Physically, the valley is really round–a hidden flat valley–something of a surprise in the rugged, oak and pine-studded Coast Range, not unlike the Hoopa Valley to the north.

Old Fort Wright, which was put here with the reservation, was abandoned in 1876 and converted to an Indian boarding school in 1883. Nothing remains of either, excepting a former officer's home.

35 *From U.S. 101, take State Rte. 162 from Longvale, through Eel River gorge to Covelo.*

Round Valley Reservation
P.O. Box 448
Covelo, CA 95428
(707)983-6126

Paskenta Rancheria. *Nomlaki (Wintun)*. (1920) Tehama Co. [Rancheria terminated and abandoned.] (See a short description of the Rancheria, p. 71.)

The Nomlaki are one of three Wintuan-speaking groups; the others are the Patwin and the Wintu. Earlier writers spoke of the Nome Cult, implying a form of religion, rather than a linguistic group. In reality, the Wintun peoples are not widely different from the other peoples of the region.

36 *The county road west from Corning on Interstate 5 passes through Paskenta en-route (unpaved) to Round Valley.*

Redding (Clear Creek) Rancheria [originally] *Wintu*. (1922) Shasta Co.

Once a Wintu community, this dry, flood plain of a creek shaded by many oaks, is now a mostly white suburb. A few ancient wooden houses remain, among modern suburban houses and trailers, homes for 11 Indian families. Nothing unusual to see.

37 *On State Hwy. 273, about 3 miles S of Redding, at Clear Creek bridge, ironically stands a plaque of State Landmark* 78, *a gold discovery site. The tract behind the plaque is the rancheria.*

Cortina Rancheria *Patwin (Wintun)*, [originally] *Miwok*. (1907) Colusa Co. (See a description of this place, p.70.)

Owing to the difficulties of getting here, I can't recommend a visit.

41 *Ten miles from Cortina Rd. (W of Arbuckle) along Sand Rd., right at a grove of trees to the main gate of a private ranch. Seventeen miles beyond to the rancheria.*

Cortina Rancheria
P.O. Box 41113
Sacramento, CA 95814

* **Grindstone Creek Rancheria** *Nomlaki (Wintun)*, *Wailaki*, and others. (1906) Glenn Co.

With the exception of a new water supply and a tribal hall, I expect that the Grindstone residents live pretty much as they have for decades – in a depressed and isolated place, but with a good hold on the old culture and ways. Modern life has made few inroads to lure the people into its culture bleach.

We find a large roundhouse at the center of these 80 acres, and a few destitute homes. Some people said they are "comfortable enough", others are bitter about never having enough to get a better home. Yet, the very existence here depends on an ugly demand of thirst (See p.68).

38 *About 3 miles N of Elk Creek on State Hwy. 162 (W of Willows, off Interstate 5), right at the confluence of Grindstone Creek and Stony Creek. Campsites at the impressive Stony Creek Reservoir.*

Grindstone Creek Rancheria
P.O. Box 63
Elk Creek, CA 95939
(916) 968-5321.

* **Colusa Rancheria (Cachil Dehe)** *Patwin (Wintun)*. (1907) Colusa Co.

The original Patwin name for this village in the Wintun is *Cachil Dehe*, and the place still bears that name. The 273 acres of the rancheria occupy a flat floodplain bordering on the Sacramento River.

The western portion (leased out) is fields of safflowers, the eastern part is a grove of ancient oaks with the inevitable tangle of vines along the river. In the center is a group of trim new suburban-like homes, surrounding a new roundhouse. Dances are held once or twice a year, and the people–old and young alike–come from many miles away and many places to dance.

39 *About 3 miles N of Colusa on State Hwy. 45, to Indian Rd.* (BIA) *155.*
Colusa Rancheria
P.O. Box 293
Colusa, CA 95932
(916)458-8231.

Rumsey Rancheria (Yocha Dehe) *Patwin (Wintun)*. (1907) Yolo Co.

Clear Lake, one of the largest natural bodies of fresh water in California, year-round sends torrents of clear water down Cache Creek, through the otherwise desiccated eastern Coast Range mountains. Rumsey Rancheria lies along this creek, its 85 acres irrigated, and its creek banks well-shaded. Hot summer visitors pass by on cool Cache Creek float trips.

The few homes are mostly modern; the valley rather secluded, except for occasional rafters along the swiftly-flowing creek. Rumsey Rancheria consists of just a few persons eking out an existence by a cold creek, in the solitude of dry mountains.

In 1982, an additional 100 acres was purchased for this group, and will be settled with housing very soon. It is located a few miles S of Rumsey, adjacent to the California Dept. of Forestry Fire Station.

40 *Road 75 at Tancred (Tan Creek) off State Rte. 16, S of Guinda (W of Woodland).*
Rumsey Rancheria
P.O. Box 18
Brooks, CA 95606.

Sherwood Valley Rancheria (Mato) *Northern Pomo* (*Mato* band). (1909) Mendocino Co. PRIVATE

Sherwood Valley is a remote, quiet, open meadow amongst forested hills. Its residents live in mobile homes or very primitive wooden ones on 292 acres. There seems to be crowding, however, by horses and people from the Sherwood [white, dude] Ranch adjacent–so much so that the residents expressly forbid trespass. Visitors may look, but not enter.

42 *From Willets, NW on Sherwood Rd, W at airport junction, go some 11 miles, over a creek (dirt road), to a corral in ruins. Stop, look, but respect privacy and do not enter.*
Sherwood Valley Rancheria
1737 S. State St.
Ukiah, CA 95482.
(707) 468-1337

Potter Valley Rancheria (Shánel) *Northern Pomo* (*Balo-Kay* band). (1909) Mendocino Co. (See description, p. 73.)

Two farms remain–both occupied by elders, one of whom is Edna Guerrero, last of the Shanel Pomo born here and a fascinating historian and archaeologist.

43 *West on Main St. in Potter Valley (N of State Hwy. 20, E of Ukiah) to Powerhouse Rd., thence S to Spring Valley Rd. The rancheria is on the W side of this intersection.*
Potter Valley Rancheria
P.O. Box 94
Potter Valley, CA 95469

* **Redwood Valley Rancheria** *Northern Pomo* (*Kacha* band). (1909) Mendocino Co.

The land is flat, pretty dry, and dotted with a few large oaks and many scrub oaks. Mountains line the edges of this rather narrow valley with its summer-dry creek. However, Redwood Valley is a center for Indian activities–there are annual dances for the entire valley area, an Indian education project, and basketmaking. A nutrition center headquartered in Ukiah serves the Valley.

Forty people live here; five families on 80 acres of now-private land. The homes are generally comfortable, but a few are very old and austere.

44 *From the town center of Redwood Valley (just NE of Ukiah, off State Hwy. 20) west (toward Willets) to West Rd., N about 2 miles to Rancheria Rd.*

Coyote Valley Rancheria *Northern Pomo.* (1909) Mendocino Co.

The original 100 acres of this rancheria are under the waters of Lake Mendocino. The Corps of Engineers "promises" an Indian museum at a lakeside site. As a result of much pressure and effort, Coyote now has a newly-acquired parcel nearby, five miles north of Ukiah, alongside U.S. 101. New housing is in progress on 58 acres.

45 Coyote Valley Rancheria
7901 Hwy. 101 North
P.O. Box 39
Redwood Valley, CA 95470
(707) 485-8723

Scotts Valley (Sugar Bowl) Rancheria *Northern Pomo.* (1911) Lake Co.

This easternmost rancheria of the Northern Pomo consists of two homes on three acres in a shady, tranquil valley along a small creek. Its residents have petitioned for a federal grant to have some of the original 57 acres returned. Their one festival is a barbeque after the annual Kelseyville softball tourney.

48 *From State Rte. 29, N of Lakeport, take Scotts Valley exit onto Hill Rd. (E), to Crystal Lake Rd., then E to Hartley Rd., then S a couple of blocks to the rancheria on the west side of the road.*
Scotts Valley Rancheria
P.O. Box 701
Lakeport, CA 95453
(707) 263-3062

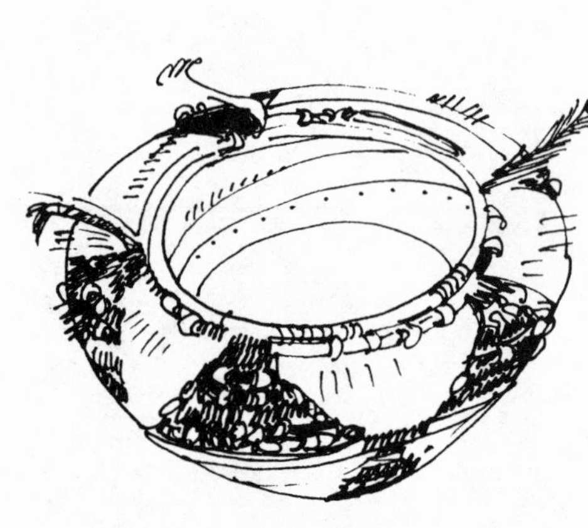

Guidiville Rancheria *Northern Pomo.* (1909) Mendocino Co.

The lower elevations of the eastern slopes of the Ukiah Valley of the Russian River are wooded with laurel; below are open vineyards. This is the setting of the Guidiville Rancheria. It once occupied 243 acres, but is somewhat smaller since its termination. Now there are four homes left, and it is the site of an annual festival with the people coming from the valley, and further.

47 *Just S of Ukiah off U.S. 101, take the road to Talmage, at its main intersection go N to the rancheria.*
Guidiville Indian Village
3071 Guidiville Rd.
Ukiah, CA 95482

Pinoleville Rancheria (Yamó) *Northern Pomo.* (1911) Mendocino Co.

Mostly non-Indian now, originally 98 acres, not scenic (see also p. 72).

46 *N of Ukiah, take Orr Springs Rd. Exit off old U.S. 101, W 2 blocks to Pinoleville Rd. The rancheria lies at the foot of a low bluff.*

Yo-Kā-Yo [Ukiah] **Rancheria** *Central Pomo.* (1881) Mendocino Co. (See description, p. 73)

The visitor would see neat homes and farms.

49 *About 3 miles S of Talmage on both sides of East Side Rd., alongside the Russian River.*

No tribal office, chairperson, or telephone (governance by three trustees).
For information, write:
Ms. Doreen Mitchell
1114 Helen Ave.
Ukiah, CA 95482

Hopland Rancheria (Shánel) *Central Pomo* (*Shókowa-ma* band). (1907) Mendocino Co.

This largest of the Pomo rancherias (2,070 acres) is situated in a region of rolling hills, sprinkled liberally with aged oaks. A few intermittent streams water the area (tributaries of the Russian River), and vineyards that were formerly hops fields line the valleys that even earlier were Indian village sites.

Homes for the 60 residents here are individually owned, and are scattered about, mostly hidden behind the hills, up small dirt roads. The land is private, so the only kind of visit I recommend is a scenic drive-through on the BIA-paved road–if you like pretty hills with broad vistas of the vineyards and Coast Range mountains.

50 *About 2 miles E of East Hopland on State Rte. 175. A BIA road (arrowhead signs) threads N among the hills and trees.*
Hopland Rancheria
P.O. Box 610
Hopland, CA 95449
(707) 744-1647

Note: Some Central Pomo people are also residents of Guidiville Rancheria (see above).

Grāton Rancheria [originally] *Southern Pomo.* (1920) Sonoma Co.

Tucked away in a forest along a creek near Sebastopol lives Mr. Frank Truvido on his one acre of "terminated" land. Some day his one acre (originally fifteen, but sold off, bit by bit, for taxes) will go to his "unterminated" daughter and once again regain Indian trust status–eligible for some federally-funded improvements. Such is the "bureaucrazy."

Mr. Truvido, originally from Tomales Bay, lives in his one-room, ancient, vertical-boarded home with his few possessions. As a former coast-dweller, he still cooks kelp–on his little Franklin stove. All around are apple ranches–and whites who covet his land. What to see? the old frame house, that's all.

51 *From Sebastopol, N on State Rte. 116 to Occidental Rd. at Molino, left past Mill Station Rd., about ½ mile to Cherry Lane. The old rancheria is on the left.*

** **Manchester** and **Point Arena Rancherias** *Central Pomo* (*Bóya* band). (1909 and 1937, respectively) Mendocino Co.

To western eyes, the Point Arena Rancheria is probably the most neatly-kept reservation in California. At the top of an ancient ocean terrace looking out over grassy fields toward the Pt. Arena lighthouse, is a small circle of homes, each with lawns and trimmed hedges. In the center of the circle children play on swings. On the hill's summit stands a new water tank, and a small clinic is available. But as Pt. Arena is modern, Manchester is the more historic; nevertheless, the same band of people lives on the 363 acres of this two-part rancheria.

At Point Arena there are three families, at Manchester, one–in several homes. (Remember, an Indian family can consist of a *lot* of relatives.) Off the road into Manchester on a quiet hillside is our ever-present reminder of times past–the cemetery. But life continues in the homes in the Garcia River Valley below. Some parcels are intensively farmed along the riverside. At the road's end rests a well-kept roundhouse, where occasional dances are held. At Chaw-Se's Big Time (p. 98), we are often treated to dances by a group of young people from here–dances beautifully executed by dancers elegantly costumed and well-trained. The people here are proud of their heritage, and are not letting it pass away.

52 *Pt. Arena–about 2 miles N of the town of Pt. Arena (on State Rte. 1), E off Windy Hollow Rd.*
Manchester–about 1 mile E of State Rte. 1 on Mountain View Rd. (toward Boonville) to a BIA *green sign, then north.*
Manchester-Pt. Arena Rancheria
284 Main St., or P.O. Box 623
Pt. Arena, CA 95468
(707) 882-2788

* **Dry Creek Rancheria** *Southern Pomo.* (1906) Sonoma Co.

High, and pretty dry, on a hillside with panoramic vistas of the Russian River and Alexander Valley, sits this very progressive rancheria–the closest one to San Francisco. Solar panels heat the new mobile home that serves as the tribal offices and community center; flowers grace the yards of most homes; a new water tank supplies the needs of the little rural community. Here, on some 75 acres (actually in ancient Wappo domain) live a number of the area's Southern Pomo people–several elderly and retired, but also a few children (who must be brought from home to school by car).

Delvin Holder, a Pomo of the Upper Lake Rancheria, supervises new construction on his home on the rancheria. (*dhe*, 1978)

53 *About 2 miles NW of "The Geysers" exit from State Rte. 128 (between Geyserville and Jimtown) is* BIA *Rd. 93 onto the rancheria.* (**Not** *near Dry Creek.)*
Dry Creek Rancheria
P.O. Box 413
Geyserville, CA 95441
(707) 433-1209

Cloverdale Rancheria (Khalanhko) *Southern Pomo.* (1921) Sonoma Co.

Amid a few vineyards on 27 acres of land live the two families who now privately own this rancheria. One family head, a Mr. Santana, is the retired postmaster of Cloverdale. The location, adjacent to local businesses, is almost flat and is in reality a suburb of Cloverdale, a pretty town in a wide part of the Russian River Valley, with low mountains of the Coast Range on both sides.

54 *Along Santana Rd. on the S end of Cloverdale (off U.S. 101).*

Upper Lake Rancheria (Xa-bé-mo-tolel) *Eastern Pomo* (*Mátuku* band). (1878, 1907) Lake Co. (See description, p. 73.)

Older homes spread over 483 acres of hillside.

59 *From Upper Lake (on State Hwy. 20) take the road to the Mendocino National Forest Ranger Station, continue about 1 mile N over the levees of a creek to Rancheria Rd., then left about ¼ mile to the road's end.*

Information:
Upper Lake Rancheria
c/o Ms. Georgianne Myers
5020 Lakeshore
Lakeport, CA 95453

Ya-ka-amá *All-Indian.* Sonoma Co. **

Some time back, Congress passed a law stating that Indians might claim any unused federal lands. This was the basis for the famous takeover of Alcatraz Island of 1969–71, and which involved Pomo people. At about the same time an alert Sonoma Co. resident informed the local Pomos that several acres of a former (1955) government radio station site were unoccupied. Some 125 acres were then occupied by the people and Ya-ka-ama vocational school was begun, after obtaining considerable government support.

Today, in a cluster of several buildings, a number of activities support local Indian education. The most popular program is one of business and clerical training. A printing and graphics shop brings in income. Research into local educational needs is an on-going program. At Ya-ka-ama is a library of taped Indian dances for cultural and historical reference.

Jim Helman, Supervisor of Prints and Publications instructs a student of Ya-ka-ama in the operation of a printing press. Ya-ka-ama is an Indian education institution near Healdsburg, Sonoma Co., that specializes in vocational programs. (*dhe,* 1979)

An 1816 watercolor by Ludovik Choris of San Francisco Bay Miwok people. (*St. Pk.*)

Attending are some 40–50 students, mostly local, who work and study an average of five hours a day. On the grounds are a ballfield, a dance ground (with arbors), and a campground for occasional events. A large Spring Fair, held on the first weekend in June draws people to dances, a softball tourney, crafts, food, and even bingo.

57 *Take State Rte. 12 (N of Santa Rosa) to Old Healdsburg Rd. to the "wye" intersection at Eastside Rd. Follow the sign (at left) to "Sonoma Youth Camp" (which you pass) to end of road, about 1 mile.*
Ya-ka-ama Indian Education
6215 Eastside Rd.
Healdsburg, CA 95448
(707) 887-1541

** **Stewarts Point Rancheria (Cu-nú-nu shinal)** *Kashaya Pomo.* (1916) Sonoma Co.

Some reservations are on plains or meadows, hills or mountains. Some are in towns, but most are rural. This one, though, is the only one deep in a redwood forest, in the heart of ancient Kashaya country. It is the Kashaya's only rancheria [approximate translation:"huckleberry heights"], although many others of this people live not far away.

The towering redwoods absorb all extraneous sounds, and the quiet solitude of these 40 acres persuades visitor and resident alike to stillness. Despite the remoteness of the rancheria, there are a tribal office building and a new elementary school, where classes in the Kashaya Pomo language are given.

Important for the continuance of the Kashaya culture are two roundhouses–dances are held about twice a month, with very special festivals of the four seasons: Strawberry (spring), Fourth of July (summer), Acorn (fall), and Christmas (winter). Also, non-Indians are usually invited to participate in these festivities. The dancers often perform their beautifully mystical rituals at other inter-tribal functions as well.

58 *From the town of Stewarts Point (15 miles N of Ft. Ross on State Rte. 1) follow the winding Stewarts Point-Skaggs Spring Rd. about 4 miles east, through the forests along the Gualala River to the rancheria–a clearing on a hilltop covered with redwoods.*
Stewarts Point Rancheria
1112 Mendocino Ave.
Santa Rosa, CA 95401
Tribal office (Sea Ranch) (707) 785-2594

* **Robinson Rancheria** *Eastern Pomo.* (*ca.* 1910, 1984) Lake Co.

Although checkerboarded with non-Indian parcels, the inevitable result of once-terminated status, the people of the tiny Robinson have again returned to their few acres to reservation status. Their homes are clustered in a small valley near Clear Lake, the source of their ancestors' life.

The hills around appear as though giant bowling balls lay under a huge carpet. On one of these hillsides above the little valley the spirits of the ancient people must still dwell–around the marked and unmarked graves of the cemetery. It was near this site that the Bloody Island Massacre took place in 1850 (see p. 22).

60 *On State Rte. 29, about 2 miles S of its intersection with Rte. 20, is Rancheria Rd. The rancheria is located right there on 43 acres. A second 100-acre parcel some 8 miles distant has been newly acquired for homesites.*
Robinson Rancheria
2000 Marconi Ave., Ste. B-2
Sacramento, CA 95825
(916) 922-4536

Big Valley (Mission) Rancheria *Eastern Pomo.* (1870, 1911) Lake Co.

Big Valley is really a flat, rich plain on the margins of Clear Lake, just to the north of the sacred Indian peak of Mt. Kanocti. In an effort to help the people of this place, one Father Luciano Osuna bought 160 acres of land in 1870 and established St. Turibus Mission here.

In 1912, the present rancheria (federal) was established, but since that time most of the land was sold upon termination, and turned into pear orchards. Nevertheless, a few of the people still live in a row of homes along the road, and have built a dancehouse to sustain their shrinking cultural roots. (The dancehouse is on private land and is off-limits to strangers.)

[Note: In Lakeport there are also an Indian Center and several centers for the betterment of life of local Native Americans.]

61 *South of Lakeport take the small lake-edge road (E of State Rte. 29) for about 5 miles. A row of ten to fifteen frame homes of the remaining residents identifies the few acres of land left.*
Big Valley Village Association
P.O. Box 993
Lakeport, CA 95453

El-ém (Sulphur Bank) Rancheria *Southeastern Pomo.* (1949) Lake Co. ★★
(See description, p. 73.)

The cultural and residential center for regional native peoples. Some roundhouse dances on weekends are open to the public. Inquire first.

62 *From State Hwy. 53, about 2 mi. S of its intersection with Hwy. 20 (SE of Clearlake Oaks), take the BIA road (green with white arrowhead) at the old mine tailings.*
El-ém Indian Colony
P.O. Box 618
Clearlake, CA 95423
(707) 998-1666

Middletown Rancheria (Callayomi) *Lake Miwok* (and *Pomo?*). (1910) Lake Co. ★

The pines of the north slopes of Mt. St. Helena (near Calistoga) shade the few remaining dwellings of Callayomi, once a big center for the Lake Miwok. Yet the 36 residents of the three families who live here do have some ambitions to better their world. Some basketry is woven here, and the chairman wants to start a public business at the edge of the 109 acres.

The site is pleasant, the clouds scraped by the mountain drop some rain here in the otherwise dryish valley. The famous old roundhouse is gone; but the residents say that, perhaps someday, another will rise.

[Note: It is imperative the visitors *never* photograph ruins of a dancehouse. In the Indian tradition of the belief of the vitality of all things, one elder told me, "You wouldn't go as a tourist into a hospital to photograph wounded people, would you?"]

66 *About a mile S of Middletown, on State Rte. 29, at Rancheria Rd.*
Middletown Rancheria
P.O. Box 572
Middletown, CA 95461

Alexander Valley Rancheria *Wappo.* (1909, 1913) Sonoma Co.

Beyond the end of Soda Rock Rd. alongside the Russian River stand some old buildings of the former rancheria, now occupied by non-Indians. The last old man's wife died, his children were all away, so Jim Adams left, possibly to rest now with his ancestors in the old Wappo burial grounds hidden (but not forgotten) in the forest near Alexander Valley road.

This rancheria, between Jimtown and Healdsburg, was the last of the Wappo reservations; but its termination certainly wasn't the last of the Wappo, several of whom are active in Indian affairs in the region around Healdsburg and Santa Rosa.

65

** **Anderson Marsh State Park** Ancestral *Pomo* land. Lake Co.

As the natural beauty of Clear Lake becomes more and more obscure from development, the difficulty of preserving it becomes more difficult. Anderson Marsh is a newly-designated preservation area. The 900-acre Park, only recently opened to the public, is the site of an old ranch, located at the outlet of Clear Lake into Cache Creek. The reeds of the marsh have been used by the native lake dwellers for centuries, and the park itself contains the remains of an ancient village site, partly excavated.

Under the guidance of some local Pomos, some model tule huts have been erected in the oak savannah adjacent to the marsh–now deserted but for the multitude of wildlife. The old ranch buildings are the site of a small museum, and serve as the center of Lower Lake Heritage Days in late October.

A visit here with a long walk around the marsh gave me a profound sense of going back in time to a tranquil meadow by an ancient quiet village.

near 63 *Entrance from St. Hwy. 53 on SW bank of Cache Creek in Lower Lake. Information available at Clearlake State Park, Kelseyville. (707) 279-4293.*

*** **Kule Loklo** Ancestral *Coast Miwok* land. Marin Co.

Kule Loklo ("Bear Valley") is the Coast Miwok name for a meadow near the Seashore headquarters–it was never a village site. But an Indian village characteristic of that people is being developed here, so that all people may feel what life was like in a coastal village before the white man.

Go into the sweathouse and imagine the pungent smoke opening your pores. Grind acorns into the Indian's staple food; watch it being cooked in a basket with hot stones; taste it. Smell the fresh tule reeds of the dwellings. Let the mystery of the dances permeate all your senses, as both Indian and other local groups perform.

The National Park Service and the Miwok Archaeological Preserve of Marin are re-creating this village, the only one of its kind in California.

The structures are built to the best of current anthropological, cultural, and archaeological knowledge. Isabel Kelly has written, "Effectively, [the Coast Miwok] people and culture have disappeared."[18] It was the Coast Miwok people who once inhabited Marin Co. and southern Sonoma Co. in the Sonoma River Valley. However, as we can see so frequently around California, descendants of supposedly "extinct" Indian groups are appearing from their long obscurity. Today, here at Kule Loklo, descendants of the early Miwok people emerge from their private lives to dance or take part in local festivals. Since the dancehouse has been scrupulously constructed following Miwok custom, local Miwok, Pomo, and Kashaya Pomo feel they can dance in an authentic setting.

The second Saturday in July has been set aside for the well-attended Annual Native American Celebration here. Also, a number of National Park Service rangers are local Indian people who take part in the celebration. They welcome your questions on Indian life.

67 *Marked trail, ¼ mi. from:*
Pt. Reyes National Seashore Visitor Center
Pt. Reyes, CA 94956
(415) 663-1092

D-Q University *All Indian.* Yolo Co. **

From all over California and many parts of the United States students come to D-Q U, near Davis, to find courses and directions not offered in any other two-year college. Here they find new directions and Indian orientation in social sciences, indigenous studies, the sciences and humanities, agriculture, and what is most properly called "appropriate technology." The latter is the study of the applications of technology to problems encountered in the many environs of Native Americans.

An average of about 200 full and part-time students live either in campus dormitories or in nearby towns. Their tuition plus Federal funding supports the "U," as it is actually known. The staff is partly volunteer and part-time, and, under a unique and beneficial arrangement the administrative staff also teaches.

The buildings themselves are to be found in the midst of open fields—the site of a former military communications station. Some buildings aren't much to look at, but they are serviceable. Along with the considerable open acreage for powwows and dances, the physical plant is used for numerous Indian conferences and gatherings.

D-Q U's name derives from both Indian and Latino spiritual names—names not publicly used, but to be kept in the mind as reminders of the ultimate dedication of the school. (The Latino groups have withdrawn for the present, owing to vicissitudes of government funding.) D-Q U was the Western center and origin of the recent "Longest Walk" on Washington for Native American rights. Continued existence of this campus has been only with great struggle.

68 *North of Road 31, about 5 miles W of Woodland, or about 2 miles E of I-505 (follow road signs.)*
D-Q U
P.O. Box 409
Davis, CA 95616
(916) 758-0470

The Indian Historian Press

A unique and unusual Indian institution, located in San Francisco, is the Indian Historical Society. This group, oriented toward all Native Americans, is primarily a press that publishes books on American Indians and the well-known magazine *Wassaja–The Indian Historian.*

Visitors by appointment only.
The Indian Historian Press
1493 Masonic Ave.
San Francisco, CA 94117
(415) 626-5236

Northern California Powwows* *Intertribal.*

Of all Indian events in California, the most emotionally charged, electrifying, visually exciting is the powwow. It is testimony to a latter-twentieth century cultural diffusion into Indian California.

Powwows are the gatherings of families, dancers in tribal dress, peoples from many tribes to the accompaniment of the incredibly stirring *drums.* A "drum" is really a whole group organized to sing and drum on the big, horizontal bass drum. In Northern California are a number of drums, usually organized by Plains, Midwestern, or Southwestern tribal peoples–"new" Californians.

Local colleges and universities seem to be the most popular and receptive places for the numerous intertribal powwows–and they are open to all interested persons. D-Q University (p. 85) hosts about one a month, and is particularly well-suited for gatherings, since the grounds are dedicated to Indian causes. Call them for a schedule.

Go and participate in a powwow. Become introduced into the world of the California Indian whose tribal heritage lies east of the Sierras.

* See also p. 140, Southern California Intertribal Activities.

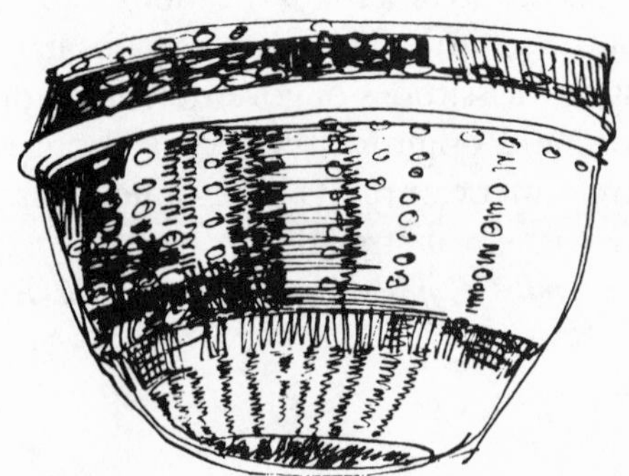

Southern Central Valley and Central Coastal, West of the Sierra Crest

Hokan Speakers*	**Penutian-Speaking Groups†**	**Shoshonean Speakers‡**
Esselen, Salinan, Chumash (and including *Tataviam [Takic?]*)	*(Plains and Sierra) Miwok, Ohlonean (Costanoan), Yokuts*	*Western Mono (Monache)*

As WE MOVE southward across the great San Francisco Bay and southward of the delta of the Sacramento-San Joaquin River confluence, there is a marked ecological change in the state–it is drier than the northern counterparts of the northern Coast Range, the upper Central Valley, and the northern Sierra Nevada foothills. The southern Sierra are reasonably green and pine-forested. Except for a narrow band of green along the Big Sur coast, the Coast Range supports a rather sparse oak population; however, the San Joaquin Valley would be desert but for the Sierra streams that meandered (today highly regulated) across it, searching for the sea.

The Plains and Sierra Miwok bands, the several Yokuts tribes, and the Western Mono (a group of Uto-Aztecan speakers who pushed west across the Sierra) occupied the Valley and foothills. The south coast (including Santa Cruz and Big Sur) mountain region was occupied by the Penutian Costanoans and the Hokan-related Esselens, Salinans, and the Chumash.

As we move southward, we also move into tribal areas more and more influenced, decimated, and often totally extinguished by early Spanish occupation. As in the north, if the reader sees no reference to the remnants of a people in present-day reservations, there is a chance that those people are culturally nearly unseen.

For instance, the Esselen of Big Sur were never a large or prosperous group, and by 1800 they were totally absorbed by the Carmel Mission, where most perished. Their southerly neighbors, the Salinans, fared a tiny bit better. Although their early culture is

* See footnote †, Northwest, p. 36.

† "Penutian" is the made-up word for "two," from Maidu and Costanoan. See footnote †, Northeast, p. 52.

‡ See footnote §, Northeast, p. 52.

The Sierra Miwok and Mono peoples of the Sierra foothills (near Yosemite Park) built tipi-like shelters of bark slabs. Cornucopia-shaped burden baskets, slung from the forehead, carried everything from firewood to berries. (Photo by Fiske, about 1870. *St. Pk.*)

Old Gabriel, one of the thousands of Esselens buried at Carmel Misson. His grave, unlike most, is well-marked. (*St. Pk.*)

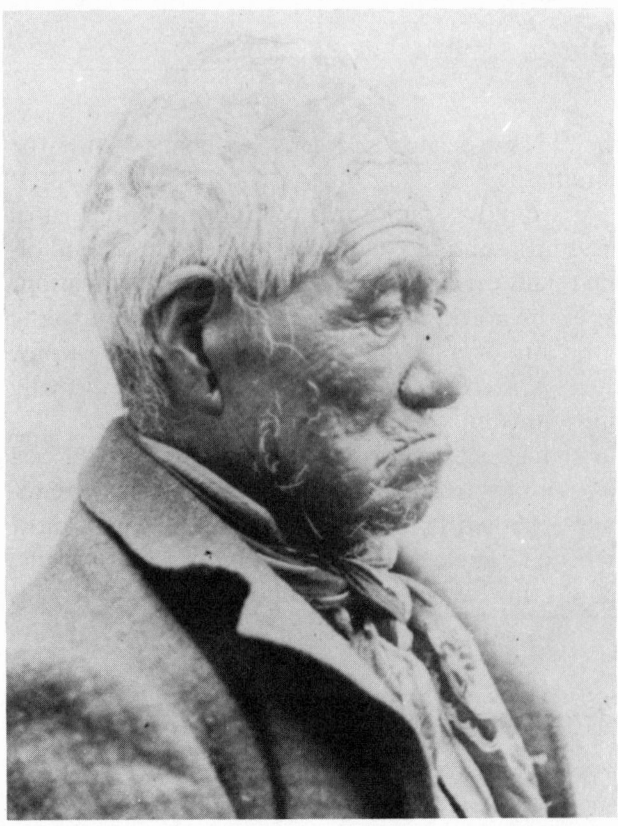

almost completely unknown, a few cultural remnants are at the Missions San Antonio and San Miguel, and even now several Salinan families are scattered about the anhydrous hills of the southern Big Sur and Diablo Ranges. These people were never given the cultural protection of a reservation, so the inevitable happened. . . .

The coastal hills, marshes, and valleys of the San Francisco-Monterey Bays, south to Santa Barbara, were abundant sources of both sea and land plants and animals for food and shelter. Lifestyles of these coastal people tended to be somewhat similar to one another and different from their inland kin. Obviously, their food was rather different, the usual acorn and game diet being supplemented by fish, shellfish, waterfowl, and sea animals.

The waters of San Francisco Bay, Tulare Lake,* and the Santa Barbara Channel are pretty quiet, so it was only natural that boats would be designed and fabricated for fishing and transport. The Ohlone tribes (Costanoans) of San Francisco Bay and the Central Valley Yokuts habiting Tulare Lake fashioned tule reed balsas [boats] like those of the Clear Lake peoples, but more crude than those of the Quechua and Aymara of Bolivia.

In the Santa Barbara Channel, several Chumash tribes built extremely elaborate seagoing plank canoes [*tomols*] from twelve to thirty feet long. These launches served for fishing and ferry alike–being used for transport to the people living on the Channel Islands.

Imagine how impressive the tomols must have been in both their design and their art. Their great hulks had been covered with a rusty red, like the bottoms of modern boats, but the prows were bedecked with *beaded* designs. In design, they were a ribless, double-ended dory, made of short planks stitched together and cemented with asphalt that oozes from the local tar pits.

The woodworking industry was so well established when the Spanish fleet came upon the area, that they named one village Carpentería, a name which survives today.

Boats, bowls, knives and arrows were the Chumash's choice works. For their bowls, they carved steatite [soapstone]. Large mines and factories produced this

*Tulare Lake is hard to find on modern maps. It lay in the center of Kings County, rising and falling with runoff of the Sierra streams. It survives today as a bird sanctuary marsh, hemmed in by dikes.

mineral, popular because it does not crack when heated, and it is easy to carve into many shapes. More than their sensitively-carved everyday working bowls, they fashioned objects for the art alone, some resembling Eskimo (Inuit) soapstone carvings. Among Chumash superlatives, basketry art must be included–especially the use of tiny motifs in the woven design.

While speaking of the Chumash arts and industries, I must also mention that the Chumash rock paintings rank among the most imaginative in the United States (see p.104). Quoting Campbell Grant: "The extraordinarily fanciful character of many of the paintings suggests that they were painted by persons under the influence of the powerful hallucinogen, *toloache* [datura or jimson weed]."

Most of the coastal peoples lived in rounded, thatched huts, unlike those structures to the north and east. Sometimes the floor was excavated, and sometimes these "huts" reached an immense fifty feet in diameter–a straw apartment flat. (Some small examples may be seen at the Santa Ynez Reservation.) Nearly all bands used sweathouses, but dancing was out-of-doors in enclosures, the weather being good most of the year.

Though not much is known of the ancient myths and religion (none is practiced today), it is known that Coyote was joined by a nautical counterpart, Swordfish. And shrines were erected to a provident deity, Shup, who was symbolized with feathers on a high pole, and to whom gifts were presented.

Life for the inland dwellers, the Plains Miwok and Valley Yokuts, was different in the extreme from that of the coastal peoples. The fact that the Central Valley flooded twice a year, with winter rains and spring Sierra snow melt, forced the Valley dwellers into migratory habits. This is not to say that the land was not provident–deer, roots, seeds, fish, and birds abounded. Indeed, fishing and fowling were the most widespread subsistence occupations.

At the northern end of this range, acorns and salmon were added to the diet, but oaks don't grow in the swampy, marshy, often salty flats of the San Joaquin Valley.

Homes here were conical, usually thatch of tule, the most common material. Many villages had an earth-covered assembly (dance) house, half-sunken, as in the north.

The Kuksu ideas seem not to have penetrated the religious life; instead, the quasi-religious use of

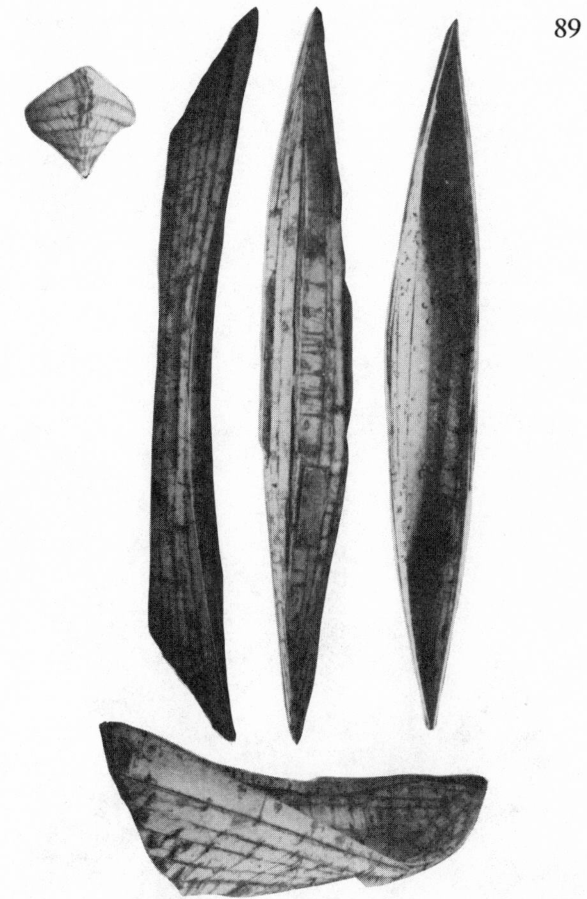

Details of a Chumash tomol (canoe), about 30 feet long. These craft were planked, fastened with sinew, and caulked with natural asphalt which oozes near Santa Barbara. The boats were seaworthy and capable of journeys to the Channel Islands, some 30 miles offshore. A surviving, decorated tomol is on public display at Santa Barbara City Hall. (*St. Pk.*)

Bob Bautista, Yokuts shaman, displays his basketry and some of his medicine equipment (*St. Pk.*, 1920)

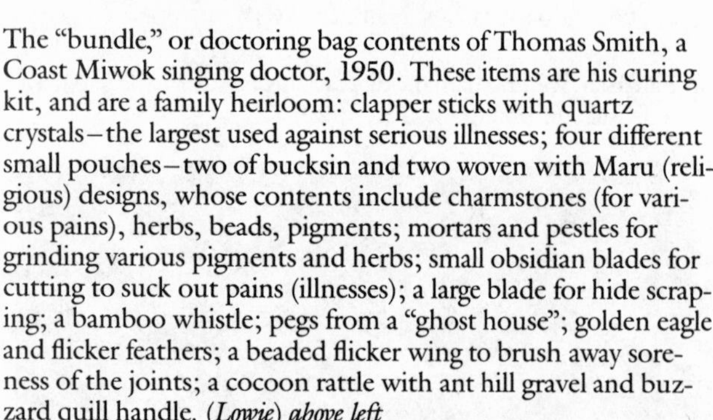

The "bundle," or doctoring bag contents of Thomas Smith, a Coast Miwok singing doctor, 1950. These items are his curing kit, and are a family heirloom: clapper sticks with quartz crystals–the largest used against serious illnesses; four different small pouches–two of bucksin and two woven with Maru (religious) designs, whose contents include charmstones (for various pains), herbs, beads, pigments; mortars and pestles for grinding various pigments and herbs; small obsidian blades for cutting to suck out pains (illnesses); a large blade for hide scraping; a bamboo whistle; pegs from a "ghost house"; golden eagle and flicker feathers; a beaded flicker wing to brush away soreness of the joints; a cocoon rattle with ant hill gravel and buzzard quill handle. *(Lowie) above left*

A mid-day shaft of light drenches a young dancer with its radiance in the Chaw-Se dance house. The occasion is the Chaw-Se Grinding Rocks Big Time, September, 1981. *(dhe) above right*

toloache became the chief foundation of a system of beliefs. (Anthropologists use the harsh word "cult," which I shall not.) As we shall see, toloache was used nearly universally in the southern half of California–the Yumans to the point of practicing "dreaming" frequently.

Both the Miwok and the Yokuts of the valley had kin in the Sierra foothills–the latter making contact with the Western Mono, and all of them living more like the peoples of northern California than either the Valley or the coast dwellers. Once again, where there were oaks, acorns were eaten; where there was bark, homes were of wood; where there were streams, there was fishing. Every people exhibited art in basketry, nearly all peoples played similar games (shinny, hand-guessing gambling, archery). Nearly all had tales of the animal spirits–Coyote, Eagle, Bear, Antelope, etc., and many family clans took on their symbols.

Now I am at Chaw-Se, an ancient village site, an oak-shaded meadow opening in the piney woods of the foothills.

Saturday evening–about sundown–the dancers take their wrapped costumes to the dance house to dedicate the house and themselves to the ceremony. Then the people may enter. The house is conical outside, covered with slabs and shingles, and is set several feet below ground level. Four tall, heavy poles support the roof beams.

We enter. Smoke from a dim fire snake-wiggles out a small hole in the top. The silhouettes of a hundred people seated on logs and pine needles line the walls and fill the space up to the rectangular dance area in the center. We have returned to the womb of Mother Earth.

A drum beat begins like the Mother heart throb. A small clutch of singers at the rear begin their chants–as they will intermittently for long into the night. The "Big Head" dancer appears from the entrance. Like sprays of fireworks or a huge dandelion, his headdress sprouts willow branches tufted with feathers, his head entirely covered with a long hat of reeds emblazoned with many-colored bird feathers. He puffs a long reed whistle. His partner arrives, with clackers in hand, a headdress of a long band of bright feathers wrapped about his forehead. We can see his face. Both dancers wear grass skirts covering long john-like leggings.

The movements are the graceful short, sharp, watchings of a deer, or a hawk–stalking, or taking care not to be stalked. After a few minutes of dancing, the leader faces the entrance of the house, as if asking for a blessing. His vision obscured, he is guided backwards into the night, like an airplane towed to its hangar. The people respond with a deep-felt "HO."

Mystical, yet informal, audience participation is requested–a simple dance at the ringside–but to do this one contributes a few coins to the collector (who also will receive from those who want to take photos). The dance is repeated several times. The drum is a plywood board placed over a small trench in the floor for resonator–it is tapped by foot or with a burlap-tipped pole.

The dance changes. This time the dimness is brightened by expert teenagers, with headdresses like deer antlers, wearing aprons of black and white feathers, occasionally flipping up the rear of the apron, like wrens or magpies or can-can dancers.

Later, standing outside in the warm summer air, the chanting, drumbeats, and smoke odor still penetrating my senses, I felt I had not yet been reborn to the 20th-century world. I found, as you may today, the Indian tradition–both ancient and adapted.

The lower foothills of the Sierra Nevada, up to about 2,000 feet, vary from rounded, grassy knolls to steep canyon-sides. Over all, there is a dappling and flecking of oaks–tall valley oaks to thorny scrub oaks. Oaks, of course, being the provider of acorns–the staple diet of most of the foothill Indian peoples.

These woodlands and meadows, rather dry in summer, except for the trickle of streams, easily yielded sustenance to the rather meagre bands of Yokuts and Mono. Then, the gold miners surged in, and most withdrew after their despoilage and ravage of the land and its people.

The Indian peoples here, as nearly everywhere, were forced to retreat to survive. Very few reservations and rancherias were provided in this region. And today's foothills land boom has made what places were reserved even more attractive to acquisitive whites. For instance, the formerly 80 acres of the Picayune Rancheria was once a casualty of termination. Only one Indian family now lives here–although they are very active in Chukchansi Yokuts affairs. As a matter of interest, the Picayune Rancheria occupies the site of a very early Indian village. Most of the extant Chukchansi still live within a few miles of here.

Another Chukchansi rancheria had existed near the town of Ahwahnee (not the one of Yosemite Park), where today there remains a burial ground, an old roundhouse, and grinding rocks. These fell into the hands of local whites for many years, but in 1978, the California Department of Parks and Recreation bought the site, evicting the former "owner."

One day I met an enthusiastic group there, planning the Wassama roundhouse restoration which had been tumbled to the ground by the former tenant. I appreciated the eagerness in the group when I recalled the Indian concept of the vitality of all things, especially ceremonial places. A roundhouse restoration can be the enabling of a miraculous recovery of a very ill being.

It's curious to me that the Chukchansi dance indoors, because it has been reported that their Valley ancestors never did. I suspect that the dancehouse may be a structure borrowed from other nearby peoples, the Mono or the Miwok.

Strange that the Yokuts were probably the most numerous group in all California, occupying the entire San Joaquin Valley and its foothills; yet today, finding bits of this once-extensive group (as above) can be difficult.

The countryside is certainly characteristic of the foothills, though Table Mountain is curious, with its flat top; while the adjacent Table Mountain Rancheria is studded with large granite boulders, like huge, moldy potatoes.

The original designation for this rancheria, 25 miles south of Ahwahnee, was for the Chukchansi tribe of Yokuts; but this is traditionally Dumna Yokuts country, and probably the truth is that the people are a mixture and remnant of the several Yokuts tribes that once frequented the valleys of these foothills. Just over the mountain once lay the hated symbol of oppression, Ft. Miller (see p.166). Today, Ft. Miller lies under the waters of Millerton Reservoir.

The 160-acre Table Mountain Rancheria nestles by some springs that water a few fields that in turn, support some cows which help nourish the residents. Although it was terminated, twelve Indian families remain in neat, small farms. There seems to be a great interest in basketball, judging from a dozen courts; a well-tended Protestant church sits in one corner. Many residents are employed by the Bureau of Reclamation at Lake Millerton. Take a drive through the paved loop road and see what a small self-supporting Indian community is like.

We go west and downslope to find one other band of Yokuts, to the Santa Rosa Rancheria, near Lemoore.

On a clear day you can see the distant Coast Range to the west or the Sierra to the east. Otherwise, all one sees is the *very* flat floor of the San Joaquin Valley. A mile or so from the rancheria, the lazy Fresno Slough meanders behind cattail and tule-lined banks, or rather, mud flats. A few miles south are the diked-in marshes of the bird sanctuary that comprises what's left of Tulare Lake. This is the country of the Táchi.

The rancheria land is, as usual, the worst of the land hereabouts. The soil is salty, practically useless for farming. Nevertheless, some people have tried small gardens. In this little 170-acre rectangle live some 30 families–people who may work the cotton fields–"tromping" or "chopping" (weeding) it, but no longer picking. Sometimes they obtain jobs in the canneries, sometimes in the vinyards or walnut orchards, but usually there's little else. Many of the homes are rundown; there is no money to fix them up. Santa Rosa isn't very isolated, so even preservation of the "old ways" is disappearing.

"In the old days we had a dancehouse," reported one lady I encountered walking with one of her ten children. "At the end of August there's a festival–baseball, horeshoes, dances–another in March. It's good for the kids. They don't have much to do. They don't like high school.

"Yes, there's some friction there between the Indian kids and the others. They generally leave for the cotton ranches. Me? I travel a lot around here, but I've only gone more'n a hundred miles twice in my 48 years."

A community center is here, and a large baseball field with a few ramadas for shade. Little else.

Snow and ice carved the Yosemite Valley; then man came to live here, then other men came to see, evicting the first tenants. Nevertheless, in one tiny corner of this vast waterfall-tasseled canyon, a valiant effort to show something of the original people is being sustained by a small crew of Native Americans.

In an enclosure behind the Park Visitor Center, local Indian people perform the daily tasks of early Indian life for the thousands of visitors–curious and indifferent alike. Around the village of four or five slab dwellings, roundhouse, and sweathouse, they and their friends grind acorns and prepare, in 70-year-old baskets, the food that was the staple of Californians for centuries.

Erected near the site of original *Awani*, the roundhouse and the sweathouse may be peered into, but not entered–for within them today a band of local Indian people hold their ceremonies. Many Miwok and other peoples from down the Merced Valley never had a reservation; they consider this place sacred and occasionally make use of the village for their assemblies.

One experience of the awesomeness of this valley, and all people of sensitivity will consider it sacred, too. There is a great spirit abroad. Go, visit the village, find some of the experience of original people here and lose the mechanical world outside. See for yourself the blend of early Indian with his environment.

Julia Parker, resident Sierra Miwok at Yosemite Park's Indian village, prepares a meal of acorn mush for the public in the old way. A replica of a Miwok shelter stands in the background. (*dhe,* 1980)

The setting–a little foothill lumbering town, too small even for the usual fast food chains. The temperature was 32° and the green hills were already neatly sliced off with snow-bearing clouds.

I gave myself a tour of the old rancheria, now all private land. But the people still live in the wooden cabins with vertical siding, and gray wood smoke dribbles out of the chimneys. I talked with busy people at the new tribal office, then went my way for dinner. It was lightly snowing.

There are two bars in town. I chose the one with the restaurant, thinking to try the one with the pool hall later. A commotion of friendly sounds came from the back room–an Indian family had finished dinner and was exchanging goodbyes with the restaurant staff. It seemed to be a good sign that the Indian-white relations here were at least OK on the surface.

A young lady slipped quietly in from the cold, sat near me at the bar. We talked. She was Cherokee, had met a local Indian man in the East, came here, he split for elsewhere, but she stayed. Tonight, she had come to the bar to get warm. Her butane had given out in the trailer, and the butane man wouldn't be back until Monday. The restaurant bar was very quiet. "How about the other bar?" she suggested.

It was 11 PM and 20°. In the pool hall bar were maybe twenty people–a general mix of Indian and non-Indian. Four guys had passed out and were draped about some chairs at the wall. Nobody bothered them. It was warm here. Nobody was uptight, conversation was banal, except for numerous comments that the lumber mill wouldn't be hiring again next week.

Another week to look forward to doing nothing, since these were all mill hands. "Party?" Only about five people were interested, bundling up into the night to an old house, black under trees. Lots of cars already there. The party was talk, more beer, and a bushel sack of marijuana. None were overindulged in. Everybody sat around a hot wood stove on piles of old clothes or rickety chairs, telling tales of what their girlfriend or boyfriend did or said last week. No plans, no dreams. A chair broke, everybody laughed. I left soon. All those cars had been there for years.

Eastward from the Central Valley I set out to explore what I could find of the peoples of the central coast. Regrettably, I found mostly archeological sites. Gone are the San Francisco and Monterey Bay peoples, extinct is the Esselen culture, gone is the Salinan culture, the Tataviam. . . .

A few Ohlone families tend their ancestors' graves at the San Jose Mission and advise on other gravesites dug up by expanding cities. A few Salinan families eke out their lives in the dry Diablo and Big Sur mountains. Alone here are the Chumash people of Santa Barbara county. You will read of their small but progressive reservation later.

An ancient site of the Costanoan or Ohlone people is to be found at Coyote Hills Regional Park in Alameda County, near Hayward. The eastern shores of San Francisco once supported one of the most dense Indian populations in the United States–some 3-5 persons per square mile. The people here were of the Ohlone culture and spoke a variety of

Costanoan languages–at this place, the Chochenyo. Nature was kind and provident, so the people found little reason to move about. Settled into villages of 30–150 persons, they tended to stay for thousands of years.

How do we know? They left garbage piles, called middens or shellmounds. The one here has been dated as far back as 380 B.C. and was continuously used until about A.D. 1800.

Of nearly a dozen, this is the only shellmound left in the Bay Area, and it has been used in the past as a student "dig," so that now one can see a cross-section of the layers of discard. Digging has been halted to preserve the rest, but found among the ashes were bones of deer, tule elk, antelope, and, of course, many clamshells.

At the site, rangers and scouts erected tule dwellings of the type common for the Bay region. At the Visitor's Center, you may find artifacts, photos, and a real tule boat, and guides to the quiet, natural beauty of this bird sanctuary-marsh.

Travelling through this region of only monuments to former native life, I ran across one striking reversal of fate.

Some years ago a sensitive and energetic Chumash man looked about him and disliked what he saw happening to his modern Indian brothers and their white cousins. After devoting many years of hard labor and stubborn effort, Grandfather, as elder leaders are often called, established a 200-acre sanctuary in the La Panza Mountains of his ancestry. He named it the Red Wind Foundation.

This retreat-like area has a purpose: to return people to the land and their spiritual roots. The forty persons living here, both Indian and non-Indian, have come from all over the United States, and have founded an almost self-sufficient community.

For sustenance are farms, animals (including buffalo), a water supply, ponds, a windmill. Around the hillsides are scattered well-made, comfortable homes, both primitive style and more modern, several tents, tipis, and wickiups. I spoke briefly with young men from Arizona cutting wood. They told me the sparse pines and oaks of this fairly dry section of the Coast Range furnish wood for building and heating. I spoke with a young woman who helped erect and staff a school. I admired a dance house and an outdoor ceremonial arena, all under the shadow of Black Mountain, in the Los Padres National Forest.

The Foundation is private and deliberately remote–it is not for the casual visitor. I mention its existence to the reader as a bright light in an often dark picture of Indian existence. Arrangement to participate must be made through the in-town offices of the Red Wind Foundation, situated in a San Luis Obispo Federal office complex, or write:

Red Wind Foundation
P.O. Box 518
Santa Margarita, CA 92506

• • •

Place names with Indian sources in Central California:

Costanoan Carquinez (*karkin*, "traders," a tribe), Ohlone (tribal name), Aptos (village name)

Miwok Tuolumne (tribal name,–*umne*, "people"), Cosumnes (*kosun*, "salmon,"+ –*umne*), Mokolumne (*mugelemne*, a place name), Omo (village name), Mi-wuk (from *Miwok*, the tribe), Awahnee (*awani*, "deep grassy valley"), Yosemite (*uzumati*, "grizzly bear"), Hetch-Hetchy (*hatchatchie*, a grass), Tenaya (a chief), Wawona ("big tree")

Yokuts Kaweah (a tribe), Chowchilla (*chawchila*, tribal name)

Salinan Jolon, Cholame (place names)

Esselen Esalen (*eslenes*, a village)

Chumash The following are place names, although slightly altered versions of the original Chumash: Anacapa (*aniapa*), Calleguas ("my head"?), Castaic (*castac*, "our eye," a tribe), Cuyama ("clams"), Hueneme ("place of security"), Lompoc, Matilija (a poppy blossom?), Mugu (*muwu*, "beach"), Nipomo, Nojogui, Ojai (*a'hwai*, "moon"), Pismo ("tar"), Sespe, Simi, Sisquoc ("quail"), Saticoy ("I have found it"), Somis, Zaca

Original populations of Central California peoples before 1830:*

Esselen 500–1,000
Salinan 2,000–3,000
Plains and Sierra Miwok *ca.* 9,000
Ohlonean *ca.* 10,000 in 8 languages
Yokuts 25–30,000 in 3 groupings of about 40 tribelets
Chumash 10–20,000 in 6 languages
Western and Eastern Mono *ca.* 4,000

* The numbers given here and in other sections are early estimates, and they are doubtless low. They are presented to show the relative populations of various groups.

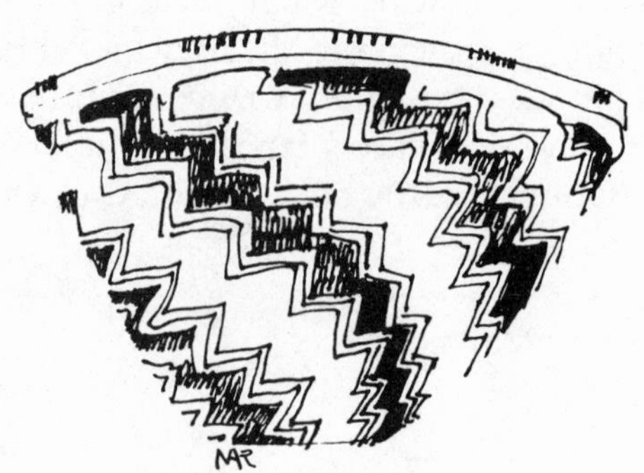

Reservation and Rancherias of the Southern Central Valley and Central Coast

Wilton Rancheria *(Plains) Miwok.* (1927) Sacramento Co. *

The land is flat, so flat that once, when it had only grass, it was called plains, and the local Miwok people were given that name. Today, on these now-irrigated plains, a variety of crops are raised, and the famous Rancho Seco nuclear power plant casts its hourglass shadow over the land.

The town of Wilton is a couple of stores and a small agricultural depot on the railroad–no more than that. And the rancheria, though terminated, has stuck together. Consisting of 39 acres, its appearance is what is almost "typical" for the small rectangles of rancheria parcels. About ten families, young and old, live here in neat, comfortable homes. Flowers, tall trees and gardens grace the community. I don't believe any ceremonies or dances are held here.

69 *From SE of Sacramento and State Hwy. 16, take Grant Line Rd. (2 mi. W of Sloughhouse) SW about 6 miles to Wilton Rd. In Wilton, Rancheria Drive leads to the place.*
Wilton Rancheria
9425 Rancheria Dr.
Wilton, CA 95693

Shingle Springs Rancheria and **El Dorado Tract** *(Northern Sierra) Miwok.* (1916) El Dorado Co.

Once, this 160-acre expanse of a few oaks and pines on low foothilly chaparral was the homesite for a few people shunted away from white society. Presently it won't support many, if any, but it could provide living space in the future.

Today, no one lives there–there is not even a road into the area. A second portion, called the El Dorado Tract, is now a freeway.

70 *Shingle Springs Drive exit from U.S. 50, N on the unpaved road about ½ mile into "developed" land (retiree cottages) alongside the reservation.*
Shingle Springs Rancheria
8024 Levering Way
Sacramento, CA 95801

Jackson Rancheria *(Northern Sierra) Miwok* (1893) Amador Co.

As the foothills rise into the Sierra Nevada, they become more and more wooded. The Jackson Rancheria lies within the woods–of oak and pine. And lumbering within its 330 acres makes it prosperous to its nine residents. What to see? A couple of remote houses up a little road.

One tribal member has been very active in construction of the new dancehouse at Chaw-Se (see p. 98).

71 *From Jackson, take New York Ranch Rd. NE to a small side road E about 5 miles S of Ridge Rd. intersection. It's easy to miss; however, their huge bingo hall isn't.*
Jackson Rancheria
2200 New York Ranch Rd.
Jackson, CA 95642

PRIVATE **Buena Vista Rancheria** *(Northern Sierra) Miwok*. (1927) Amador Co.

In the early days after its establishment, this place was a well-known ceremonial center, though only 70 acres. Today, all is in private hands, and only two structures remain–watching over a lonely burial ground.

A few low hills rise off the flats, but the once-gently rolling fields are now torn and scarred with the open wounds of coal and clay strip mines. And over what's left are scattered the metal and plastic of mobile homes–cheap land on the defaced countryside. The rancheria alone is an oasis.

72 *South of State Rte 88 near Ione lies the junction corners of Buena Vista. The rancheria is adjacent to an active coal strip mine, about a mile on south. Don't enter; the land is private, and the residents are not cordial to outsiders.*

Sheep Ranch Rancheria *(Central Sierra) Miwok*. (1916) Calaveras Co.

Take a winding road through the forests and the hills, through lumbering and mining communities, and find the settlement of Sheep Ranch. Find the schoolhouse (not difficult), and next to it find the 0.92 acre of this little rancheria, a postage stamp on the great parcel of the foothills. Its one resident doesn't even live here year-round. One wonders why the great white father even bothered.

A neighbor says the little government-plywood house, with a cat, is host to lively parties. He spoke kindly of his neighbor, who apparently spends some time in Tuolumne (see below).

74 *About 5 miles from Murphy's (just off State Rte. 4 NE of Angels Camp).*
Sheep Ranch Rancheria
Sheep Ranch, CA 95250
(See also Tuolumne Rancheria.)

*** **Chaw-Se, Indian Grinding Rocks State Park** *(Northern Sierra) Miwok*. Amador Co.

Several hundred years ago the ancestors of the present-day Miwoks found a flat meadow in the generally hilly, wooded foothills. Acorns showered from the tall oaks, a continuously-flowing stream gave water for drinking and acorn preparation, and several outcroppings of smooth granite projected from the ground, like the bald heads of buried gray giants.

The granite made a great place for grinding and washing the acorns, with space left over for chipping in some favorite designs and figures. There are literally dozens of grinding holes on the rocks and many of the petroglyphs are quite distinct, even after hundreds of years of weathering.

The local Miwok people have been called upon to add to this mystical site some of their early cultural heritage. Some primitive homes, made of slab, have been constructed, but most importantly, a roundhouse that is used by them for presentation of dances to the public, both Indian and non-Indian, has been carefully erected. It is the largest in California.

The "Big Time" celebration is held on the third weekend in September. All during the weekend, there is barbeque, Indian football (something like soccer plus hockey with a big, mushy ball), many other games and many other foods. Crafts are sold, conversation is exchanged, and

A Shake Head dance performed in the Chaw-Se dancehouse at Big Time, 1980. This dance is a more secular one, and sometimes may be photographed. (*dhe*) *left*

**

A Big Head dance photographed by A. L. Kroeber in 1910. Dance costumes used today have changed only in the materials used for some parts of the headdresses. The Big Head is a sacred dance, conceived in a dream centuries ago. Its dancers may be photographed these days only when dancing is not in progress. (*Lowie*) *right*

hundreds of Indians from miles around come to camp-meeting and to be together. (See also p. 91.)

73 *8 miles E of Jackson at Pine Grove, on State Hwy. 88, take the road to Volcano, N about 1 mile to the Chaw-Se entrance. Camping. Museum of Miwok culture open 9–5, Wed.–Sun. (209) 296-4440.*

Tuolumne Rancheria *(Central Sierra) Miwok* and *Yokuts*. (1910) Tuolumne Co.

The Tuolumne, the largest of the several Sierra Miwok rancherias, is the administrative and ceremonial center of its people. Oak forests creep to the edges of the small fields that form the large clearing in the center of the rancheria. While the fields are small, essentially small gardens or pastures, they do provide some additional support for the residents.

Of importance here are a medical dental-clinic, a fine tribal council building, and a dancehouse which fronts on a festival arena. Tuolumne features an acorn (and barbeque) festival open to the general public, the second weekend in September.

Next to some of the homes, which are quite scattered over the 336 acres, the people maintain a few individual sweathouses. It is obvious from the festivals and structures that the old traditions are kept here. Even the school has a club for the Indian children.

76 *About a mile out of Tuolumne on the road north connecting the town with State Rte. 108, is the rancheria sign (E).*

Tuolumne Rancheria
P.O. Box 696
Tuolumne, CA 95379
(209) 928-4277 (Health Center)

Chicken Ranch Rancheria *(Central Sierra) Miwok*. (1908) Calaveras Co.

In an old gold-mining foothill region, where the lonesome steam whistle of the Sierra Railroad still echoes, a few of the people are left from a once-terminated but recently restored rancheria. Today it is a mixed suburb of Jamestown, hardly a metropolis, but a suburb's a suburb. Most Indian activity outside of family life centers around the Tuolumne Rancheria a few miles east.

In 1985, the rancheria tribal income has been supplemented in a most unusual and lucrative manner. High-stakes bingo is offered here; however, since a number of outside authorities frown on such activities, it will be interesting to see how long this one can survive.

75 *From State Rte. 108, on the western city limit of Jamestown is Chicken Ranch Rd., which leads to the top of a hill and the Indian parcels remaining.*
Chicken Ranch Bingo
Jamestown, CA 95327
(209) 984-3000

*** **Ahwahnee Village, Yosemite National Park** [original territory of the] *Southern Sierra Miwok*. (1930s) Mariposa Co.
(For a description of this fascinating place and its people see p. 93.)

The native facilities here are used by both local Miwok and Paiute peoples. The adjacent Indian Museum is usually open daily. Its dioramas and collection of basketry, ornaments, and tools is excellent.

77 *Visitors Center of Yosemite National Park.*

** **North Fork Rancheria** *Western Mono* (or *Monache*). (1916) Madera Co.

The rancheria is a small, peaceful settlement of 80 acres of cabins and small homes scattered under the trees of a mountainside. Visit the *Sierra Mono Museum*, between North Fork and South Fork. It is also the tribal council headquarters for area residents and features excellent descriptive tableaux.

Note: The *Sierra* Mono people are separated from, but related to, the desert Eastern Monos across the mountains to the east. The Eastern Mono peoples have no reservation home and are widely scattered.

78 *Museum, 1 mile from North Fork on the road to South Fork. Rancheria, take Rd. 22 south toward Mammoth Pool, ½ mile past lumber mill to Cascadel Rd. 233, then ¼ mile to BIA Rd. 209 (dirt) at a church.*
North Fork Rancheria
Intertribal Council of California, Inc.
P.O. Box 275
North Fork, CA 93643

Big Sandy (Auberry) Rancheria *(Western) Mono.* (1909) Fresno Co.

Big Sandy occupies some 245 acres of a quiet foothill valley. The homes are scattered around the community–on several parcels of a few acres each, and today individually owned. There appears to be little "tribal" activity, only the family connections which seem to keep Indian consciousness alive.

79 *From the town of Auberry, about 4 miles up Huntington Lake Rd. to a Sierra National Forest signpost, left to the valley floor, signs to (Baptist Church) Mission Rd.*
Big Sandy Rancheria
P.O. Box 337
Auberry, CA 93602

Cold Springs Rancheria *(Western) Mono.* (1914) Fresno Co.

Of all the Sierra reservations, Cold Springs is the most hidden and remote. Green mountains surround the beautiful, secluded valley. Small homes, some mobile, others old, hide beneath the many trees, trying not to interrupt the expanse of green. I'm told that there aren't any dances, roundhouses, or other specially Indian events, just a quiet life on the 101 acres.

As I was leaving one moonlit evening, a shadowy figure in a long black cloth coat, bed roll nestled under one arm, glided up the dark road, attracting only the comments of the neighborhood dogs. Deer bounced across my path as I mounted the steep lane out of the valley.

80 *South of Tollhouse, on State Rte. 168, to Burroughs Valley Rd., go 5–6 miles E to Watts Valley Rd. (don't take it). Left on (unmarked) Sycamore Rd. across meadows, down a grade.*
Cold Springs Rancheria
P.O. Box 209
Tollhouse, CA 93667
(209) 855-2326

Picayune Rancheria *Chukchansi Yokuts.* (1912) Madera Co.
(See description, p 92.)

81 *Picayune Rd. (Rd. 417) leaves State Rte. 41 about 2 miles S of Coarsegold, and about 1 mile down the road is the rancheria, now private property.*

Wassama (Ahwahnee) Roundhouse *Chukchansi Yokuts.* Madera Co. **
(Details on the roundhouse and the tribal office, p. 92.)
This Ahwahnee roundhouse is not to be confused with the dancehouse in Ahwahnee Village, Yosemite Park.

82 *From State Hwy. 49, turn NE for ½ mile at the Ahwahnee Post Office to the Round House Ranch gate.*

Table Mountain Rancheria *Chukchansi Yokuts.* (1916) Fresno Co. *
(See description, p. 92.)

83 *Go 4 miles NE of Friant on the east shore drive of Lake Millerton to Table Mountain Rd. (loop through the rancheria).*
Table Mountain Rancheria
P.O. Box 243
Friant, CA 93626

Santa Rosa Rancheria *Táchi Yokuts.* (1921) Kings Co. *
(A description of the last refuge of the Tachi can be found on p. 92.)

84 *Between Lemoore and Stratford off State Hwy. 41; between Jersey and Kent Avenues, and W of 17th Ave.*
Santa Rosa Rancheria
16835 Alkali Dr.
Lemoore, CA 93245
(209) 924-1278

Tule River Reservation *Yokuts, Western Mono, Tubatulabal, Kitanemuk*, and others. **388** (1873) Tulare Co. ***

The Tule River Reservation was one of the first reservations in California, and because it was so early, became a refuge for the wreckage from numerous southern Sierra and Central Valley peoples. The most numerous were various tribes and dialectal bands of the Yokuts, the people of the southern San Joaquin Valley. Many of the other peoples from the Tehachapi region are quite few in number, and owing to their proximity to each other, have intermarried, effectively diminishing the variety of tribal influences.

The setting of the Painted Rocks Cave on the Tule River Reservation is in the rounded rocks of the foothills, where the cold Sierra streams plunge into the Central Valley. (*dhe*)

The reservation is the second largest in the state, at 54,116 acres, occupying the Tule River Valley between the lowest part of the foothills up to the Sierra forests of seven thousand feet altitude. Lumbering has been one of the most valued income producers, but now that the sawmill is closed, logs are brought down more sporadically.

The lower elevations, where most of the 375 residents live, consist of rocky, nearly treeless, dry and mountainous slopes. A number of small farming operations with horses, cows, sheep contribute to survival. Fortunately, there is room to spread out, and in many places the people live in new, modern, wooden homes.

Clustered about the population center are a striking new tribal office/library/community center (including a museum, until recently, when some items were stolen); a firehouse; medical, dental, and optical health services; a church, a school, and a small store.

Tule River holds no regular dances nor (to my knowledge) has a dance-house, but the festival of San Juan is celebrated at the rodeo grounds on the Saturday nearest June 24th.

For visitors there are two campgrounds, one known for summer fishing upriver, the other, the Painted Rocks Campground. Painted Rocks–accessible, well-protected, and accompanied by interpretive signs–are magnificent examples of ancient Southern Sierra pictographs. Several walls of a cave are painted in fantastic and realistic designs in white, yellow, red, and black. The colors have been preserved well for hundreds of years, and represent animals and geometric designs, most probably for shamanistic purposes.

Outside the cave, the Tule River tumbles over granite, and the numerous oaks of the valley once supplied the ingredients for the old grinding rocks there. I stayed a while to explore this placid, rustic setting and found a setback in time of many years.

This is a region of archaeological interest. The hills around Porterville bear a number of pictographs (rock paintings) and petroglyphs (carvings)–examples of early California art. High in Inyo National Forest above the reservation I stumbled upon grinding rocks–in a pine forest. Obviously, the early peoples here brought acorns up from the torrid summer valley for summer "campouts".

86 *From Porterville, take State Rte. 190 to Highway J-42 to the reservation. Two all-service campgrounds.*
Tule River Reservation
P.O. Box 589
Porterville, CA 93257
(209) 781-4271

Coyote Hills Regional Park *(Ohlone) Costanoan*. Alameda Co. **

(A description of this archaeological site may be found on p. 94.)

Coyote Hills Regional Park, near Fremont and Newark, CA. Guided tours Saturdays 2 PM to the shellmound; self-guided tours of the marsh, year-round; Visitors Center open 8:30–4:30. (415) 471-4967.

Santa Ynez Reservation *Chumash*. (1901) Santa Barbara Co. *

There are two centers of Chumash activity. One is in Santa Barbara for the benefit of Indian residents of that area. The other is this reservation, situated on 100 acres of an original "grant" by the Bishop of Monterey to Chumash families living near the Santa Ynez Mission.

The reservation, in the Santa Ynez Valley below a 3,000-foot mountain range, is growing remarkably. Several older homes and a large number of atypical new HUD homes dot the banks of willow-lined Zanja de Cota Creek. At the entrance is a very large, handsome tribal office, community center, and office for a large, commodious public trailer park.

Next to the center is an interesting old adobe home, and across the creek from the campground is a reconstruction of a typical ancient Chumash camp–made of tule reed.

88 *Adjacent to Santa Ynez (E of Solvang), just south of State Rte. 246. Nearby is the old Misión Santa Ynez (see p. 155).*

Santa Ynez Reservation
P.O. Box 517
Santa Ynez, CA 93460
(805) 688-7997

** **Chumash Painted Cave** Santa Barbara Co.

In the midst of the dry Santa Ynez Mountains above Santa Barbara are dozens of small caves bearing ancient multi-colored paintings and carvings, known only to a few archaeologists, local hikers, and the Chumash Indians. The caves are of a yellowish sandstone, reminiscent of those of the famous Mesa Verde in Colorado.

One of these is accessible to public view. Although the cave is barred to protect it from vandals and is usually rather dark, its brilliant colors of reds and yellows, whites, and black are as vivid as when they were painted.

Look at these fantastic spoked cogwheels, centipedes, striped humanoids, and eerie animals. Imagine yourself in a trance with a shaman–perhaps introducing you to the secrets of power–power with natural things and the animals of the hunt which will be your sustenance.

The real reasons for the paintings being there are unknown, or untold. Apparently, they were created between 1000 and 1800 A.D., and are reputed to be one of the most beautiful examples of Indian rock art in the United States.

near 88 *From Santa Barbara and State Rte 154, go east on Camino Cielo Rd. off Rte. 154 two miles to Painted Cave Rd. Turn right, go past a huge "Painted Cave" sign about one mile through a very winding one-lane road in a wooded area alongside a stream to the cave.*

Southern California and East of the Sierra Nevada

Hokan Speakers*
Washo (Lake Tahoe Region)
Ipai, Tipai, Kumeyaay (Kamia) (All three formerly called *Diegueño*)
Quechan
Halchidhoma
Hamakhava (Mohave)

Uto-Aztecan Language Speakers†
Shoshonean: Northern Paiute-Bannock, Owens Valley Paiute, Eastern Mono, Shoshone (including *Death Valley, Panamint, and Koso peoples*), *Chemehuevi (Southern Paiute), Kawaiisu*
Takic: Gabrielino-Fernandeño, Luiseño-Juaneño, Cahuilla, Cupeño, Serrano-Vanyume, Kitanemuk
Tubatulabal: Tubatulabal

ONE GLANCE at the map and it might be said that this is the region of the Indians of Dry California. And, as always, the climate and ecology subjects the inhabitants to certain similar ways of life, but not all ways. As we see from the variety of language families, differences go far back into the past of these peoples, as well as differences provoked by local geography.

What is this land? An ocean at the western extremity, warmer than in the north, a coastal zone of small and large marshes (among which today ply boats and ships of Marina del Rey of Los Angeles and the harbors of Long Beach and San Diego). Mountains which rise to 10,000 feet and scrape winter rains and snows from the wind. Chaparral-flecked hills that shelter oak-tufted stream beds. Deserts that are among the driest and hottest in the world; high plains that do not detain the hot and cold wind. Rivers that bring streams of water to their deep, highly

* See footnote †, Northwest, p. 36. Judging from their places on the map, it is believed the Hokan speakers may have been in California first, then were split and pushed aside and southward by Penutian speakers. Finally, it appears that the Uto-Aztecans penetrated from the east, completely separating the once-similar language groups.

† Three groups of languages comprise the California Uto-Aztecans: the Shoshonean (or Numic), the Takic, and the Tubatulabal. The Shoshone affiliation is widespread, including the Shoshone tribes, the Utes/Paiutes, and even the Comanches. The language of several Takic peoples was extinct (owing to the missions) long before they were known by Westerners.

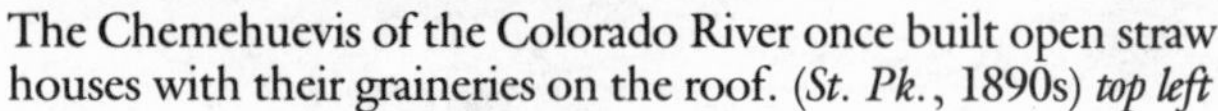

The Chemehuevis of the Colorado River once built open straw houses with their graineries on the roof. (*St. Pk.*, 1890s) *top left*

Mourners at a Hamakhava (Mohave) cremation ceremony in 1926. (Photo by E. H. Kemp. *Lowie*) *top right*

The Washos, living in the high and often cold deserts of California and Nevada, were highly skilled in weaving blankets of rabbit skins. (*St. Pk.*) *middle right*

Like this family, many Hamakhavas lived in wood and mud homes from the 1880s until only recently, when government aid and land development vastly improved their well-being. (*St. Pk.*, 1890s) *lower left*

colored valleys and canyons–and end there. This is Dry California.

Who were here, who were the early peoples? As we look first at the northern part, then toward the south, we see an increasing complexity and structuring of life and village organization, as well as formalized rituals. As A. L. Kroeber observed, there are fewer dances, less use of the dancehouse, less regalia and paraphernalia, and an "increase of personal psychic participation, of symbolism and mysticism, of speculation or emotion about human life and death, and of intrinsic interweaving of ritualistic expression with myth."[14]

Many of the people here, especially in southwestern California, followed Chi-ngich-ngish, erecting to his spirit small, sacred temples with a small skin and feather image. Around the image were ornamentations with elegant geometric sand paintings of symbolic spiritual references to the heavens and earth.

Here, too, the shamans had more power and functions than those of the north–they might be rainmakers as well as doctor-priests; they might transform into bears; they might use hypnosis; or they might use something like the voodoo of Haiti and Brazil, casting spells upon others.

We find climatic differences among the peoples. "Changes in attitude with changes in latitude," said Jimmy Buffet. The peoples of the north, though restricted in movement by weather and climate, were interlinked by an "elite" of multilingual traders and religious leaders. Traders disseminate the goods of diverse cultures.

More importantly, the religious leaders established a vast network among groups, allowing the great religions to spread and enabling intertribal alliances to keep the peace.

In the south, trade was common, mutual traditions shared, and people were accustomed to move about more freely; but paradoxically, intergroup conflict was more widespread, possibly because the religious network was less extensive.

To those not ready for the desert, it can appear a hostile place, but to its inhabitants, it was home, and they found ways to deal with it. The Paiutes and Shoshones of the Owens Valley, the Mojave Desert, and the ranges and basins around Death Valley weren't many in number, but they were there. They found the rare water, they painted magnificent pictures on the dry rocks, they lived in temporary brush and frame houses, for they were frequently on the move. Before the horse, people traveled on foot.

Other peoples on and around the southern slopes of the Sierras (the Kawaiisus and Kitanemuks) and in the southern coastal mountains (what is now the metroplex of Los Angeles to San Diego) were fortunate to have more water–and more grass for seeds, piñon pines for nuts, oaks for acorns, animals for game, and for those directly on the coast, fish and shellfish.

These people lived variously under what has been described as large, thatched domes, or less imposing conical structures or in summer, simple open sheds (examples at the Morongo Reservation, p. 138). Sweathouses were known here, and were earth-covered. Large ceremonial dancehouses were used, and there was often a fenced-in temple. The further south and east one goes, the more skilled were the potters. Cahuillas, Yumans (lower Colorado River peoples), and the Hamakhavas (Mohaves) showed the greatest proficiency, with their artistry in pottery and basketry coming from a Southwestern Hakataya influence. North of the southern Sierra, pottery apparently was not made–inventive basketry took over its function.

Meanwhile, over along the Colorado River, peoples such as the Hamakhavas, Chemehuevis, and the various Yumans were living their lives somewhat differently from their neighbors across the desert. Owing to their source of being–the huge River in the desert –they were a bit more sedentary, although there seems to have been a good bit of shifting of territories up and down the river.

These peoples acquired many of their modes of life from further east and south: (1) earth-covered dwellings, likely related to the pueblos and kivas or wattle-and-daub (interlaced branches or reeds covered with mud, as seen at the Ft. Yuma Reservation Museum, p. 125); (2) pottery making and decorating; (3) cultivation of corn, squash, and beans–the only intensive agriculture known in California;* (4) a "dreaming" form of inner religious experience; (5) a more "political" tribal organization with a sense of a whole people, more like the central U.S. peoples.

Over Dry California, then, ranged three rather distinct groups: (1) the coastal peoples usually related in

* The territories of the Colorado River and desert peoples support few or no oaks for acorns.

Desert dwellings of sod-covered roof and a brush wind shield, like this one of the Colorado River, were made of readily available materials. Though more primitive than homes of planks or thatch, they served to protect the inhabitants from wind and weather, and for a semi-nomadic people, they were easy to construct and easy to leave. (*St. Pk.*)

Yuman (Quechan) women of the lower Colorado River were, in 1890, proud of their beauty-enhancing body marks. Tattooing was a common practice throughout California. Clothing in the scorching climate of this region was pretty scanty. (*St. Pk.*)

language and customs to those further north, (2) the Shoshoneans who were more kin to the Great Basin peoples, and (3) the Colorado River Hokan speakers, with traits borrowed from further east. Each group adapted a set of ancient customs to their ecology, but differentiated by following their own individual inclinations over the centuries.

From the wet winter storms of the Pacific, first the Coast Ranges, then the mighty Sierra Nevada wring rain and snow. Little moisture is left for the eastern slopes–it is desert, just about where Nevada begins. So it isn't too unexpected that the government "found" this type of land appropriate for Indian habitation. We're in Washo and Paiute country. Washo bands were, in the old times, fairly stationary, living near the mountains east of Lake Tahoe that sustain the growth of greenery coloring the fertile Carson River Valley.

Washo families live about the valley today. Solitude reigns over their desert, with seven ice-cream-cone peaks of Alpine County as a backdrop to the newly-organized Washo California community near Woodfords. The Indian land is pure desert, but with the evidence of hope for the future–a network of paved roads, water, and electricity; and an already functioning tribal center and child education group.

The Hoopa Valley of the Trinity River, Humboldt Co., contributes to the needs of some 1500 Indian people.

The palatial estate of Gen. Mariano Vallejo, built in 1834 and worked by local Indian labor. Petaluma, Sonoma Co.

A residence, formerly the Indian Agency school, Ft. Bidwell Reservation, Modoc Co.

Battles were fought for the salt from this spring, Colusa-Butte county line, near Stonyford.

The grave of Old Gabriel, a faithful Carmel Mission parishioner for many years.

One of many ancient Chumash cave paintings in the mountains east of Santa Barbara, naturally protected by luxuriant poison oak growth.

Painted Rocks Cave on the Tule River Reservation lies at the edge of the oak-lined river, as it tumbles from the Sierras.

The San Miguel Mission courtyard, which many hundreds of Indian people once called the vital center of their village.

Ancient Shoshone shamans carved thousands of rocks in the Owens Valley of Inyo Co. Most of these glyphs were designed for rituals to enhance success in hunting.

Los Coyotes Reservations, San Diego Co., in winter, is a place of great solitude and serenity.

The bridge over the San Luis Rey River on the Pala Reservation, San Diego Co., bears a footpath from secluded homes in the hills to the village of Pala.

The Serrano people's tribal center on the San Manuel Reservation lies at the foot of the scenic San Bernadino Mountains.

Ancient native designs on the walls of the chapel of the Asistencia on the Pala Reservation.

Ceiling designs of Mission Dolores, San Francisco, among the few remnants of the original natives of that city.

Many of the contestants dancing at the annual California Indians Days celebrations in Sacramento belong to tribes far to the east, north, and south of California.

Paiutes of Walker Valley already have their new village, Camp Antelope, 25 miles south along U.S. 395. A few years ago, the United States Department of Housing and Urban Development used an old military plot of land for the construction of 32 homes for a number of Indian people who had been living in grossly inadequate places along the eastern slopes of the Sierra. Camp Antelope's houses are arrayed about a desert hillside, overlooking the oasis-like Walker River Valley, and with vistas of lofty mountains to the west.

The community looks like a HUD suburb–most homes are alike, but some are beautifully tended with gardens, others are already run-down and ill-kempt, depending on the mind of the keeper. Nevertheless, the project is exemplary. I have seen many HUD reservation homes. There appear to be about 2 or 3 house plans; one or two bedrooms, universally made of those new, brown plywood sheets. Though sturdier than 50-year-old clapboard boxes, and comfortable with upkeep, I wonder what they'll be like in ten years.

It takes a lot of homeland attachment and spectacular Sierra scenery to overcome the desire to flee a destitute existence. The Indian people of Bridgeport have not fled. My first visit to the Bridgeport Reservation in 1979 was a shocker–the majority of the people were existing in dilapidated clapboard houses more than half a century old. Five years later, one can find one or two of those run-down houses, but now totally deserted. Today there are thirty new homes on the 40-acre reservation on a mesa-land overlooking the old town of Bridgeport and its lake.

The occupants of these new homes and trailers have one of the most enviable spots in California–a wide, round, 6,700-foot-high valley, Bridgeport Lake as its heart, and surrounded by 10,000-foot peaks. Finally, a people who have suffered privation for so long have a decent community to call home. The people do have occasional gatherings here, around the thatched ramadas lining the edge of their recreation field.

Now, travel on down U.S. 395 past Mono Lake, drying up because of Los Angeles' thirst and political power. The lake was sacred to the Eastern Mono people, now scattered and without reservation land. Go east through pine-rimmed glass craters, where Mono and Paiute and Shoshone once picked up the natural obsidian glass for making the finest arrow points. They traded this essential resource far and wide for hundreds of miles. Find yourself at mile-high Benton Hot Springs. Look south.

One new home sits lonely upon a desert hillside, a few abandoned wooden shacks have tumbled into the tumbleweed, and the White Mountains tower above it all, silently, as they always have. Down the hill, the hot springs settlement ghosts away, with a bizarre general store whose proprietress said of the Benton Paiute Reservation, "There ain't nary a soul lives there now." When the electricity gets hooked up, maybe a soul or two *will* live there, once again.

We are here at the upper end of the Owens Valley, a region which early natives found suitable for sculpting thousands of petroglyphs and pictographs.

Unfortunately, I am not at liberty to divulge locations of these marvelous, mystical, and magic markings; and I hope my readers will understand why. Even some later Indian people didn't appreciate their heritage–as one early guidebook says: "About 1888 the Paiute went on a rampage and destroyed many of the markings, which were made, they said, 'by evil little men who crept from the rocks at night.'" Later whites have destroyed others for less worthy reasons.

The Paiute people of Owens Valley were promised 66,000 acres of the valley for a reservation in 1910. Land which, of course, was theirs to begin with. However, thirsty Los Angeles "bought" the land and the cascading waters of Bishop Creek and the Owens River from the local farmers to build the Los Angeles Aqueduct in 1913.

The 875 acres of the Bishop Reservation, with 872 acres of Big Pine, Ft. Independence, and Lone Pine Reservations to the south, are all that's left of the grand promise. Early guidebooks speak of the great fertility of the Owens Valley. The few farms that are left reveal what it must have been. The Bishop Reservation retained some water rights, as numerous irrigation ditches gurgle water into green pastures.

The Reservation, as most of the base of the Owens Valley, sits on the high river floodplain, un-rained upon, a region of sagebrush and rounded stones. Although the Valley is nearly 4,000 feet in elevation, it lies low between the Sierra Nevada and the White and Inyo Mountains–both ranges towering 10,000 feet above.

In this extraordinarily tranquil setting, the people of the Reservation (Paiutes from this valley, Shoshones from over the Whites in the Panamint Valley) have lived, farmed, and done the tasks of survival. Homes on the reservation are spaced in parcels–like tiny farms. Cows and horses graze, along with other farm animals.

Invited to a local church social, I found, to my mild surprise, that the food was good Mexican-style cooking. I don't know what I *should* have expected. I also heard from one of the parishoners that local bars were full of alcoholic Indians, and that their only salvation was the church. Looking around later that night, in a friendly local bar with a good all-Indian country-western band, I realized that the parishoner was wrong on *two* counts. (Earlier, I had looked in on a staid Forest Service party–nearly all white. Just one more bit of evidence of the work-and-play separation of our society.)

I enquired about Indian history in the local schools. It seems as though "the course" is given only intermittently (though this may change).

I had a strange sense of lack of overall community here, as if most families existed independently of each other. For instance, I thought it unusual that the young lady at the Indian Education Center seemed to know little of the history of the area or little of the activities of the community, especially Indian activities. Perhaps that is a problem of being young–one's own history is relatively unimportant compared to the big problem of growing up.

Ironic as it is, several California reservations occupy the land of the conqueror. In 1862, at Fort Independence (**349**) in the center of the

Owens Valley, the U.S. Army dug some caves in a dry wash embankment for the enlisted men to stay in (some are still here), and put up tents for the officers, who later moved into wooden quarters (one remains). The Fort, or "Camp" as it was then called, was to subdue the inordinately active Paiutes, who had a certain attraction for their Valley homes. It was soon abandoned, but later occupied by the local Indian people in search of a place to call home. Today a few of the people make a scant living on 356 acres of the old Fort grounds. Pastures are green from an irrigation ditch. A couple of ancient buildings shelter some families, newer homes, others. It is very quiet.

The sawteeth of 14,500-foot Mt. Whitney loom right down into the Owens Valley upon Ft. Independence; the clouds pass over, very high, seldom even watering the Inyo Mountains, just to the east. To understand the words "splendor" and "grandeur" and why the Paiutes wanted their Valley, go five miles up the road toward Kearsarge Pass. Look back and lament their loss.

To develop or not has become a serious question. Is tribal self-sufficiency, rather than termination and allotment to private individuals a worthwhile goal? Those groups which have elected development have always required external financial support–sometimes a single grant, sometimes continuing support. And that support has not always been easy to obtain.

In the north, only the large reservations have had any chance of on-reservation self-help programs: lumbering, some fishing, a little tourism.

The reservations of southern California are nearly all much larger in size than the dozens of tiny rancherias of the north. Once barely self-sufficient, as most of the land is practically desert, the technology of irrigation has increased the commercial value of several lands immensely. Further, the scarcity of *any* land in California is augmenting its desirability, especially in the national rush to the "sun belt."

"Develop" can take two faces: agricultural or tourist. Although it may seem that groups of destitute people would jump at the chance to make money, there are deeper principles involved. The concept of working the land to make it pay is very foreign to native traditional uses. The relation of an Indian to the land is not one of forcing it to yield, but rather a cooperative effort in which nature supplies, and the individual or group takes only what is immediately needed.

Above and beyond, or because of this basic ethic, the Indian has been a reluctant modern style farmer, often hesitating even to harm Mother Earth with a hard steel plow. Once the land is tilled and despoiled, is *used*, it no longer can bear the former, old relationship.

Possibly the strongest reason for slow development, until recently, is that the economic backing and marketing techniques to start large scale farming has not been available. The Colorado River peoples are among those most pressured by the dilemma, since their claims to water rights are now usually acknowledged. The "use it or lose it" doctrine has not always applied.

Traditionally these river tribes have been cautious and prudent agriculturalists, with appreciation of the stewardship of the land. However, the urgency of survival has dictated a departure from the old ways.

Go to the Fort Mojave Reservation in Needles. One finds a business-like bustle at the tribal office that administrates the many acres leased to agri-businesses. The income has enabled the children to have a decent library and gym; it has enabled the tribe to pull down hot, stuffy cracker-boxes and build more than 150 substantial homes on tree-lined streets; and it has given the people a reasonable standard of living.

Similar agricultural transformation has been accepted on the huge Colorado River Reservation and the Ft. Yuma Reservation, both of which sit astride the Colorado River. Nearly 100,000 acres of once open desert are under cultivation at the Colorado River Reservation, irrigated with a complex of 250 miles of canals. Ft. Yuma's irrigation complex was begun in 1934, and has been expanded recently. During winter months, a large greenhouse and hydroponics business provides tomatoes, cucumbers, and other vegetables for national consumption.

In 1938, as the backwaters of the newly-constructed Parker Dam on the Colorado River began flooding the rich, flat lands south of Mohave Canyon, the residents of this remote stretch of river, the Chemehuevis, began to disperse. Some went to Los Angeles, some to Parker, Arizona, and a few remained on the dry, forbidding, higher terraces nearby.

Things have radically changed for them in the last dozen years. Between 1970 and 1982, more than $6 million of development has been achieved on the reservation, now the banks of Lake Havasu, those backwaters of Parker Dam. Since the sandy, sloping, and mountainous land is unsuitable for agriculture, development has been in the form of recreational facilities for the general public – long-lease, fully-equipped homesites, marinas, campgrounds, a motel, restaurant, store, and even a passenger ferry to Lake Havasu City, Arizona, and London Bridge, across the river. These sun belt developments have enabled the Chemehuevis to become highly self-sufficient, so much so that many dispersed families are returning to their homeland.

Although it is good to see the welfare of the people improving, with "progress," little time is left for tradition – no dances or festivals are held here. There *are* activities for the Chemehuevi people, but they are held to the south at the Colorado River Reservation. What will happen to the Chemehuevis as a people, a tradition, when "civilization" takes over?

Archaeological sites might be expected in the ancient places of the Colorado River, and they are indeed here. Though generally not available to the general public, such features as petroglyphs, pictographs, grinding rocks, turquoise mines, and sleeping circles (wind and weather protection) abound. The most spectacular antiquity in the area, however, is an historical landmark called "Giant Desert Figures" or "Indian Intaglios" (see p. 124) adjacent to the southwest border of the Colorado Reservation.

Of late, pillagers loaded with booze and beer, bikes, buggies, and bullets have been intentionally desecrating many of these desert sites. The outrage upon the native heritage never seems to cease.

To the north of this site is a mysterious furrowed field, called a "Rock

Maze", an antiquity of the Hamakhava (Mohave) people, near the Needles (see p. 123).

The Cahuilla have always been a desert people. But the desert has changed, and so have the Cahuilla. Who would have guessed in 1875 that the desert would be as popular as it is today? So long as it has any water, there are demands for the land. With some irrigation, large tracts of Torres-Martinez Reservation have been leased; with a few water pipes for residents, Agua Caliente has profitably leased or sold its resources, the Reservation being a large part of the City of Palm Springs and the historic Palm Canyon.

But most of the Cahuilla desert lands remain as they always have, and are increasingly an ecologically unspoiled island. The most publicly active Cahuilla center is the Morongo Reservation. It is the home of the Malki Museum, a repository for Cahuilla artifacts and the site of festivals, ceremonies, and barbeques.

I had the distinct honor of visiting the former director of the museum, Mrs. Jane Penn. She came from her sickbed to tell me of names. "Malki," she said, "was a sly way for the people here to fool the Indian agents, who asked what their tribal name was. In reality, 'Malki' means 'dodging'. Even 'Morongo,'" she added with a twinkle, "is a misnomer." In their haste to name the place, the agents gave it the name of a family who lived some distance away. With Mrs. Penn's untiring help, this museum has become one of the more complete museums of local Indian cultures in California. [Jane Penn died about a year after I spoke with her.]

The government-abrogated treaties of 1851 set aside as reservation a huge swath of the southern Coast Range in Riverside and San Diego Counties from the present Interstate 10 to the Mexican border. Today over thirty smaller reservations comprise all that actually became Indian land.

Very little of this barren mountain and desert countryside is habitable without expensive or unobtainable irrigation. So, although they form an undisturbed preserve of Indian territory, several lands are unoccupied: the Augustine (hot desert), Ramona (high chaparral), Twenty-nine Palms (rocky desert), Capitan Grande and Mission Reserve (barren mountains), and Inaja-Cosmit (remote valley) Reservations. Cuyapaipe and La Posta have fewer than ten residents between them.

A few Southern California reservations have adopted a decided no-develop policy, notably Pechanga and Cahuilla. Most of this region's peoples are quite content to exist with moderate, small changes, consisting only of improved housing and community facilities.

The striking exception in this region is the Agua Caliente Reservation, which is a large chunk of Palm Springs. Looking about the city, realizing that much of what I see is Indian land, it is easy to see that even finding an oil field here would have been less fortunate for the tribe. (Oil spoils the land forever.)

The Indian people of southern San Diego County were once called "Diegueño" by the Spanish, after the San Diego Mission. In actuality,

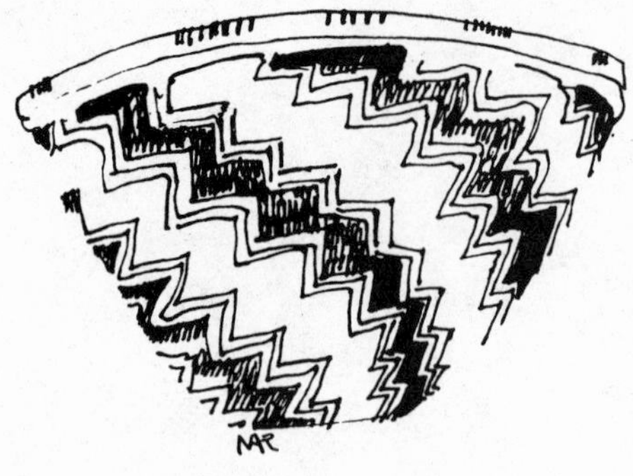

two culturally similar groups traditionally occupied this land, the Ipai and the Tipai. In recent times the Tipai, especially, have used the name Kumeyaay or Kamia for themselves.

The Kumeyaay people have a long history of fierce independence. Even when Spanish troops were rounding up natives for the coastal missions some 200 years ago, many fled to these desolate hills to escape and evade. The same was true of their avoidance of the U.S. Cavalry. Recently several steps have been taken to emerge–such as considering a federal housing project and planning for a regional Indian museum at Campo, their population and administration center.

Some residents of Campo and five neighboring Tipai reservations exercise a right that few other Native Americans possess–dual United States and Mexican citizenship. The original territory of these peoples straddled the political division of these two modern nations, so why would their descendants not be free to move about from homes of relatives on either "side" of the border?

The Kumeyaay continue ancient cultural ties with the Colorado River peoples, who, in earlier times would often move toward the Jacumba Mountains through the dry Imperial Valley to avoid the blistering heat. Occasional fiestas are held at Campo, usually tied to church festival days such as the All Saints Day Barbeque. Many older tribal customs are still kept, such as the use of the "Diegueño" language. Archeological sites in the area are known, but since they are undeveloped and unprotected, they must remain confidential.

The Kumeyaay people are located on Campo, Cuyapaipe, La Posta, Manzanita, Sycuan, and Jamul Reservations. The bands (or tribes), although geographically practically adjacent to one another, maintain considerable independence, owing in no small part to their historic isolation and rivalry. Consequently, though in a similar ecologic region, and bearing a common history, temperaments among the bands vary vastly.

All through these valleys and mountains I see the ancient with the old and with the newer. The oldest is the undisturbed land–the bare mountains and the piney mountains, the clumps of oak where they can find water, the stiff green-gray chapparal, the brown and red rocks. I see the older things–the fish traps dug on the banks of a lake from a cooler, wetter age, rocks carved by long-gone ancestors. I see old churches and missions with their burial grounds–the clapboard chapels of Sycuan and Campo and Jamul, the Spanish missions of Santa Ysabel and Pala. And I see the flower-decked adobe homes of La Jolla and Pauma, the many little wooden houses erected so long ago, where generations have been born. And I see new mobile homes and new government-built homes, and cars, and sometimes horses.

These are part of what the Indian environment is today. To know the Indian people of today, go to some of these places to better understand their life.

Come along to the Pauma Valley–the valley of the San Luis Rey River and its tributaries, lying in the shadow of Mt. Palomar. The valley is very Indian. On the north, orange orchards stripe the gentle western slope of the mountain. The Pauma Reservation is a settlement that has much of the character of a Mexican village: a few houses clustered about an earth-brown stucco chapel and dissolving adobe walls.

Two miles down the road the scene changes as we pass the Rincon Reservation. Things are more active here–we find a cluster of buildings that have an architectural unity with the grand countryside, housing services that improve the quality of life and living: health, fire protection, education, tribal affairs, personal services action. All are signs that the people are striving hard to better themselves.

Throughout Southern California the mania for crashing about through fields with motorcycles and four-wheel drives has been a serious problem. The people here want none of it, so they have posted militant prohibitions on off-highway travel, another sign of awareness.

East, up the valley, we go back in time. In California there are two *La Jolla*'s [pronounced *hóy-a*]. The word, a corruption of Spanish for either "the jewel" or "the hollow" fits both places. One is near San Diego and does not concern us here. The other, La Jolla Reservation, hugs the wooded, southern slopes of Mt. Palomar and descends in cascading terraces to the cool forests of the upper reaches of the San Luis Rey River. Along the creek, the Reservation has provided the public with campgrounds, which have excellent access to stream fishing. The campgrounds here and at nearby Los Coyotes are superb locales to explore and experience these ancient Indian lands.

Almost hidden in the flanks of the mountain are the scatter of homes, many with orchards and small cattle ranches. From the highway, a careful eye can pick out several adobe homes with yards adorned by flowers and cacti. The quiet, undeveloped beauty of these shady acres truly makes this a jewel.

At the valley head, Lake Henshaw covers the lush marshes that once sustained bands of Luiseño, Ipai-Tipais, and the Cupeños, whose permanent village of Kupa was by the bubbling hot springs. The hot springs (Warner's Hot Springs) at the edge of Los Coyotes have occasioned several episodes of relatively recent history. Originally the center of Cupeño life, the springs and adjacent fertile lands were appropriated by the San Luis Rey and San Diego Missions. Later, one Jonathan Trumbull (*alias* Juan José Warner) acquired possession and established a ranch here in 1844, giving succor to Col. Stephen W. Kearny (on his way to take Los Angeles from the Mexican Army, 1846), and later to Butterfield stages passing east-west.

During this time the Indians had been "allowed" to live nearby, and somehow felt this their land. But, by a California Supreme Court decision in 1903, they were removed in one of the State's many "trails of tears" to Pala Reservation. Meanwhile, a resort was built at the springs, and today, the valley's water quenches throats and yards of San Diegans. But that isn't all. One day I visited the reservation, the friendly, soft-spoken tribal spokesman was seeking police to investigate the shooting-up of his home by some trigger-happy white. This in 1979! When will it end?

In spite of their past tribulations, some 60 Cahuillas now live (mostly in summer) on the spacious 25,000 acres of low mountain-land above the hot springs, and have made part of their magnificently scenic homeland available to the public for year-round camping and exploring. Follow the paved, winding road leading up into the mountains overlooking the Valle de San José and Mt. Palomar in the distance. At the top of a hill, further in, sits a tiny, solitary chapel with its separate bell tower, reminding me more of Peru than California.

From Los Coyotes, up over the hillcrest to the south continues more Native history at Santa Ysabel. This pleasant place has been a well-known center of Indian activity for many years, owing to the presence a mile down the road (Hwy. 79) of the Santa Ysabel Asisténcia (see p. 130), founded here in 1818, and rebuilt in 1924. The adjoining cemetery, Campo Santo, dates back to the 1820s.

The reservation spreads over the slopes and woodlands on the northeast side of the road, overlooking the fertile valley feeding the Sutherland Reservoir. It is in just such valleys, so characteristic of the southern Coast Range, that with a little creative dreaming I see the blue smoke from the hearths of native villages layering the air. Not now. The native homes only overlook the valleys. The best land is no longer theirs.

Several times I have camped in the Pala valley, feeling the coexistence of two civilizations. A quaint suspension footbridge crosses the river from a cool oak grove to the heat of a brick kiln. Amid the very old homes, a young man remarked on one resident's collection of five shiny new Camaros: "The finest on the rez." I have the lasting image of an old man leading his saddled horse and dog across a road made white by dust blown from large, whirring quarry trucks.

In the midst of the metropolitan colussus of greater Los Angeles, a remarkable feat of survival of a tribal group of California Indians is even today developing. The Smithsonian's 1978 *Handbook of North American Indians* declares that as of 1900 "Gabrielino culture is now only in the minds of a few people."[18] This is news to some 1500 descendants of the original Gabrielino and Fernandeño groups from the San Gabriel and San Fernando Valleys.

In 1983, having read accounts such as the one above, I was surprised to find a newspaper article about an ancient Gabrielino village site near El Segundo. It was being dug up for a new Hughes Aircraft complex, yet the excavation was being carefully observed by a *local Gabrielino*, present to make certain any burials were not disturbed. (None were found.) Soon thereafter I noticed that the new Santa Monica Mountains National Recreation Area (SMMNRA) was preparing a cultural center near Thousand Oaks (see p. 139) for Chumash and Gabrielino peoples. It seemed that Gabrielino people must still be around.

I then located the SMMNRA Gabrielino guide, who enlightened me on the situation of his people. The native people of 1900 had disappeared from sight by retreating into isolation. Their isolation was into that of a rapidly expanding metropolis, where they could, at the very least, maintain family ties, often using the San Gabriel Mission as another basis of contact.

Many of the early remembered traditions continue to be practiced by a small core of elders (though some are very infirm). Gatherings tend to be within the extended families, though some larger meetings are held in halls. The Gabrielinos annually hold a fiesta at the San Gabriel Mission on the 3rd of September, and hold a powwow at the end of June, gathering their people mostly from the San Gabriel and San Fernando Valleys. The cultural center site at the SMMNRA (called *Satwiwa*) may soon be ready for ceremonies. Remarkable activities for 1500 people who have been considered "culturally extinct."

A similar resurrection of identity among groups of the Southern Sierra-Tehachapi region is happening. Just as I was about to accept the anthropologists' writings of the "disappearance" of the Kawaiisu and Tubatulabal peoples, I learned of a powwow in Tehachapi. From a leader at that gathering, I learned of a newly-formed council representing some 400 Indian families who live scattered about that region.

He told me of a number of families living in secluded areas of those rugged Sierras that still speak the old language–in fact, they hardly know English. The groups of this region identify themselves as branches of Paiute: Kawaiisu (Tehachapi), Tubatulabal (Kern River/Lake Isabella), and Koso (China Lake area). Since linguists consider the Paiute and Shoshone languages as Uto-Aztecan, this self-description is quite logical. The people themselves maintain close ties with the Paiute groups of Owens Valley.

Their annual late-June powwow is held in a high, cool, green mountain valley called Indian Hills near Tehachapi, whose remote location lends a special spirituality to the ceremonies.

Although I write this with caution, I don't think the same story can be told for the other peoples between Los Angeles and Tehachapi–the Tataviam and Kitanemuk. The Army roundups of the 1850s seem to have cleared this region of natives and their cultures. These peoples, as well as some Tubatulabal, were removed to the Tule River Reservation, where their few descendants live today.

On the Ancestral Homelands map, you may find one group along the Colorado River I have not mentioned–the Halchidhomas. Their tribal narratives tell that, owing to pressure from other peoples from the north and south, they began a retreat from this region long before 1830, possibly as early as the 1500s. They migrated up the Gila and Salt Rivers of Arizona and became partially amalgamated with Maricopa groups to the east. Their descendants now live near Tempe, Arizona, and their old lands along the Colorado are today occupied by the Chemehuevi people.

Characteristic of many emerging groups, two southern California groups are presently seeking formal tribal recognition from the BIA–one in San Juan Capistrano and another in San Luis Rey. "Recognition," even though without land, greatly facilitates a tribe in obtaining government assistance and many title benefits.

Finally, one group of Indian people who once were at least occasional residents in extreme southeastern California areas are the Cócopas. However, today their reservation is in Somerton, Arizona, near Yuma, in the center of their ancient lands.

Place names of Eastern and Southern California with Indian origins (often with Spanish spellings):

Gabrielino Malibu ("deer"), Pacoima ("running water"), Cahuenga, Cucamonga ("sandy place"), Topanga, Tujunga ("mountains") (*–nga*, "place of"), Azusa ("skunk")

Shoshone Shoshone (*tso* + *sóni*, "curly head"), Tecopa (*tecopet*, "wildcat"), Pahrump ("rock spring", from *–pah*, "water"), Ivanpah ("good water"), Nopah ("no water"), Piute and Paiute (from *pah-ute*, "water Utes," i.e., those on the wetter sides of the mountains), Inyo ("dwelling place of a great spirit")

Tipai Jamacha (a wild squash), Jamul ("foam", a village name), Jacumba ("hut by the water"), Guatay ("large"), Cuyapaipe (*cui-apaip*, "rock lie on"), Cuyamaca (*ekwi-amak*, "rain above"), Otay ("brushy", a village name), Sycuan (a kind of bush)

Washo Tahoe ("lake")

Other names Aguanga, Cahuilla ("leader"), Coso ("fire", a spelling of the *Koso* Shoshone), Chemehuevi (tribal name, corruption of *Në-wë-wë*), Mohave or Mojave (corruption of *hamákhava*, "three mountains"), Mono (from *monache*, "fly people"), Morongo (Serrano family name), Olancha (tribal place name), Pala ("water"), Pechanga (place name), Palomar, Soboba (place name), Temecula ("rising sun"), Temescal (Aztec for *tema* + *calli*, "bath house"), Tehachapi (Kawaiisu for "frozen creek"), Yucaipa (Serrano for "wet or marshy land"), Yuma (Quechan for "sons of the river")

Original populations of Southern and Eastern California peoples before 1830:*

Peoples of Eastern California:

Northern Paiute/Bannock, Washo, Owens Valley Paiute, Shoshone, Kawaiisu, Chemehuevi, Halchidhoma, Hamakhava (Mohave), Quechan. California total about 5,000, more in Nevada and Arizona

Eastern and Western Mono 4,000

Gabrielino-Fernandeño up to 5,000

Luiseño-Juaneño 5,000

Cahuilla 6,000

Cupeño 500

Serrano-Vanyume and Kitanemuk 3,000

Tubatulabal 1,000

Ipai and Tipai, including some of Baja California 2,000–3,000

*These early estimates are known to be low.

Reservations East of the Sierra Nevada and the Mojave Desert

Alpine-Washoe Reservation *Washo* (*Wáshoe*). Alpine Co. (See comments, p. 108.)

In the mid-1970's a sturdy tribal council hall and education center was put up on a plot of 80 acres in a field on the desert. A well was dug, streets laid out and paved. This is today the home for 44 families–people from the adjacent Dutch Valley. Some 300 Indian families live in the valley now.

89 *From Woodfords (on State Rte. 88, S of Lake Tahoe) go E about 2 miles to the only road SE before the Nevada state line. Go S about 1 mile over a creek and to the top of the next mesa.*
Washoe Tribe of Nevada-California
Stewart, NV 89437

Camp Antelope *Intertribal*. Mono Co. (See description, p. 108.) *

90 *Off U.S. 395 at Coleville, Eastside Lane (S side of town), 1 mile to Camp Antelope.*
Camp Antelope
Coleville, CA 96107

Bridgeport Indian Colony *Northern Paiute*. (1974) Mono Co. (See description, p. 109.)

Stand by one of the now empty paintless little cabins here, looking at majestic mountains, and try to imagine what a zero-degree winter across these 40 acres must be like. This, too, is all a part of Indian existence in California.

91 *From State Rte. 182 (close to the intersection with U.S. 395 in Bridgeport), take Aurora Canyon Rd. The reservation is immediately to the S of this road.*
Bridgeport Indian Colony
P.O. Box 37
Bridgeport, CA 93517
(619) 932-7083

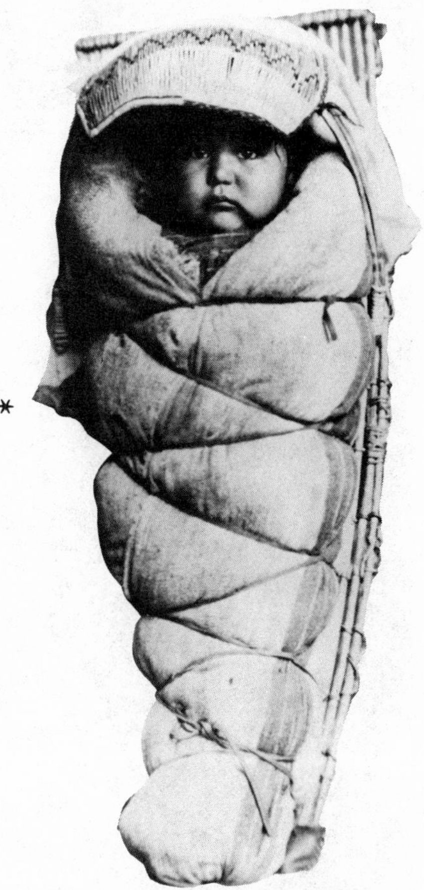

Washo children were well-bundled from the cold winter winds of the Great Basin desert, 1905. (*St. Pk.*)

Benton Paiute Reservation (Utu Utu Gwaitu) *(Owens Valley) Paiute*. (1915) Mono Co. (See description, p. 109.) *

92 *From State Rte. 120 (W of Benton) at Benton Hot Springs, 1 mile S up the dirt road. The reservation lies at the S side of the road. (160 acres.)*
Benton Paiute Reservation
P.O. Box 1525
Bishop, CA 93514
(619) 873-7448

Bishop Reservation *(Owens Valley) Paiute and Shoshone*. (1912) Inyo Co. (See earlier description, p. 110.) **

I recommend a visit to the Bishop Reservation if you are passing this way. The setting is unusual–dry valleys and green mountains. The reservation itself is not greatly unusual, but appreciate that here are a hunting and a gathering people, used to the range, that have only recently been forced to settle in a farming lifestyle. Realize, too, that 65,000 acres were taken from them only 70 years ago.

The most striking building houses the new tribal offices and community center complex. Crafts and artifacts of the Paiute and Shoshone

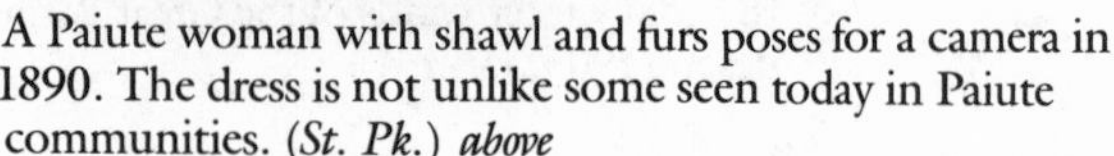

A Paiute woman with shawl and furs poses for a camera in 1890. The dress is not unlike some seen today in Paiute communities. (*St. Pk.*) *above*

The Paiutes of the Owens Valley, like the Chumash of the Pacific coast, made shelters of a "haystack" type in the early 1900s. (*St. Pk.*) *top right*

The Red Rock petroglyphs, near Bishop, contain hundreds of carvings. The setting is a large rock outcrop on a flat plain between the towering Sierra and the White Mountains. The amphitheater aspect with animals and other figures indicate that this was a ceremonial site dedicated to the hunt. (*dhe,* 1979) *middle, lower*

peoples are displayed in their new museum, open April to October. You'll also find a day care center, an historic old tribal office, and a couple of clapboard churches that have served some of the people for many years.

93 *West side of town of Bishop. State Hwy. 168 passes through it.*
Bishop Reservation
P.O. Box 548
Bishop, CA 93514
(619) 873-3584

[Note: The Bishop Chamber of Commerce can provide directions for a Petroglyph Loop Drive in the area, in which the visitor may see a number of ancient rock carvings devoted to ritual and the hunt.]

Big Pine Reservation *(Owens Valley) Paiute* and *Shoshone*. (1912, 1937) Inyo Co. *

What is said of the Bishop Reservation previously in terms of its setting in the spectacular Owens Valley may be said also of Big Pine. Here the valley is narrower; the mountainsides don't slope, they plunge.

The reservation consists of a scattering of homesites in rectangular parcels, occupying most of the eastern side of the town of Big Pine. Many homes have been newly erected under the auspices of OVIHA, the Owens Valley Indian Housing Authority.

A few horses can be found on the rather dry 279 acres; but mostly there is simply a small community, a gathering of people of like background.

94 *On U.S. 395, in the town of Big Pine, both sides of Bartell Rd. (E of highway), and tribal offices on U.S. 395 near Blake Rd.*
Big Pine Reservation
814 S. Main
P.O. Box 384
Big Pine, CA 93513
(619) 938-2121

Fort Independence Reservation *(Owens Valley) Paiute*. (1915) Inyo Co. (See earlier description, p.110.) *

To gain a wider understanding of the history of the local Native peoples, the Paiutes and the Shoshones, visit the *Eastern California Museum* on Grant St. in town. Intermittently open, the Indian campgrounds along U.S. 395 are in a magnificent place to spend time.

95 *About 2 miles N of the town of Ft. Independence on U.S. 395. Take Schabell Rd. about 1 block (to cave sites in a dry wash). Reservation extends over both sides of U.S. 395.*
Ft. Independence Reservation
P.O. Box 67
Independence, CA 93526
(619) 878-2126

Lone Pine Reservation *(Owens Valley) Paiute and Shoshone*. (1937) Inyo Co.

As what is left of the Owens River dribbles towards its end in Owens Lake, it passes Lone Pine. It is lonely, but only if one doesn't care for grand mountains, quiet, desert, and solitude. The railroad ends here. Pack trips begin here, often on Indian horses.

The reservation of 237 acres is rather new (1937). A number of new homes were constructed by OVIHA. In the town of Lone Pine is a trading post at 137 S. Main. Try their pinyon nuts, once a staple of these peoples.

96 *On U.S. 395, just S of Lone Pine–tribal office on W side of the highway.*
Lone Pine Reservation
Star Route 1
1101 S. Main St.
Lone Pine, CA 93545
(619) 876-5414

Death Valley Timbi-Sha Western Shoshone Band (1982) Inyo Co.

Sometimes government action moves very slowly; it wasn't until 1982 that the BIA formally recognized this little group of Western Shoshone people that has managed to survive borax miners, 20-mule wagon trains, and government takeover.

These people are direct descendants of the original inhabitants of Death Valley, whose history is depicted in the Park's Visitor Center.

Though this has always been *their* land, they must pay the Federal Government a token $5 a year rent, an obvious scheme to show who's the "real" owner.

near **97** *You can find this band of tenacious people on 40 acres, called the "Indian Village", within the Monument.*
Timbi-Sha Western Shoshone Band
P.O. Box 108
Death Valley, CA 92328

Kern Valley Indian Council *Kawaiisu, Tubatulabal,* and *Koso Paiute, Yokuts,* and others. Kern Co. (See p. 117 for description.)

near **86** Kern Valley Indian Council
P.O. Box 168
Kernville,CA 93230

** **Fort Mojave* Reservation** *Mohave (Ha-mäk-ha-va).* (1870) Clark Co., NV, Mohave Co. AZ, and San Bernardino Co., CA

Many of the peoples along the Colorado River in California still occupy some of their traditional tribal lands. This is true for the nearly 400 Hamakhavas living on some 38,000 acres of their reservation, which lies in three states.

At the north end of the reservation is the site of old and hated Fort Mojave (see p.168). Nothing is left but sidewalks to nowhere. Beyond the southern end of the reservation, along Interstate 40, are the remaining acres of an ancient furrowed field, called Rock Maze (see below)–the field has mystical powers to the Hamakhavas.

The spacious tribal office-library-community center and gym are situated at the north edge of Needles, CA. On the Arizona side of the river are several public RV parks. The southern boundary of the reservation is also the boundary of the Havasu National Wildlife Refuge, a wide, flat marsh of the Colorado River. The reservation itself covers an even wider flood plain, flat enough for intensive farming (see also p. 111).

* Note the different spellings of the Fort (from the Spanish) and the name for the people (English transliteration), both a corruption of "Hamakhava."

Dances are open to the public in September, and the tribe supports a famous marching band that tours all over the U.S.

98 *In Needles, take the River Rd. Exit from I-40, south 4 blocks on W. Broadway to I-40 overpass. North to tribal offices in Needles. Maps of the reservation are available there. The casual visitor can drive the length of the reservation along Arizona State Rte. 95 from Topock to Bullhead City, Mohave Co., Arizona.*

Ft. Mojave Tribe
P.O. Box 798
Needles, CA 92363
(619) 326-4596

Rock Maze San Bernardino Co. **

At the south end of the Ft. Mojave Reservation (see previous entry) are about two acres of a field that appears to be plowed or furrowed in a maze-like fashion. From the north, the Colorado River has been flowing through a wide flood plain, but here it hits narrows caused by needle-like projections of rock.

The mazes were "discovered" by the first whites in the area, and most have been rather miraculously preserved. Legend has it that they were created to confuse and entrap evil spirits pursuing spirits of the dead floating down the river. Until recently the Hamakhavas have been using this holy place for funereal ceremonies. Some of the field has disappeared, but, thanks to the efforts of many people, the adjacent Interstate and pipelines have bypassed it.

near 98 *East of Needles, take Park Moabi Exit off I-40. At mile 1.7, keep to left and at mile 1.9 ("Road Closed" sign), before a pipeline pumping station, find a parking lot for viewing the maze.*

Intaglios, or **Desert Carved Figures** Providence Mountains State Park, San Bernardino Co. *

About 40 miles W of the Colorado River at the State Park can be found several figures scooped into the desert varnish by ancient shamans. These mysterious figures, as those along the Colorado River (see p. 124), were probably intended for hunting and religious purposes.

Chemehuevi Reservation *Chemehuevi* [Ché-me-way-vĭ] *Paiute* or *Në-wë-wë*. (1870s, 1930s) San Bernardino Co. *

Although lying in the ancient territory of the Chemehuevi, much of this reservation as such is relatively new. (See pp. 111–112 on the development of this and other reservations.)

Developed only along the Colorado River bank, the reservation occupies some 28,000 acres of mostly dry desert and dry mountains, and possesses a number of archaeological sites. Birds, coyotes, and wild burros roam free; but an excess of the donkeys causes great problems with destruction of the few trees and spoilage of wells and water holes.

New project offices and a wildlife protection and security office are near the new boat landing, but council offices and most Indian homes are located on a secluded northern end of the reservation. A visitor gets no feeling of "Indian-ness" here, but the realization that human needs are being cared for as never before is a welcome one.

99 *An un-numbered turnoff with sign to "Lake Havasu", on U.S. 95, about 17 miles S of Needles. Proceed E about 15 miles to a guardhouse at boat landing. Maps of the reservation are available at the Reservation project office.*

Chemehuevi Tribe
P.O. Box 1826
Havasu Lake, CA 92363
(619) 858-4531

*** **Colorado River Reservation** *Mohave (Hamakhava), Chemehuevi (Nëwëwë), Hopi, Navajo (Diné).* (1865) Yuma Co., AZ, and San Bernardino and Riverside Cos., CA.

Around 1865 several bands of peoples from southeastern California and western Arizona were settled into a sixty-mile portion of the Colorado River, which is the ancestral home of the Halchidhoma people. After World War II, they were joined by a large group of Hopi and Diné.

Although the reservation's 2500 residents present a melange of five peoples, the languages and cultures of each are currently practiced—dances are held periodically; potters and basketmakers are active; cultural classes are available. You will find an excellent library and museum in the Parker (Arizona) headquarters amid the large complex of tribal offices and community center. National Indian Day, the last Friday of September, is observed in a big way on the Reservation, with thousands of people coming long distances to participate. A campground is available for public use year-round.

The Bureau of Indian Affairs (BIA) and other governmental agencies also maintain a large complex of health, housing, and maintenance facilities a mile south of Parker. In and around the several communities on the reservation, there is an air of the progressive spirit of expanding agricultural areas. For persons wishing to find a feel of a large Native American community, this is probably the most impressive in the southern California area, although the headquarters lie just across the river in Arizona.

Visitors to this area should experience the striking ancient Giant Figures gouged into the desert floor centuries ago, located on the southwestern edge of the reservation (see below). (See also comments on reservation development, p. 111.)

100 *Extending S for 60 miles on both sides of the Colorado River from Earp, CA (State Rte. 62 and U.S. 95) and from Parker, AZ, to near Ehrenburg (BIA Rd. 1). Reservation offices and museum are about 2 miles S of Parker on Agency Rd., past the BIA-hospital complex, in modern buildings. Reservation maps available there.*
Colorado River Tribes Administrative Office
Rte. 1
Box 23B
Parker, AZ 85344
(602) 669-9211

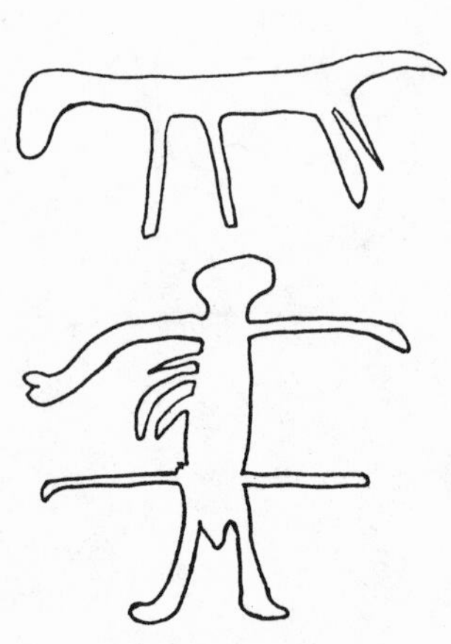

*** **Giant Desert Figures** or **Intaglios**. Riverside Co. **101**

Off U.S. 95, 15.3 miles N of Interstate 10/U.S. 95 intersection in Blythe, are found several huge figures (95 to 167 feet) on a mesa, "carved" into the desert pavement. The "pavement" is of small dark brown pebbles resting on a light-colored sand, the "carving" is as though scooped with a shovel. The figures are of stylized animals and hunters. Since early survival depended largely on finding game, it is presumed that these figures were made by shamans to better the fortunes of hunters.

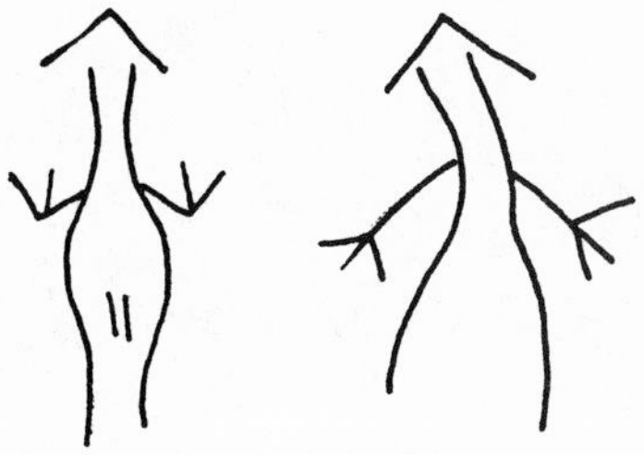

Fun-loving despoilers have defaced some of the [now-protected] surface with jeeps and dirt bikes, but the figures still appear almost newly-made, although pre-dating all local Indian knowledge of their origin. (See also *Smithsonian Magazine*, September, 1978, and *New West Magazine*, January 29, 1979 for articles on the deliberate defacement of Indian antiquities, this included.)

Ft. Yuma Reservation *Quechan* and others. (1883) Imperial Co. ***

In 1781 the Quechans (one of the Yuma language groups) and their allies of the lower Colorado River launched an assault on the year-old Spanish mission and fort at what is now Ft. Yuma. These peoples were ungrateful for the servitude offered them by the Spaniards. They were successful in maintaining the independence won in this battle–even though under considerable pressures from all sides–until the American invasion around 1850, when freedom was lost.

After many skirmishes and struggles, a reservation was established in 1884 at the site of the old mission. An Indian agency and a new church were erected on the California prominence overlooking the city of Yuma, Arizona. Today the refurbished buildings of the old fort (see p. 169) and agency school appropriately are in use by various tribal offices. The old Officers' Mess Hall (1851) is a museum (open only sporadically); adjacent to it has been erected a wattle-and-daub home in the ancient Quechan style. Just below the museum is a venerable Protestant mission. On the same hill are the tribal chambers in an attractive new building.

In 1934, a large irrigation complex was begun that crosses the Reservation. Only lately, however, has full advantage been taken of the water rights, resulting in much agricultural development. During the winter months, a large greenhouse-hydroponics business struggles to provide tomatoes, cucumbers, and other vegetables that are sold nationally, but it suffers from Mexican competition.

Around the 8,800-acre reservation are several trailer parks, picnic sites, and campgrounds. As in *all* reservations, tribally-issued licenses are required to fish in the many canals.

The life? Busy, quiet. One day I found an elderly Quechan man searching for a horse, property of an Indian dreamer-lady who had walked the animal all the way from Oregon, only to lose it here. I found at a club in Winterhaven a good Indian band playing country/rock music–a style that is very popular among the Indian peoples of California. Annual powwow is during September Indian Days, and the first week in March is the time for a powwow in Winterhaven hosted by San Pascual School.

101 *Off I-8, the Winterhaven Exit (from west) will lead to a road N toward Imperial Dam/Picacho. A few hundred yards down the highway is the road up the hill to the tribal offices (maps available), museums, and old missions.*

Quechan Tribal Council
P.O. Box 1352
Yuma, AZ 85364
(619) 572-0213

• • •

Reservations of Southern California, West of the Mojave and Colorado Deserts

* **Campo Reservation** *Tipai* (other names: *Kamia* or *Kumeyaay, Southern Diegueño*). (1893) San Diego Co. (For a discussion of the Kumeyaay people, see p. 114.)

The 15,000-acre Campo Reservation lies high on a 4,000-foot plateau in the Laguna Mountains east of San Diego, endowed with powderings of winter snow and cooler breezes in summer. The hills are rocky and naturally covered with chaparral, but many clearings offer grazing and small-farm land; taller oaks shade the valleys.

On the north part of the reservation are a motel, store, and trailer park in Live Oak Springs (some non-Indian owned). The tribal administrative center is on the south end of the reservation, where one finds a beautiful new community center, health services, and tribal office, adjacent to an exceptionally colorful old church and Indian cemetery. A visit to this site might give one a good experience of the patterns of life in the Kumeyaay community.

I might add here that "Ipai" and "Tipai" as seen in this text are early names for these peoples, and they are the names used today by cultural anthropologists. "Kumeyaay" is the name used by many people today.

102 *Tribal offices are located on a hillside on Church Rd., right alongside State Rte. 94, between Campo and Jacumba. Some dirt roads traverse the reservation, but it must be remembered that this is private property!*

Campo Reservation
Box 1094
Boulevard, CA 92005

Quero Santo, Ipai-Tipai of Mesa Grande, in dancing costume, 1907. Performance of original dances is rare in this region, owing to near-extermination of the custom by the Mission padres. (Photo by T. T. Waterman. *Lowie*)

Manzanita Reservation *Tipai* (or *Kumeyaay*). (1893) San Diego Co. PRIVATE

The Manzanita, named for the brushy bush so common over drier California, occupies a 3,580-acre rectangle of infertile upland valleys and meadows in the western part of the Carrizo Desert.

Homes of the residents are widely scattered, tucked behind boulders and hillsides for protection from the uncompromising summer sun. As residents have been troubled by inconsiderate and trespassing scofflaws, they prefer no off-road visitors.

103 *East of San Diego, Live Oak Rd. from Live Oak Springs is a southern public access road to parts of Anza-Borrego State Park, passing through the reservation, but heed the preceding sentence. Information*:
Chairperson • Manzanita Reservation
P.O. Box 1302
Boulevard, CA 92005
(619) 478-5028

La Posta Reservation *Tipai* (or *Kumeyaay*). (1893) San Diego Co. PRIVATE

Under the shadow of 6,270-foot-high Mt. Laguna and at the eastern edge of Cleveland National Forest lies this 3,672-acre park-like highland. La Posta has occasional residents, who value and guard their privacy. The one entry road is dusty or muddy, and is fenced off from intruders.

104 *The almost vacant countryside with grand vistas of mountains and valleys, E of San Diego, may be seen only by taking the Posta Rd. Exit N off I-8 (the same exit S is Hwy. 80 E to Live Oak Springs). Vistas from a nearby hilltop overlook. Information*:
Chairperson • La Posta Reservation
P.O. Box 984
Boulevard, CA 92005
(619) 478-5523

Cuyapaipe [Kwía-pipe] **Reservation** *Tipai* (or *Kumeyaay*). (1893) San Diego Co.

The pines and evergreens of the south slopes of Mt. Laguna spread their cover onto the remote lands of the Cuyapaipe. As with much other reservation land, this place was at one time considered nearly valueless, but the real value, solitude and fastness, has been preserved for nearly a century. Its 4,100 acres, as is true of several nearby reservations, is not "developed".

One can only walk in–on paths that are known only to the two or three residents and a few locals of Mt. Laguna. The land is as it was from the beginning–it is beautiful.

105 *In the forest southeast of the mountain resort of Mt. Laguna. Information*:
Chairperson • Cuyapaipe Reservation
P.O. Box 187
Campo, CA 92006
(619) 478-5289

Sycuan [Sī-quań] **Reservation** *Tipai* (or *Kumeyaay*). (1875) San Diego Co. *

At the head of a narrow, chaparral-coated valley, surrounded by a scatter of sun-seeking white developments, lies this, the oldest reservation of the Kumeyaay.

The center of activity is on a small hill overlooking the several older homes and trailers. Nearly hidden by a clump of trees is a pretty clapboard chapel; nearby is a bingo hall and a couple of randomly-parked fire engines–for combatting the frequent summer brush fires. The new community center and tribal offices for the 640-acre reservation are on the hill, too. Down the far slope of the quiet valley is the ever-present reminder of the past, the cemetery.

106 *East of El Cajon on I-8, take the Alpine-Tavern Rd. Exit, go S on Tavern Rd. to Dehesa Rd. Then about 3 miles to the Dehesa Fire Dept., right on paved road past a cattle guard.*
Sycuan Reservation
5441 Dehesa Rd.
El Cajon, CA 92021
(619) 445-4073

* **Jamul Indian Village** *Tipai* (or *Kumeyaay*). (1912, 1975) San Diego Co.

Sixty-five years ago a small band of Tipai found themselves six acres upon which to settle–a tiny plot in the rolling hills east of the town of Jamul. The village is a bit cluttered, and the houses old; nevertheless, there is a feeling of great community.

The winter Sunday I first arrived, the sky was cold and wet, the one dirt road nearly impassable. But in the air was a feeling of excitement–these friendly people were meeting in their ancient tribal hall to hear what new things their newly-attained status was to bring them. The village had just become a full-fledged reservation, and everyone seemed pleased that 65 years of "squatting" and tenacious endurance was finally being rewarded.

Incidentally, whatever else progress brings to Jamul, I hope the picturesque church and tribal hall will be preserved as tributes to the labors of the past.

107 *East of San Diego on State Rte. 94, one mile E of the Jamul junction with Proctor Rd. and one block E of Jamul Fire Station.*
Jamul Reservation
14191-A Hwy. 94
Jamul, CA 92035
(619) 697-5041

** **Viejas (Baron Long) Reservation.** *Ipai-Tipai.* (1939) San Diego Co.

The upland plateaus and wide valleys of the Coast Range east of San Diego were regions inhabited in the past by rather impermanent bands of Native Americans–small groups that camped for a year or two or less, while foraging for the local plants and animals. The 1,609-acre Viejas Reservation occupies the end of one such valley. Oaks dot the valley floor with open green to brown pastures. Farther up the slopes of the low mountains, scrub oaks appear, then give way to chaparral and live granite rock.

The Spanish named it El Valle de Las Viejas ("The Valley of the Old Women"), for when a party of them approached the valley, searching for persons to populate the coastal missions, they found only old women. The men had fled to hide and fight another day.

Today, back in the oaks of the valley head, an RV park and campground is run by the residents for the general public. The management can point out Ma-Tar-Awa, an ancient archaeological site – a place frequented by those earlier roving groups of people.

Note: The Viejas and Barona Reservations keep very close ties, and jointly control the large Capitan Grande Reservation.

108 *East of San Diego, from I-8, the E. Willows Rd. Exit (between Descanso and Alpine).*
Viejas Reservation
P.O. Box 908
Alpine, CA 092001
(619) 445-3275

Barona Reservation *Ipai-Tipai.* (1932) San Diego Co. *

The Barona, like the Viejas, occupies one of those wide, rather fertile, highland valleys of the Cleveland National Forest area. This is not the unproductive wasteland pawned off on powerless people – here are several ranches, much cleared land, some small farms, clusters of comfortable homes, a large tribal office and community center, gymnasium, rodeo grounds. Here also is an attractive Mission-style chapel with meeting hall and ball ground. (5,181 acres.)

All in all, you will find signs of some prosperity and comfort as you drive the eight miles of Barona/Wildcat Canyon Rd.

109 *Northbound: from El Cajon, State Rte. 67 to north side of the arroyo in Lakeside, right onto Willow Rd., sharp right at creek, left at Wildcat Cyn. Rd., then about 5 miles through reservation on Barona Rd. Southbound: from Ramona, San Vicente Rd. 5 miles to Wildcat Cyn. Rd., right to Barona.*
Barona Reservation
1095 Barona Rd.
Lakeside, CA 92040
(619) 443-6612

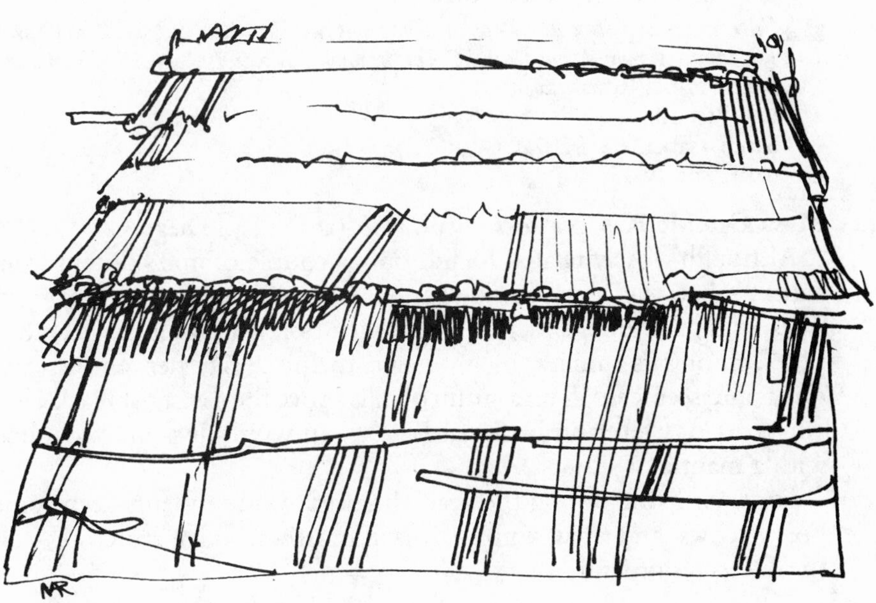

Capitan Grande Reservation *Ipai-Tipai.* (1875) San Diego Co.

While driving through the Barona Reservation, the large, bare mountainous region seen to the east is the uninhabited Capitan Grande. This 15,753-acre mass of dry mountain was judged incapable of habitation by the bands which now are in the lower, wetter, more fertile valleys.

The Capitan Grande, situated in the center of the Cleveland National Forest, west of the 6,500-foot Cuyamaca Peak, is bisected by El Capitan Reservoir. It is jointly controlled by the people of Barona and Viejas.

110 *North of Alpine (off I-8), flanking the upper stretches of El Capitan Reservoir.*

Inaja-Cosmit Reservations *Ipai-Tipai.* (1875) San Diego Co.

These are two parcels of rather remote and inaccessible land under the silhouette of Cuyamaca Peak. At present there are no permanent inhabitants of these 852 acres, although some remodeling is underway on Inaja. Deep winter snows and lack of facilities make these locations inhospitable to all but the hardiest.

Many years ago, I am told, there were residents on Cosmit, and once there were fiestas and dances. Time has changed modes of existence.

111 *West of the intersection of State Rte. 79 with County Road S-1, N of Cuyamaca Reservoir, 7 miles S of Julian.*
Spokesperson
Inaja-Cosmit Reservations
P.O. Box 102
Santa Ysabel, CA 92070
(619) 765-1993

* **Santa Ysabel Reservation** *Ipai-Tipai.* (1875) San Diego Co.

(See p. 154 for a description of the early mission asisténcia and its location.)

The homes on these 15,527 acres are mostly older ones, as are the tribal and educational buildings. An old wooden structure standing near the highway is for the Indian equivalent of ceremonies like "wakes and showers," one resident told me. November 14th is the big feast day for the mission, founded in 1818.

112 *Entrance is E off State Rte. 79 on Schoolhouse Cyn. Rd., ¼ mile N of Mesa Grande Rd. intersection and aobut 2 miles N of the town of Santa Ysabel (NE of Ramona).*
Santa Ysabel Reservation
P.O. Box 126
Santa Ysabel, CA 92070
(619) 765-0845

PRIVATE **Mesa Grande Reservation** *Ipai-Tipai.* (1875) San Diego Co.

Although closely related to and only a couple of miles distant from Santa Ysabel, the Mesa Grande band is one of those groups that cherishes a singular independence. The reservation land itself has been disputed among its families. In any event, the place is rather remote, very quiet, and scenic, high on a group of hills above the forests of Black Canyon (part of Cleveland National Forest). In winter it is often covered with a mantle of snow.

For their living during the year, the thirty-odd residents keep some horses, cows, and a few simple farms in mostly wooden structures–on the 120 acres of land.

113 *From State Rte. 79, 1½ miles N of Santa Ysabel, go W on Mesa Grande Rd. about 5 miles to intersection with Black Canyon Rd. at several abandoned stone buildings. Black Canyon Road, a steep, winding, dirt road, passes through an unoccupied portion of the reservation in the National Forest. The habitations, on* private land, *are off a paved farm road 0.7 mile E of this intersection.*
Mesa Grande Reservation
Mesa Grande Star Rte.
Santa Ysabel, CA 91070

San Pascual Reservation *Ipai-Tipai.* (1910) San Diego Co.

Although one of the later-acquired reservations in southern California, much of the reservation has been removed from its original location. The original site is now occupied by Lake Wohlford and by an organization dedicated to the preservation of nature, the San Diego Wild Animal Park. Compensatory land is now in five parcels, totalling 1,500 acres, on the dry, scrub oak hills east of Valley Center. At least the lake provides the residents with some water that they would not otherwise have had.

Indian activity is centered at the new Tribal Hall and education center, marked with a fine carved-wood sign.

114 *Take the Lake Wohlford exit from Highway S-6 on the north end of Valley Center, about 1½ miles to the San Pascual Tribal Hall sign.*
San Pascual Reservation
Box 365
Valley Center, CA 92082
(619) 749-3200

Pala Reservation *Luiseño, Ipai,* and *Cupeño.* (1875) San Diego Co. ***

Groups from three distinct people live on the Pala Reservation: the Luiseño are named for their proximity to Misión San Luis Rey, including also people from Misión San Juan Capistrano (earlier called Juaneño). It is ancient Luiseño territory upon which Pala is located. The Ipai (earlier called Diegueño, from Misión San Diego) are descendants of people brought here from several miles to the south. The Cupeño are people whose fathers were tragically dispossesed of land in and around what is now Los Coyotes Reservation (see p. 135), about 40 miles to the east of here.

In several ways, mainly family customs, ceremonies, and language, the three groups maintain some distinctiveness to this day. Intermarriage, proximity, and common religion have tended to blur most differences, however.

The village is very interesting, consisting of a large assemblage of older houses gathered about the reconstructed Pala Asisténcia (p. 154) **243**, decorated with ancient Indian motifs and flanked by the Indian cemetery. In the village center are also small stores and the Cupa Cultural Center, focus for activities of the Cupeño people, and an adult learning center. Further out in the 11,600-acre reservation are a ballpark, school, and various HUD-type homes, mobile homes, and small farms.

Some income is derived from a large quarry, a brick kiln, and a full-service campground. Cupa Days Festival is the first week in May.

115 *The village of Pala is at the intersection of Highway S-16 and State Rte. 76, about 25 miles E of Oceanside.*

Pala Reservation Tribal Office
P.O. Box 43
Pala, CA 92059
(619) 742-3784

Mission Reserve Reservation (*Luiseño*). (1903) San Diego Co.

The 9,500 acres of this rocky, chaparral-covered uninhabited mountain adjoin the east side of Pala Reservation and are administered jointly by the Pala and Pauma Reservations. Who knows what some early bureaucrat thought when he assigned such an uninhabitable rock for a reservation.

116

Rincon Reservation *Luiseño or WASXAYAM.** (1875) San Diego Co.

Probably the best term for this reservation is "bustling." Although the reservation is more than a century old, the people have put up new buildings housing a Health Service, an Indian Action Team, a fire department, and an Indian Education Center and Tribal Hall, entitled WASXAYAM POMKI ("Place of the Washxayam"–the Luiseños' name for themselves).

Scattered over the 3,960 acres are old and new homes, athletic fields, Catholic and Protestant chapels, and, in this green valley of spectacular vistas of Mt. Palomar, orange orchards, small farms, and even prickly pear cactus cultivation.

Signs marking the reservation boundaries bear prohibitions against trespassing off the highway, so roads and buildings are strictly for persons on business. However, as of 1985, the public is invited to bingo on weekends.

117 *Both sides of County Rd. S-6, about 10 miles NE of Escondido. Signs mark entrance to reservation lands.*
Rincon Reservation
P.O. Box 68
Valley Center, CA 92082
(619) 749-1051

** **La Jolla Reservation** *Luiseño.* (1875) San Diego Co.

State Highway 76 passes through La Jolla and its forest, welcome in this dry region of brush and chaparral. Two campgrounds run by the reservation offer shelter to the visitor and an opportunity to enjoy the cool San Luis Rey River.

At milepost 40, a small dirt road leads up the mountainside to the reservation center–a small mission with its ancient Indian cemetery, a tribal center, and recreation fields. (See also p. 115 for a further description of this peaceful, 2,828-acre reservation.)

118 *About 2 miles E of the Mt. Palomar Observatory road on both sides of State Rte. 76*
La Jolla Reservation
Star Rte. 2
P.O. Box 158
Valley Center, CA 92082
(619) 742-3771

* Orthography is tribal.

Pauma-Yuima Reservations *Luiseño.* (1892) San Diego Co. *

The area of this pair of reservations totals nearly 6,000 acres. Yuima is high on the Mt. Palomar slope; it has no residents. Pauma's ninety-odd residents live along Pauma Reservation Rd. by a chapel and brand-new Spanish-style tribal hall, all set in orange groves and crumbling adobe ruins (see p. 114).

119 *On Pauma Reservation Rd., off State Rte. 76, 1½ miles N of the town of Pauma Valley (30 miles E of Oceanside).*
Pauma-Yuima Reservation
P.O. Box 86
Pauma Valley, CA 92061
(619) 742-1289

Pechanga Reservation *Luiseño.* (1882) Riverside Co. *

The broad, highland mountain basin sometimes watered and sometimes inundated, by the Temecula River accommodates several ranches, some housing developments, and the Pechanga Reservation. However, the 4,094 acres of Pechanga are almost totally undeveloped. All "development" is strictly individual, with some comfortable homes, many tiny ones, and some clutter. The roads are mostly unpaved, winding around the old clapboard chapel on a low hillside and the picturesque old wooden tribal hall.

The residents want it this way–they'd rather not be saddled with paved roads and bulldozed countryside. Since this is the way it has been for a century, why change? On the west side of Highway S-16 lies the Pechanga burial ground and the remains of Juan Diego, hero of Helen Hunt Jackson's novel *Ramona*–an exposé of the terrible Indian conditions of the last century.

120 *Pechanga Rd. (47,000-block) off County Rd. S-16, just S of the intersection with State Rte. 79 (at Rancho California).*
Spokesperson
Pechanga Reservation
P.O. Box 1014
Temecula, CA 92390

Cahuilla musicians, William Levy and his brother, before their home near Indio, 1907. (*Lowie*)

Soboba Reservation *Luiseño* and *Cahuilla* [Ka-wé-a]. (1883) Riverside Co. *

Where the San Jacinto River at one time spread out over this wide valley, its currents cutting terraces at the edges of the low mountains, the Soboba stretches its 5,036 acres. Although first a Cahuilla reservation, most of the people who live here now are Luiseño, quite a distance from their original territory and the other Luiseño reservations.

Along the rocky mesa are a few horse ranches, some elderly homes, an old chapel and cemetery, and fine offices in the AHMIUM tribal hall and education center. Here, as well, are located dental and medical clinics. There are some archaeological displays in the new hall–relics retrieved from the hills and mountains of the area.

Soboba is the site for occasional powwows; a few miles away at Ramona Bowl, in April and May of every year has been enacted the Ramona Pageant–a story of the terrible struggles of southern California's native population in the last century.

121 *East on Main St. in San Jacinto, across the arroyo to Soboba Rd., right 1 mile to tribal center.*
Soboba Reservation
P.O. Box 487
San Jacinto, CA 92383
(714) 654-2765

* **Hemet Maze Stone** (557) Riverside Co.

Before the days of perserving an artifact by not disturbing it, the State of California installed a bronze plaque on this large granite boulder, bearing an incised pictograph maze, about 1½ by 2 feet, probably an ancient Cahuilla relic.

near 121 *Five miles W of Hemet off State Rte. 74, on California Ave. 3 miles N to small park.*

* **Cahuilla Reservation** *Cahuilla* [Ka-wé-a]. (1875) Riverside Co.

Many high, upland plains of the southern Coast Range are dry, as is the Cahuilla Reservation. At 4,000 feet, it is relatively cool–between the towering hulk of Mt. Palomar (6,126 ft.) to the west and San Jacinto Peak (10,800 ft.) to the east. The Cahuilla people here are one group among many who have preferred to allow their 18,272 acres to remain much as it always has been.

The scrub brush, granite boulders, gentle hills, and dry washes support about two dozen persons on a few widely-scattered ranches. A few dirt roads wind about the desert-like landscape; the silence broken only by the wind, a few birds, and the whine of high-speed motors on the highway.

A primitive old schoolhouse in a clump of pines beside the road is now the tribal hall. I took refuge behind a large rock at the adjoining burial ground one windy day to feel the spirits. They were there.

122 *Four miles W of the settlement of Anza on State Rte. 371 (about 30 miles W of Palm Desert).*
Cahuilla Reservation
P.O. Box 185
Aguanga, CA 92302
(714) 658-2711

Ramona Reservation *Cahuilla*. (1893) Riverside Co.

Out on that big plain mentioned earlier in the Cahuilla Reservation (above), lie 560 uninhabited acres of this reservation. It is administered by the Hamilton family of the Cahuilla people.

123 *Access by dirt road, NW from State Rte. 371, about 1 mile W of the intersection of State Routes 371 and 74.*

PRIVATE **Santa Rosa Reservation** *Cahuilla*. (1907) Riverside Co.

Ten miles east of here in the Coachella Valley lies one of the hottest, driest deserts in California. But the 5,000-foot altitude of this valley is watered by some rain and snow snatched from the clouds passing around nearby 8,000-ft. Santa Rosa Peak, one of several in the San Bernardino National Forest.

The 11,093 acres of the Santa Rosa Reservation are thinly populated, with a few ranch houses scattered along a dirt road in a long, narrow valley. The mountainside are dashed with Jeffrey, sugar, and yellow pines,

as well as other greenery–refreshing after seeing much desert in the surrounding lowlands. Beautiful as it is, the people want to keep it that way, so have subtly suggested that the public stay away by erecting a series of unmistakable NO TRESPASSING signs.

124 *Private road about 4 miles E of intersection of State Routes 371 and 74 (E of Palm Desert). Rte. 74 actually passes right through the reservation, but there are no signs indicating it.*
Spokesperson
Santa Rosa Reservation
325 N. Western St.
Hemet, CA 92343

Los Coyotes Reservation *Cahuilla* [originally *Cupeño*). (1889) San Diego Co. **

(This accessible, picturesque location is described on p. 115.)

In a high valley on Los Tules Rd., the Banning ranch house serves as tribal hall.

125 *Warner Springs, on State Rte. 79. Entrance sign on the highway, 6 miles to campground* via *Camino San Ignacio and Los Tules Roads.*
Los Coyotes Reservation
P.O. Box 249
Warner Springs, CA 92086
(619) 782-3269

Torres-Martinez Reservation *Cahuilla.* (1876) Riverside Co. *

In the last century, in the course of making large land allotments (e.g. railroad grants, national forests, public lands, certain Indian reservations), it was popular to set aside alternate sections of land, that is, every *other* square mile (640 acres). That is why the Torres-Martinez, Ft. Mojave, Morongo, and Agua Caliente Reservations look like checkerboards (see Map II inset).

In this very flat, hot, dry (if it's without irrigation), scrubby portion of the Coachella Valley, the Cahuilla people have elected (or have been forced by economics, as in many other places) not to develop much of their checkerboard reservation. In the midst of shady, stately rows of date palms with citrus groves on all sides, chocolate brown mountains rising up close by, the Torres-Martinez remains much as it always has been, a desert. More than 10 sq. mi. lie under the waters of the Salton Sea, flooded by accident in 1905.

A Cahuilla woman stocks her elevated granary of acorns in the rocky mountains of southwestern California, about 1900. Higher elevations of this portion of California support the growth of large acorn-bearing oaks. Acorns are known to be the most efficient vegetable-to-animal protein conversion known. (*St. Pk.*)

Except for a few primitive homes and garden plots and the tree-shaded ruins of the old government Indian Agency (a national landmark), there is only greasewood scrub . . .

A few employed people seem to work the land of others, not their own 24,823 acres.

The Indian Agency ruins are interesting in their decrepitude. In the same yard under some palms is a little brick tribal hall with grinding rock relics out in front. A baseball field adjoins.

126 *North of the Salton Sea, off 66th St., between Mecca and Valerie Jean at a point halfway between Hwy. 86 and 195, is the paved entrance, S, to ancient palms of the Agency.*

Torres-Martinez Reservation
963 E. Charles St.
Banning, CA 92220
(619) 894-6204

** **Fish Traps** Riverside Co.

In the prehistoric days when the Mohave Desert had water, and the Salton Sea, the Imperial and the Coachella Valleys were Lake Cahuilla, some of the early Cahuilla Indians were fishers. But their fishing methods were unique.

Taking full advantage of a rock slide at the edge of the old lake, they arranged the large, loose stones to form fish corrals two or three feet deep at the water's edge, whence they drove the fish to an ultimate capture. It is remarkable that this process must have been carried out over many years, as the lake level dropped, for the traps are to be found from the highest level down some twenty to thirty feet.

The old beach levels of ancient Lake Cahuilla are quite evident; up against the mountainside is the rock slide in which the traps are to be seen. Do not disturb the loose rocks!

near 126 *From State Rte. 86 at Valerie Jean (8 miles S of Coachilla) take 66th Ave. W to Jackson St., then go N two blocks.*

Augustine Reservation *Cahuilla.* (1893) Riverside Co.

Lying between 54th Ave. and Airport Blvd., State Route 86 and Van Buren Street, south of Coachella, is nearly a square mile of uninhabited chaparral, called a reservation. Yet, it *is* reserve land, an ecological preserve.

Cabazon Reservation *Cahuilla.* (1876) Riverside Co.

Cabazon shares with Agua Caliente the dubious distinction of being an urban reservation–a real oddity in California.

There's not much to look at–but the 1,452 acres (in two parcels) is extremely neat, made up of a collection of newer trailers under four or five shade trees in the middle of the desert fields at the edge of town. That's it. But a new tribal hall is here, along with HUD housing for its 25 members. Bingo in '86.

128 *Go east on Interstate 10 access road off State Rte. 111, right at the Coachella city limits, over the SP tracks, first left (N), 0.5 mile to the trailers-in-a-grove.*

Cabazon Indian Reservation
83-180 Requa Ave. #9
Indio, CA 92201
(619) 342-2593

Agua Caliente Reservation *Cahuilla.* (1896) Riverside Co. *

Many centuries ago, the Cahuilla found the springs that greened one of the few native palm stands in the West. From watering holes like this have come the life source of all desert peoples. But in the 1930s, a life force alien to this desert came here–the wealthy, who wanted a winter playground. Thus, an Indian reservation came to be in the middle of one of the richest communities in the state, Palm Springs.

How do you tell reservation from the rest of the town? Sometimes you can't. On some of the nearly 50 squares totalling 24,463 acres, the Indian homes are the more modest, on other squares, everybody looks the same. On some squares, the non-Indians have bought out the Indians (whose land is probably forever lost), on other squares at the edge of town, there's nothing at all. On some squares the locals lease the land itself for their own buildings–making this one of the richest reservations in the state.

The tribal office is a big, new building, partly rented by the BIA. The people used to have elaborate dances for the public once a year. No longer–"progress" and urbanization have taken their toll on the ancient culture.

129 *Palm Springs.*

Agua Caliente Reservation
441 S. Calle Encilia
Palm Springs, CA 92262
(619) 235-5673

*** **Morongo Reservation** *Cahuilla, Serrano* and *Cupeño.* (1877) Riverside Co.

The Morongo is one of the few reservations in California that is impossible to miss. Interstate 10 passes right through it at Banning and San Gorgonio Pass (2600 feet). Signboards point out the local cultivation of *jojoba* (a soap-yielding plant) and the Malki Museum (see p. 113 for more comments on this fine museum).

The 32,248-acre reservation is a well-developed community of some 300 persons, with a good-sized health clinic, tribal offices and a newish hall, substantial homes, ranches, farms, and an historical Moravian church dating back to the 1890s. Hollywood and TV films are made here occasionally. Bingo is offered.

In May the residents present a festival and barbeque with some ceremonies and dancing centered around the adobe museum, which is situated in the dry, often windy, open fields looking up to the towering 10,800-foot San Jacinto Peak.

Morongo has been home for Cahuillas, Serranos (from the north of here), Cupeños (from Los Coyotes and Pala), and Chemehuevis (from the Colorado River area).

130 *Field Rd. exit from I-10 at Cabazon is the road to the Malki Museum. Potrero Rd. is where the tribal offices are.*
Morongo Reservation
11581 Potrero Rd.
Banning, CA 92220
(619) 849-4697

Twentynine Palms Reservation *Chemehuevi-Luiseño.* (1895) San Bernardino Co.

This 402-acre rocky hillside reservation, originally established as a Chemehuevi refuge (far from their Colorado River home), now under BIA-designated Luiseño control (a long distance from their home) currently has no residents. A few persons live in the area, however, who use the land occasionally for gatherings.

On Adobe Street in the town is a well-kept Chemehuevi burial ground – the graves traditionally unmarked.

132 *Adobe Rd., S of State Hwy. 62, to a corner of Joshua Tree National Monument.*
Twentynine Palms Reservation
Jesse Mike
Gen. Delivery
Palm Springs, CA 92262

* **San Manuel Reservation** *Serrano.* (1893) San Bernardino Co.

The early Serrano people lived among the peaks, valleys, and deserts of the San Bernardino Mountains, from Victorville to Twentynine Palms. Most present-day Serranos are still in that region – living on or near two reservations, San Manuel and Morongo.

The 653 acres of San Manuel are arrayed along a foothill of the San Bernardino Mountains near Riverside. The approach to the hill is lined with ancient eucalyptus, which shade the Mexican rancho-style Serrano Cultural Center at the base of the foothill. On the slopes above are a group of older homes, a few adobe ruins, an ancient functioning *acequia*

[irrigation canal], some storehouses, and the quiet of a burial ground–all with vistas of mountains to the north and the valley of San Bernardino to the south.

The cultural center displays some articles of archaeological and ethnological interest. Educational and tribal functions are also held in the building. Outdoors are athletics fields and games areas.

133 *In Highland, take Highland Ave. to Victoria Ave., go uphill to the Center.*
San Manuel Reservation
5771 N. Victoria Ave.
Highland, CA 92346
(714) 862-2439

Satwiwa *Chumash* and *Gabrielino.* (1978) Rancho Sierra Vista, Santa Monica Mountains National Recreation Area, Ventura Co. *

Within the Rancho portion of this huge National Park, a segment of the Park has been dedicted as an American Indian Natural area. Its name is Satwiwa, and it is sponsored by the National Park Service and the Friends of Hutash and Tugupan. "Hutash" is Chumash for Mother Earth, and "Tugupan" is Gabrielino for Sky.

Satwiwa is a remote location set aside for the appreciation of the countryside, and for Native Americans to perpetuate their traditions in a place of spiritual beauty. Come, park, walk the land through relatively untouched ecological areas. Mountain lions and golden eagles live here.

Access from Ventura Fwy. (U.S. Hwy. 101) at Wendy Dr., W of Thousand Oaks. West on Potrero Rd. to Rancho Sierra Vista–continue to trailhead and Satwiwa.
Santa Monica Mountains N.R.A.
22900 Ventura Blvd.
Woodland Hills, CA 91364
(213) 888-3770

Calico Early Man Site San Bernardino Co. **

In 20,000 B.C., the Mojave Desert was wet, and was inhabited by distant ancestors of the California Indians. In 1942 A.D., San Bernardino County Archaeologist Ms. Dee Simpson, and later, Dr. Louis S. B. Leakey, took an interest in the culture of these people, mainly because Ms. Simpson had discovered the site of a stone tool factory belonging to them. The public is invited to tour this superb archaeological "dig" and displays of thousands of arrowheads, mallets, choppers, scrapers, lance heads, etc. Wednesday through Monday, 8–5.

Fifteen miles NE of Barstow, access by Minneola Rd. exit from Interstate 15.

Sherman Indian High School *All-Indian.* (1902) Riverside Co. **

An Act of Congress of 1891 for the "Relief of the Mission Indians" included the founding of a boarding school, Sherman Institute, under the direction of the Indian Service (now the Bureau of Indian Affairs). To this residential school, a hospital was added in 1902 which lasted until 1964. A United States Public Health Service clinic remains at the school.

The Institute was moved in 1911 and has lost some of its original 80 acres; it underwent many trials of poor leadership and instruction in the 1920s and 1930s. Only two of the original buildings remain–the old administration building now a museum.

Several years ago, California students were excluded as a result of a policy of forcing this state's Indian students into local schools. It was presumed that the local schools were adequate, but this proved to be an error. For a time only out-of-state students were admitted.

This comprehensive, accredited school receives Indian students of high school age and provides them, if eligible, with funds for both education and board. Today, in its many modern buildings, some 600 students augment their basic high school curricula and sports with a special Native American direction. Pride in being Indian is of prime importance.

134 Sherman Indian High School
9010 Magnolia Ave.
Riverside, CA 92503
(714) 351-6332

Southern California Intertribal Activities*

Today, in southern California, intertribal functions are most commonly found at powwows. From all parts of the south, including urban areas, the people have organized four *drums,* each drum being responsible for a powwow.

A "drum" is an organization devoted to the perpetuation of Indian customs, especially dancing and all the ceremonial aspects that go with it, such as singing and drumming. At the powwow, the actual large drum will be played by a number of members. Usually, at least two groups, each playing a different type of rhythm, will participate. Often, some individual tribal groups will present dances of their own. Other social events may be included at the powwow, as well. (Usually, the interested public is invited, and the announcements can be found at local Indian centers.)

In the south, as throughout the state, All-Indian rodeos are popular. The constestants are all Indian, and the public is invited to attend.

During the past twenty-five years, California has become the home of thousands of Indian people from further east. Consequently, the larger powwows and gatherings have taken on a decided color from Southwest and Plains peoples. Perhaps this is the beginning of a new, latter-day amalgamation and change of Indian cultures.

***Talking Leaf*: "The Los Angeles Indian Newspaper"**

Since 1935, *Talking Leaf* has been one of the major Indian voices of Southern California. The paper's voice, with seriousness and dashes of humor, speaks messages of importance from many tribal sources to Native American and non-Indian peoples alike.

I find the paper fascinating–excellent feature articles, good cartoons, Indian news from all over North America, national calendar of events, a directory of (urban) Indian Center services.

Location and Subscription address: Subscription, $10/year
Talking Leaf
1610 W. 7th St.
Los Angeles, CA 90017
(213) 265-0769

* See also p. 86, Northern California Powwows.

Former Trust Land Rancherias

Terminated and abandoned during 1960–70, these are presently not under Indian or U.S. Government control.

Rancheria	*County*	*Original Tribal Designation*
Alexander Valley (burial ground remains)	Sonoma	Wappo
Cache Creek	Lake	Southeastern Pomo
Chico (burial ground remains)	Butte	Maidu, Wailaki
Colfax	Placer	undesignated
Indian Ranch	Inyo	Shoshone
Lower Lake	Lake	Southeastern Pomo
Lytton	Sonoma	Pomo
Mark West	Sonoma	Pomo
Mission Creek	Riverside	Cahuilla
Nevada City	Nevada	Maidu
Paskenta	Tehama	Nomlaki
Ruffeys	Siskiyou	Shasta
Strathmore	Fresno	Yokuts
Strawberry Valley	Yuba	undesignated
Taylorsville	Plumas	Maidu

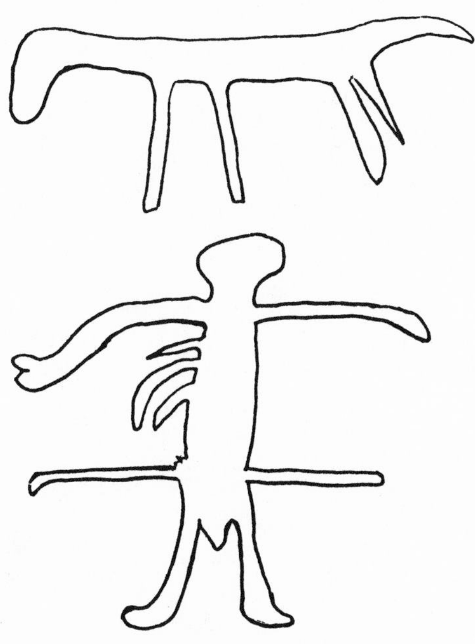

And for the Past, I pronounce what the air holds of the red aborigines.
The red aborigines!
Leaving natural breaths, sounds of rain and winds, calls as of birds and animals in the woods, syllabled to us for names;
Okonee, Koosa, Ottawa, Monongahela, Sauk, Natchez, Chattahoochee, Kaqueta, Oronoco,
Wabash, Miami, Saganaw, Chippewa, Oshkosh, Walla-Walla;
Leaving such to The States, they melt, they depart, charging the water and the land with names.

Walt Whitman, 1865, from *Leaves of Grass*,
[Whitman was a clerk in the Indian Bureau in 1865,
but was discharged for writing immoral poetry.]

PART THREE

Special Problems of the Indian in California Today

Ca. 1900. *St. Pk.*

E.W. Gifford, 1922. *Lowie.*

Panorama Magazine. St. Pk.

dbe

dbe

dbe

dbe

dbe

dbe

Relationship with the Larger Society

WHAT IS THE RELATIONSHIP between the Indian and the white – both personal and public? I have observed a range of attitudes on both sides from warm to hostile, with apparently no common reason for any one attitude. However, as in most of our society, the greatest antagonism seems to be between widely divergent income groups.

Of course, discrimination exists at all levels and in all places; it is the subtle form of hostility. I need not give examples. Allow me, though, to illustrate with some comments, the variety of attitudes from some California rural areas:

Rohnerville Rancheria resident: "Hassles with the local police and local Indian kids aren't uncommon."
Smith River, Gusha Community Center employee: "This is a nutrition center for anybody who needs us."
Cortina, nearby rancher: "I'm not particularly interested in their [new residents] having big parties, but I wouldn't mind seeing good residents like they've been for a good many years."
Warner Springs, Los Coyotes Reservation Spokesperson: "I'm looking for the person who shot up my home last night."
Bishop and Ft. Bidwell Forest Service employees: "Not many Indians work for us. They don't trust *any* government agency."
Laytonville Cahto: "We don't want people to come to stare."
Paskenta waitress: "How come the government gives them [two terminated Nomlakis] a trailer and don't give us none?"
Sheepranch neighbor: "They're good people, but they give some lively parties."
Santa Rosa Rancheria resident: "There's some friction between the Indian kids and others. So they generally leave school"
North Fork Mono: "Everybody's in the same [unemployment] mess here. Nobody looks to see who's Indian."
Lake Havasu Chemehuevi: "I got along fine with 'em [Whites]. After all, they're rentin' from *us*."

Health problems have been neglected for a long time, but recent efforts at providing at least a local health clinic have resulted in many new facilities. An idea of the distribution throughout the state can be seen from this list, itself incomplete:

Tsurai and Hoopa (Humboldt Co.)
Anderson (Shasta Co.)
Ukiah and Round Valley (Mendocino Co.)
X-L Ranch (Modoc Co.)
Susanville (Lassen Co.)
Tuolumne (Tuolumne Co.)
Lakeport (Lake Co.)
Oroville (Butte Co.)
Santa Rosa (Sonoma Co.)
Tule River (Tulare Co.)
Clovis (Fresno Co.)
Bishop (Inyo Co.)
Morongo (Riverside Co.)
Pauma Valley (San Diego Co.)
Santa Barbara (Santa Barbara Co.)
Parker, AZ (Eastern Riverside and San Bernardino Cos.)
Ft. Yuma (Imperial Co.)
Ft. Bidwell (Modoc Co.)

The feeling of worth and the rewards of effort begin where they should, with the young. This declaration is at Hoopa High School. (*dhe,* 1978)

Facilities consist of as little as a part-time clinic, to dental and eye clinics. The goal is health care approaching that of the local communities–it has not yet been achieved.

Employment will continue to bedevil Native Americans; whether from lack of skills, motivation, location, or education. In the north, what little employment there is centers mostly in the lumbering industry. For the Indian laborer (and others), the tasks are often hazardous and dangerous. Few of the older persons do not have some degree of disability from accidents in the forest or in the mills. Other jobs are mostly temporary and highly dependent on the status of the economy–the Indians being the most susceptible to job loss.

It has become imperative for many to devise some sort of activity, if for no other reason than to stem the boredom. Horsemanship has become one such activity, and one can find a number of all-Indian rodeos around the state in summer. Concentrated (and sometimes funded) efforts in restoring ancient customs, rituals, art, work, dance traditions, are among other such activities.

Commercial fishing and farming have not always been in the Indian's repertory, but as some land is made more arable by irrigation, we are seeing many acres turned into larger farms (see p. 111). The same goes for tourism, mostly in providing and maintaining campgrounds and occasionally mobile home parks (see p. 123, 128).

Religion is a problem. This may be an unusual statement, but I have seen patronizing missionizing which gives both Protestant and Catholic a suspicious name. And I have also seen some militant religious activity restrict destructive drinking habits. More importantly, I have seen the revival of the old ways and customs and revival of Indian pride give the same result without threat of damnation.

The question of choosing a religion or not (and which one) is a definite problem of conscience, for the reservation Indian is subject to greater pressures to choose *something* than those Indians living independently or in urban areas.

It is toward the young that some far-seeing concerned elders are looking for cultural continuance. In the past, it was enough just to practice the old ways. But now it is necessary to teach and to show and to tell.

In the dancehouses I see many children; on the dance arena I see many young adults. All about, I see the younger Indians seriously striving to learn the old ways, proud and glad to be who they are. And only in this way will the culture continue–with the elders as the source of knowledge and guidance, and the children, the teens, the young adults as the avid learners.

Current Land Issues

Of all the states, California has had the best reputation for being an easy place to live–temperate climate, leisurely life, available food, cheap energy. The swelling population expects these to continue, and for this population, land is becoming ever harder to obtain. The earth is being pushed harder and harder to produce.

Against this, the Indian is pushing back with renewed claims to original and treaty land rights. Let me recall and mention a few of the more recent issues.

In Elk Creek, Glenn Co., I have mentioned (p. 68) the continuing drama of water versus Indian land. One recent submergence of Indian land occurred near Ukiah with the Coyote Valley Rancheria (p. 72). The local tribal Pomo group held together remarkably well until new land was obtained. They were lucky in that numerous relatives lived nearby.

Also in Pomo country lies Rattlesnake Island, at the south end of Clear Lake. The land on this hitherto undeveloped island is a traditional Pomo ceremonial site. Nevertheless, a developer laid claim and has announced his intention to build on this place, but not without much protest, especially from the El-em Pomo community. We await the outcome.

Along the Pit River tributaries in Shasta Co. lie vast forests of timber. Some years ago, the Pacific Gas & Electric Co. laid claims to this land of the Pit River people. The struggles to retain the rights to the land near Roaring Creek Rancheria have been intense, resulting in occasional campaigns, occupations, and arrests (see p. 56).

Another struggle involves the Yurok claims to their control of the Klamath River fishing rights and their loss of control of the lower Klamath margins (p. 41).

Some years ago, the California legislature put forward laws regulating development or exploitation of (1) traditional Indian land and (2) land upon which significant Indian artifacts or burial grounds may have been found during excavation. With regard to the first law, the Karok people of Del Norte County have been protesting a massive enlargement of primitive logging roads between the towns of Gasquet and Orleans (the GO Road). Proposed routes would desecrate some remote and secluded Karok sacred grounds in Six Rivers National Forest. It appears the GO Road may go through, but with modified routing, thanks to the loud protests raised.

Much further south, in a large undeveloped tract of Los Angeles, of all places, remains of an ancient Gabrielino village were uncovered during development excavation. Work was halted until the significance of this site could be determined. A spokesman for Hughes Aircraft, the developer, told me that since there were no burials, the historic significance was greatly diminished. Yet, the protests of the organization of local Gabrielino descendants provided the initial stay of erasure of one more bit of our heritage.

In Southern California, land issues are not often a problem, owing to the relatively permanent status of reservations, as contrasted to the problems of small rancherias in the north (p. 72ff.). The problems looming largest in the south are those of land use (see pp. 111–112), and a form of environmental protection may be seen in the nondevelopmental aspects of Augustine, Pechanga, and Inaja-Cosmit, for example.

Mother Earth *is* the land. The land was the one resource of the early Native Californian. To be a good custodian of what remains is imperative.

The Urban Indian

The majority of the Indian people of California reside (at least temporarily) in towns or the larger cities. Many of these persons have come to California from other states, perhaps as many as half the state's estimated Indian population of well over a million (including numerous Latin Americans). Owing to this, and the fact that cities do not perpetuate specific cultures of various peoples, this book cannot treat in a meaningful way with urban Indian institutions that are not oriented toward those California cultures.

Since it certainly is not my wish to ignore the large urban population, I do want to include here a few of the institutions within the cities which serve the urban Indian. Some, serving urban and rural areas alike, are listed on p. 29. Other than giving descriptions of a few urban educational institutions, I must rely simply on the soulless device of lists.

Indian education within towns and cities can be provided through the very important Johnson-O'Malley program, which contributes supplementary funds for children three years old up to high school age. Johnson-O'Malley is directed by the Bureau of Indian Affairs, and its administrators may be found in Los Angeles, Sacramento, San Diego, San Jose, San Francisco, and several other smaller cities and towns in the state. Parents of prospective students, for example, would first contact their tribal council or urban American Indian Center. Eligibility (by tribal membership and being one-fourth Indian, among other things) would be established, then BIA would supply assistance in the nature of room, board, transportation, and other expenses.

It's not as easy as it sounds–especially dealing with governmental forms, requirements, etc. For instance, take the urban Indian who was born in the city. BIA wants a tribal affiliation, which means some sort of "belonging" to a tribe. Papers of Indian-ness and original tribe must be produced, even if difficult to find. So perhaps this person needs educational assistance and is entitled to it, but has spent a large portion of life not being Indian, but being a city-dweller. . . . Instead of benefactor, BIA becomes the big, prying, bureaucratic slug. The motivation to push through this is not bestowed on most of us.

Within some cities, such as San Francisco, El Cajon, San Jose, and Redding, a number of special educational facilities may be found for Indian children and adults. A typical school which I visited in San Francisco is supported by Title IV of the Indian Education Act of 1972 and provides basic educational aids for more than 500 students. One group, kindergarten through grade 12, receives needed supplementary education–tutoring and outreach programs in basic subjects–to aid the students in their present schooling. Another program assists adult students in their preparation of the GED (high school diploma). Both groups may take advantage of cultural enrichment studies–Indian history and culture.

An entire secondary education program may be provided under a (BIA-directed) scholarship program like the partial assistance described above; or, occasionally, at such schools as Sherman Indian High School (p. 139), or the private Indian school at Pala Reservation or Stewart, Nevada.

The BIA also steers and directs deserving students into employment assistance through training, career development centers, or direct employment.

Higher education programs are offered at the one Indian college in California, D-Q U (p. 85).

Native American Studies programs may be found at a number of California universities: State Universities at Long Beach, Los Angeles, Fullerton, Northridge, Sonoma, San Francisco, Hayward; and the University of California at Berkeley, Santa Cruz, Davis, and Los Angeles.

Educational opportunities exist, but still the problems of motivation and appropriate employment upon graduation remain–problems enough for nearly everyone, but especially for Native Californians.

Latin American Indian Events in California

The economic magnet that is California pulls from the south as well as from the east and north. This attraction is making California temporary or permanent home for hundreds of thousands of persons of Indian descent from south of the border. Indian history to the south has had many parallels to that of the U.S.–persecution, subjugation, economic privation, personal oppression, land loss. Yet, like here, many islands of tribal identity manage to maintain their cultures.

For the same social and economic reasons that exist in the U.S., many Hispanics have been reluctant to acknowledge their Native heritage. These attitudes are slowly being put to a retreat, as Indian pride and consciousness and power build.

In California, a surprising number of Latin American immigrants and workers identify with a tribe, such as Mixtec, Mayan, or Yaqui, etc. The vast majority of these people must return to their tribal territories in order to take part in festivals, dances, and other tribal occasions. However, today in California, a few of the better-represented Mexican tribal groups have organized to sponsor regular fiestas and gatherings. Four centers with such activities are Sacramento, San Francisco, Los Angeles, and San Diego. These groups present dances primarily from (but not restricted to) the central region of Mexico–Aztec, Mixtec, etc. Sharing in or attendance at one of these events is to participate in an intensely satisfying and exciting ceremony. The sponsoring dance groups and their leaders in each area are listed below. Please see the Calendar of Events for the dates and places of their annual functions.

Sacramento

Danza Quetzalcoatl
Chuy Ortiz, capitán
3402 – 7th Ave.
Sacramento, CA 95817
(916) 739-1105

San Francisco Bay Area

Xitlalli (resident company of Mission Cultural Center)
Francisco Camplis, capitán
Macuil Ortiz, maestra
501 Hanover St.
Daly City, CA 94014
(415) 586-0435

Los Angeles & Orange Co.

Xipe Totec
Lazaro Arvizu, capitán
(714) 774-9803

Flores en Aztlán
Josefina Gallardo, capitana
(213) 664-6433

San Diego

Danza Mexicayotl
Mario Aguilar, capitán
(619) 422-6433

Reference Matter

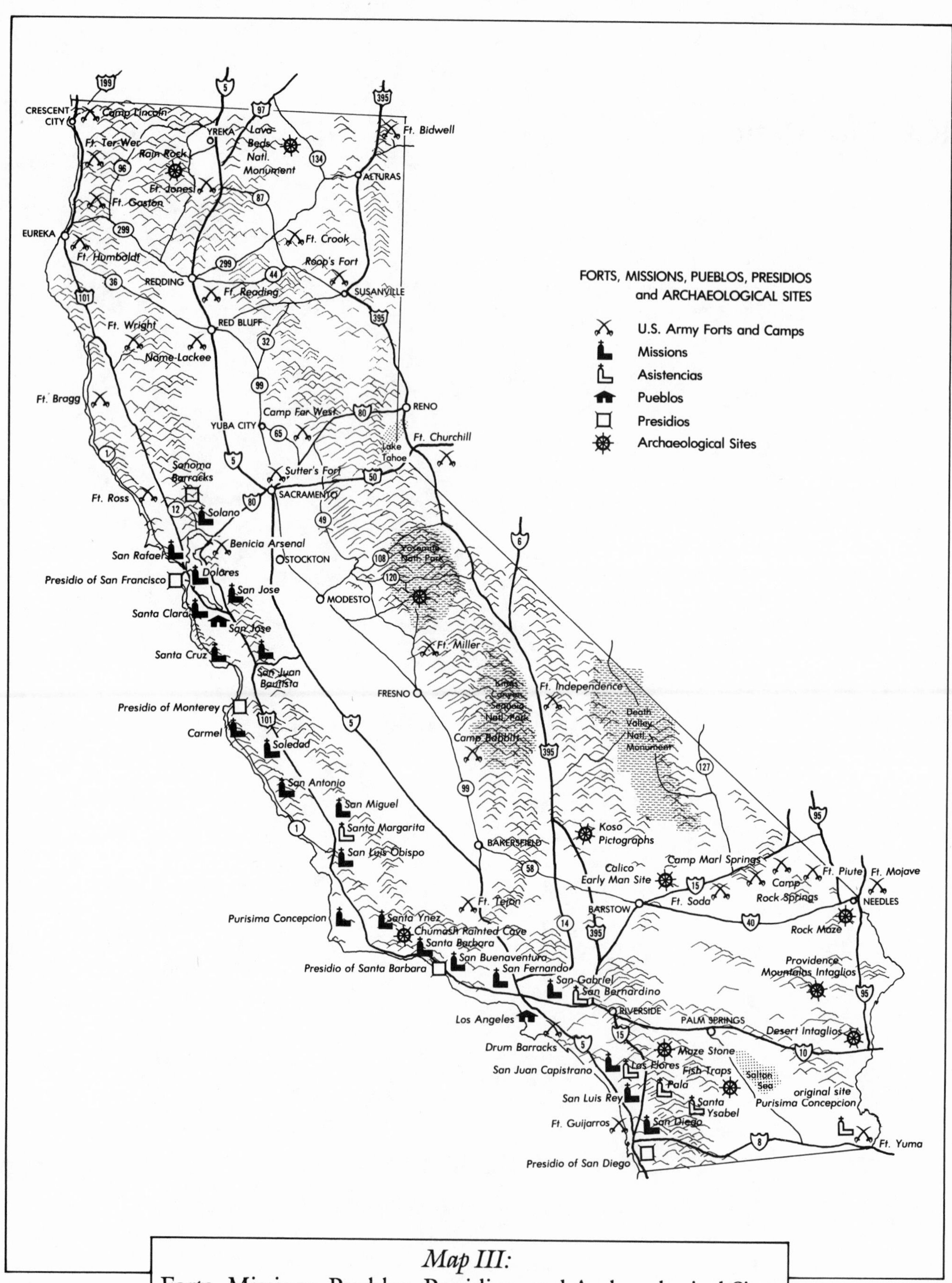

Map III:
Forts, Missions, Pueblos, Presidios, and Archaeological Sites

Appendix A
The Missions, their Asisténcias, the Presidios, and the Pueblos, 1769–1834

Other places were undoubtedly settled at this time–by Spanish immigrants, by the foot soldiers, by traders, even the padres themselves; however, this listing is based on places that had significant direct effect on the Indian population in or around the establishment.

These are only the shortest of sketches–the history of the missions is detailed in numerous other places. The order of listing is south to north, so that the reader might find them more easily–to pay homage to the thousands of native Californians and padres who lived and died there.

Numerous other missions to the Indians, but not ones of the original "Chain of 21," still exist on reservations. Most are mentioned in the section discussing that reservation.

As elsewhere in this book, the numbers in **boldface** type (e.g., **242**), refer to California Historical Landmark numbers.

1769 **Misión San Diego de Alcalá • 242, 52** **
(Indian name, *Nipaguay*)
Though the original site was at the Presidio, the mission was moved some distance away, so as to remove the neophytes from the coarse army types (a policy followed at all the Presidios). Several times destroyed by Indian attack, earthquake, and neglect, today it is a beautiful church overlooking the Mission Valley of San Diego. Museum.
Founder: Fray Junípero Serra (Franciscan).
Indian peoples: *Tipai, Ipai, Kameyaay* (once all lumped under the term *Diegueño*).

1769 **Presidio de San Diego • 59** (Indian name, *Cosoy*)
Of the site of the original fort at Old Town, San Diego, the only remnants are the tile floor of the chapel and some crumbling adobe walls in a green and tree-shaded park. This was once the headquarters for the Spanish army occupation of the entire southern region of Alta California.

1780 **Misión Purísima Concepción • 350** **
(See also p. 156)
Located at Fort Yuma (Imperial Co.), the original buildings were destroyed in an Indian revolt, 1781. The mission was not rebuilt until 1922, as St. Thomas Church, part of the Ft. Yuma Reservation. The first mission name was transferred to the coastal Santa Barbara Co. site.

Indian peoples: *Quechan, Halchidhoma, Halyikwamai* [formerly all called *Yumans*], *Cócopa* [from Arizona].

** 1818 **Asisténcia de Santa Ysabel • 369** (Indian name, *Elenaman*)
Located one mile N. of Santa Ysabel, on State Rte. 79 (San Diego Co.), it was a branch, or *visíta*, of Misión San Diego. A pretty chapel and an Indian cemetery remain. Feast Day (see Calendar).

Indian peoples: *Ipai, Tipai, Cupeño, Cahuilla, Luiseño*(?).

* 1798 **Misión San Luis Rey de Francia • 239**
To be found at San Luis Rey (San Diego Co.), the church is a well-restored pastel jewel set in a jade of grass. It probably never looked so good as today.

Founder: Fray Fermín Francisco de Lasuén, Serra's successor as President of the Alta California missions.
Indian peoples: *Luiseño, Gabrielino.*

*** 1816 **Asisténcia de San António de Pala • 243**
At the Pala Reservation on State Rte. 76 (San Diego Co.), this is one of the most interesting chapels with original Indian designs on the walls and ceilings. Hundreds of Indian people still worship there. The chapel cemetery contains curious gravemarkers with personal possessions. It was an adjunct of Misión San Luis Rey.

Founder: Fr. António Peyri.
Indian peoples: *Luiseño, Cupeño, Cahuilla.*

1823 **Asisténcia Las Flores • 616**
In Camp Pendleton (San Diego Co.) today, it was a branch of Misión San Luis Rey, and was built for use as a way-station between San Luis Rey and San Juan Capistrano.

** 1776 **Misión San Juan Capistrano • 200**
Situated in the town of San Juan Capistrano (Orange Co.), this beautiful place once bustled with the arts and industries of the local native. Now it is famous for its swallows which arrive annually on March 19th (St. Joseph's Day). The tourists leave; the quiet settles in.

Founder: Fr. Serra
Indian peoples: *Luiseño* (formerly called *Juaneño*), probably *Gabrielino.*

* 1830 **Asisténcia de San Bernardino • 42,** and the **Zanja • 43**, (Indian name, *Guachama*)
On Barton Rd. in San Bernardino. This was a branch of Misión San Gabriel, with an irrigation system (zanja) built, as always, with Indian labor. Small museum.
Indian peoples: *Gabrielino, Cahuilla, Serrano.*

** 1771 **Misión San Gabriel Arcángel • 158**
In San Gabriel on Mission Drive, today this is a parish church with rather Arabic architecture of short towers and buttresses. It was once one of the largest missions. Gabrielino festivals.

Founder: Fr. Serra.
Indian peoples: *Gabrielino, Serrano*, probably *Tataviam and Vanyume, Kawaiisu.*

1797 **Misión San Fernando Rey de Espanã • 157** **

To be found on State Rte. 118 in San Fernando, what remains of the mission is the old convent; there is a new church, and the gardens are tropical and nearly silent, a refuge from Los Angeles.
Founders: Fr. Lasuén and Fr. Francisco Dumetz.
Indian peoples: *Gabrielino (Fernandeño), Chumash, Tataviam, Kawaiisu.*

1781 **El Pueblo de Nuestra Senora la Reina de Los Angeles de Porciuncula • 144** (Indian name, *Yangnah*) *

The second of the "towns" founded by the Spanish (the first was San José) with Indian help, as usual. Located near Los Angeles' City Hall, the tourist-oriented Olvera Street is part of the original pueblo.

1782 **Misión San Buenaventura • 310** *

On Main and Figueroa Streets, Ventura (Ventura Co.), only the church structure and a little garden remain of the buildings twice hit by fire and once by quake.

Founder: Fr. Serra
Indian peoples: *Chumash, Yokuts(?), Kawaiisu.*

1782 **El Presidio de Santa Bárbara Virgen y Martir • 636** *

The remains of this fort are just off Anacapa St. in Santa Barbara. Some excavation is presently being undertaken of the old Presidio walls. The most interesting intact part is the old guardhouse. After abandonment of the Presidio proper, the Covarrubias family rancho enveloped the entire Presidio lands. The Covarrubias adobe is an excellent present-day museum.

1786 **Misión Santa Bárbara • 309** **

On a high hill in Santa Barbara, at Los Olivos and Laguna streets, this is a beautiful, stately place, actually constructed in 1815—with Indian labor. It also has an elaborate irrigation system and a museum. The cemetery contains the graves of 4,000 Chumash. Display of artifacts.

Indian people: *Chumash* (formerly called *Canalino*).

1804 **Misión Santa Ynéz** (also spelled **Inés**) **• 305** *

This small mission is in Solvang (Santa Barbara Co.) at the south end of town, not far from the present Chumash reservation (see p. 103). In it are some local relics; outside are fields and impressive mountains.

Founder: Fr. Estévan Tapis.
Indian people: *Chumash.*

1787 **Misión La Purísima Concepción • 340** ***

On State Rte. 246 near Lompoc (Santa Barbara Co.), this is probably the most complete mission remaining, and one of the few

built without fortifications. It also has an elaborate water system and a museum. Subjected to a month-long Indian revolt in 1824, this is the second mission of the same name (see p. 153).
Founder: Fr. Lasuén.
Indian people: *Chumash.*

* 1772 **Misión San Luis Obispo de Tolosa · 325**
At the center of San Luis Obispo, at Chorro and Montgomery Streets, a few restored parts of one of the oldest missions remain, overlooking a small creek.
Founder: Fr. Serra.
Indian peoples: *Chumash, Yokuts.*

ca. 1831 **Asisténcia de Santa Margarita · 364**
Near Santa Margarita (San Luis Obispo Co.), this was a way-station and granary for Misión San Luis Obispo.

*** 1797 **Misión San Miguel Arcángel · 326**
Along U.S. 101 in San Miguel (San Luis Obispo Co.) the entire aspect of the mission gives one a feeling of the earlier era–the town is small, the hills are dry. The small cemetery conceals the hundreds of Indians buried there over a few short years. Museum.
Founder: Fr. Lasuén.
Indian people: *Salinan.*

*** 1771 **Misión San Antonio de Pádua · 232**
Situated in the mountains six miles from Jolon at the entrance to Fort Hunter-Liggett (Monterey Co.), the setting is picturesque and remote; the buildings have not been altered for tourists–it's pretty much as it was, including the water works (now dry).
Founder: Fr. Serra.
Indian peoples: *Salinan, Yokuts, Esselen.*

1791 **Misión Nuestra Señora de Soledad · 233**
To be found three miles southwest of Soledad (Monterey Co.), all that remains are a plain reconstruction of a chapel and many crumbling walls in a field.
Founder: Fr. Lasuén.
Indian peoples: *Salinan, Yokuts, Esselen(?), Costanoan.*

*** 1770 **El Presídio de Monteréy · 105**
The ornate chapel is all that is left of the old Presidio, except some stone walls (Church St. at Camino El Estero, Monterey). The chapel was also part of the first mission. With U.S. military occupation, a redoubt was added in 1847 (still there, with antique cannon). The post is still active. A museum on the grounds includes a number of Rumsen Costanoan Indian artifacts.

*** 1770 **Misión San Carlos Borromeo del Rio Carmelo · 135**
Located in Carmel (Monterey Co.). This extraordinarily beautiful mission was originally founded in Monterey (see above) in the

Presidio, but moved in 1771, because of the rowdiness of the soldiers. Once again, the tiny cemetery only hints at the graves of thousands of the local Indians buried there.

Founders: Frs. Serra and Juan Crespi
Indian peoples: *Esselen and Costanoan* (mostly *Rumsen*).

1797 **Misión San Juan Bautista • 195** **

Right in the town of the same name, near Hollister (San Benito Co.). The colorful chapel is strongly buttressed against the many earthquakes of the San Andreas fault that occur here. Parts of the old town coexist with the mission. Once the largest of the missions, it also bears some 4,000 Indian graves. In September and March, Indian festivals are held.

Indian peoples: *Costanoan, Yokuts*.

1791 **Misión la Exaltación de la Santa Cruz . 342**

On High and Emmett Streets in Santa Cruz, a diminutive replica is all that one sees at the site of the original mission, destroyed in two quakes.

Founder: Fr. Lasuén.
Indian peoples:*Costanoan, Yokuts*.

[*Villa de Branciforte* **• 469,** an adjacent pueblo, was founded at the same time, but without an Indian population.]

1777 **El Pueblo de San José de Guadalupe • 433**

The old town center was at Jefferson School, San Jose. Though the first pueblo, it was not immediately populated by a large number of Indians–they preferred to remain in nearby rancherias.

1791 **Misión Santa Clara de Asís** *

First site: **• 250** Kifer Rd. and De La Cruz Blvd. (Indian name, *Soco-is-uka*)
Last site: **• 338** Alameda and Lexington St. (Indian name, *Gerguensun*), both in Santa Clara (Santa Clara Co.). After the first site flooded, two other sites were chosen, the last subjected to two quakes. As a result, of the orignal buildings, only cloisters remain–adjacent to several buildings of the University of Santa Clara.

Founders: Tómas de la Peña, Joseph Murgíria.
Indian peoples: *Costonoan, Yokuts, Plains Miwok*.

1797 **Misión del Gloriosísima Patriarca Señor San José • 334** *

Located on State Rte. 238 near Fremont (Alameda Co.). Strangely, the mission isn't in the town of San Jose, but several miles northeast. The church was recently totally restored, but with one older cloister as a museum. The Indian cemetery nearby is tended by local Ohlone (Costanoan) people. Where once was the mission compound is now an ancient grove of olives.

Founder: Fr. Lasuén.

Indian peoples: *Costanoan (Ohlone), Yokuts, Plains, Lake and Coast Miwok.*

** 1776 **Misión de San Francisco de Asís** (or **Misión Dolores**) **· 327**

A rather oddly-colonnaded building is all that is left of the mission establishment that once covered huge tracts in what is now San Francisco. The chapel bears original Indian-painted designs on the ceiling beams.

Founder: Fr. Serra.

Indian peoples: *Costanoan* (*Ramatush*, and others), *Miwok, Patwin*.

* 1776 **El Presidio de San Francisco · 79**

The military station in San Francisco has been headquarters for all military activity in northern California since Spanish times—through Mexican and Yankee rule as well. One Spanish building remains, now the Officers' Club, whose entrance is flanked by two 1673 Spanish cannons from Lima, Peru. See also p. 166.

1817 **Misión San Rafael Arcángel · 220**

Fifth and Court Streets, San Rafael (Marin Co.). A very plain reconstruction of the chapel; nothing else remains, but modern buildings are all around.

Founder: Fr. Ventura Fortuni.

Indian people: *Coast Miwok*.

** 1823 **Misión San Francisco Solano · 3**

Located on the Central Plaza, Sonoma (Sonoma Co.). Under independent Mexico, this mission was the last to be founded in the "Chain of 21", more as a political gesture toward Russia than from religious zeal. The beauty of the chapel is in its simplicity; the cloisters hold grape arbors, framing the entrance to a museum.

Founder: Fr. José Altamira.

Indian peoples: *Coast Miwok, Patwin (Suisun), Wappo.*

(A description of the *Sonoma Barracks*, put up about the time as the mission, may be found on p. 165.)

Appendix B
Notable Historical Ranchos

Early Northern California

Year Founded	*Historical Landmark No.*		*Founder*
1820	**246**	**Rancho San Antonio** (San Leandro, Alameda Co.)	Don Luís Peralta
1833	**18**	**Rancho Petaluma** (Petaluma, Sonoma Co.)	Gen. Mariano Vallejo
1835	**241**	**Rancho Las Positas** (San Leandro, Alameda Co.	Robert Livermore
1835	**509**	**Rancho Laguna de Los Palos Colorados** (Moraga, Contra Costa Co.)	Don Joaquín Moraga
1836	**564**	**Rancho Caymus** (Yountville, Napa Co.)	George C. Yount
1839	**525**	**New Helvetia** (Sutter's Fort) (Sacramento Co.)	Capt. John Sutter
1840		**Rancho Rincoñada de Los Gatos** (Los Gatos, Santa Clara Co.)	José Hernandez and Sebastian Peralta
1845	**534**	**Rancho Los Putos** (Vacaville, Solano Co.)	Juan Peña and Manuel Vaca
1846	**12**	**Rancho de La Barranca Colorado** (Red Bluff, Tehama Co.)	Gen. William B. Ide
1846	**10**	**Rancho Buena Ventura** (nr. Cottonwood, Shasta Co.)	Maj. Pierson B. Reading
1846	**206**	**Rancho Los Robles** (nr. Lemoore, Kings Co.)	Daniel Rhoads
1847	**426**	Ranch at Kelseyville (Lake Co.)	Andrew Kelsey and Charles Stone
1847	**331**	**Rancho de Las Mariposas** (Bear Valley, Mariposa Co.)	Col. John C. Frémont
1849	**329**	**Rancho Chico** (Chico, Butte Co.)	Gen. John Bidwell
1850s		Ranch in Fresno Co.	Maj. James D. Savage

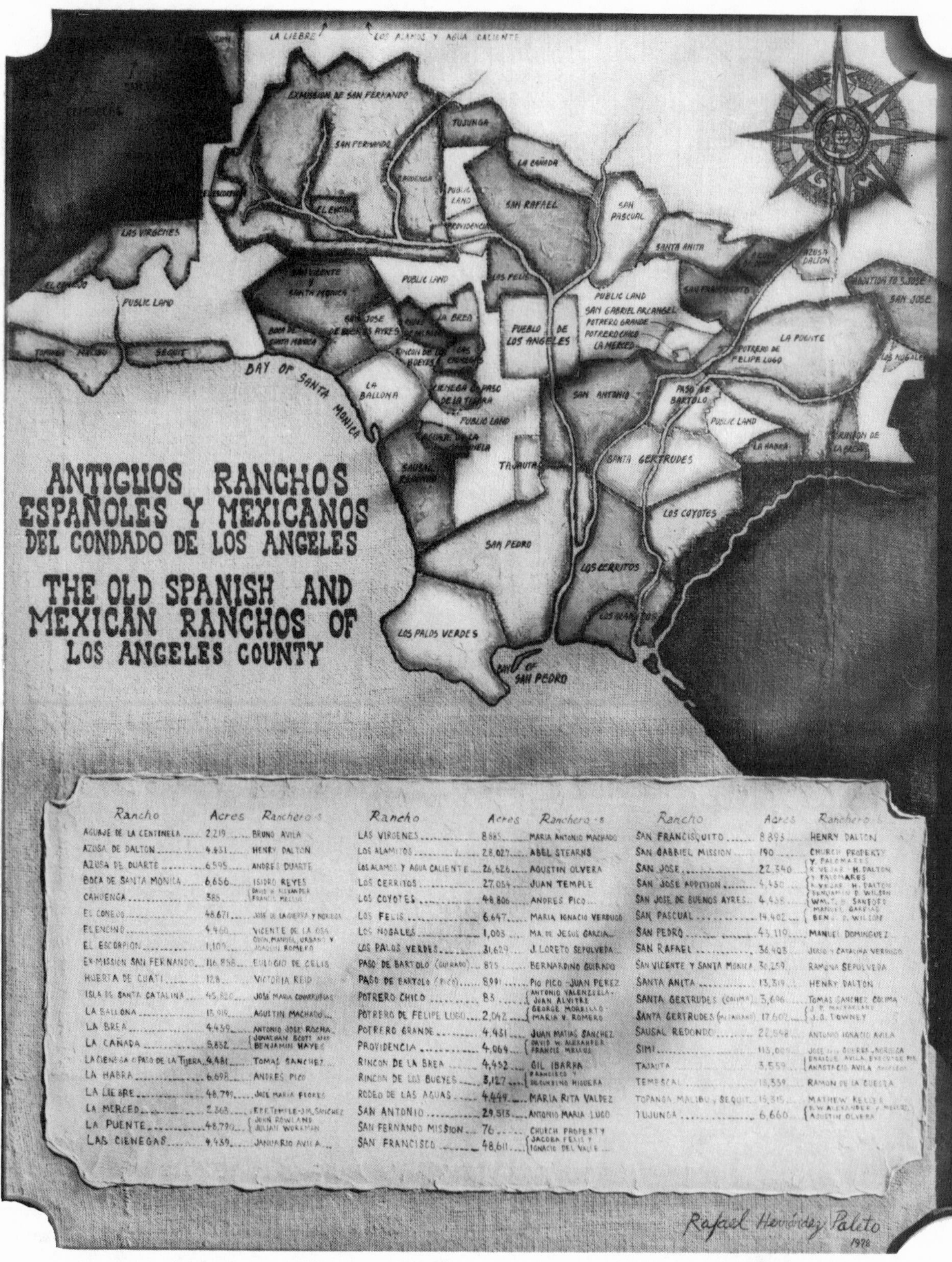

A map of the ranchos existing in Los Angeles Co. around 1840 appears in an ice cream store on Olvera St., the site of the original pueblo of Los Angeles. (*dhe,* 1978)

Early Southern California

Year Founded	*Historical Landmark No.*		*Founder*
1784	**235, 637**	**Rancho San Rafael** (Glendale, Los Angeles Co.)	José María Verdugo
1784		**Rancho Los Cerritos** (Long Beach, Los Angeles Co.)	Manuel Nieto
1810	**226**	**Rancho Santa Ana** (Santa Ana Canyon, Orange Co.)	Don Bernardo Yorba
1817	**308**	Covarrúbias Adobe and Rancho (Santa Barbara Co.)	Don Domingo Carillo
1818	**383**	Rancho/adobe (Palos Verdes Hills, Los Angeles Co.)	José Sepúlveda
1828		**Rancho Santa Margarita** (San Fernando, Los Angeles Co.)	Pio Pico
1834	**362**	**Ranchito Romulo** (San Fernando, Los Angeles Co.)	Rómulo Pico
1836	**227**	**Rancho Santiago de Santa Ana** (Costa Mesa, Orange Co.)	Diego Sepúlveda
1839	**368**	**Rancho Santa Anita** (Arcadia, Los Angeles Co.)	Hugo and Victoria Reid
1839	**553, 556**	**Rancho San Francísco** (Los Angeles and Ventura Cos.)	António del Valle
1840	**372**	**Rancho San José** (Pomona, Los Angeles Co.)	Don Ygnácio Palomares
1842	**199**	**Rancho Cañada de Los Alisos** (El Toro, Orange Co.)	Jose Serrano
1842	**528**	**Rancho San Bernardino** (San Bernardino)	Diego Sepúlveda
1843	**425**	**Rancho Cañada de Los Coches** (El Cajon, San Diego Co.)	Apolinaria Lorenzana
1844	**311**	**Warner's Ranch** (Warner Springs, San Diego Co.)	Juan Warner
1844	**102**	**Rancho Jurupa** (Riverside, Riverside Co.)	Louis Rubidoux
1849	**689**	**Rancho El Encino** (Encino, Los Angeles Co.)	Francisco Reyes

Appendix C
Military Posts of Northwest California

Please see comments in Appendix C, p. xvii.

Fort Humboldt, Eureka, about 1885, established for control of the Hupa and their neighbors, and the Eel River tribes. Only one of these buildings remains. (*St. Pk.*)

** **Fort Humboldt · 154** (1853–66) Humboldt Co.

The terrain along the Eel River here is rugged, the forests dense, the climate chilly and damp. It drove one commandant, Gen. Ulysses S. Grant, to drink–so goes the legend. Because the local Indians so loved this, their land, the Army spent 13 years here driving them out of it.

Ft. Humboldt was the headquarters of northwestern California's Army activities, but the only Indians who saw it closely were some 300 prisoners, jammed into a stockade. It was not needed after the Civil War.

Remnants: Two restored wooden buildings on the old parade ground–now part of a logging museum. This site is unloved and shunned by the local Indians.

On U.S. 101 at the south city limits of Eureka.

* **Camp Lincoln · 545** (1862–69) Del Norte Co.

The Tolowas, Yuroks, and Karoks felt the terrible pressures of the company of soldiers based here–here to guard the invading miners and settlers.

Remnants: Commandant's home–now a private farm house against the forest front, overlooking lush, green fields.

Three miles off U.S. 101 or 1 mile off U.S. 199, just north of Crescent City (markers on U.S. 101).

Ft. Ter-Wer • 544 (1857–61) Del Norte Co.

One of those little posts for "containment" of the local Yuroks on the lower Klamath River. Poorly sited, the location has been completely washed out several times by floods.

Ft. Gaston • (1858–92) Humboldt Co. *

(For details, see p. 43, Hoopa Valley Reservation.)

Ft. Jones • 317 (1852–58) Siskiyou Co.

For six years two companies of dragoons harassed the Karoks and Shastans attempting to defend their homelands.

There are no remnants, only a bas-relief brass marker featuring covered wagons and stockades.

One mile S of Ft. Jones on the old east-bank Scott River road to Etna.

[Note: Ft. Dick is the name of a town in Del Norte Co., but it apparently never had even an encampment.]

Military Posts of Northeastern California

Ft. Bidwell • 430 (1866–97) Modoc Co. *

(See Ft. Bidwell Reservation, p. 59.)

Ft. Churchill • (1860–71) Nevada (See p. 167.) **

From this large post in Nevada, troops were occasionally dispatched into northeastern California.

Roop's Fort • 76 (1854–64) Lassen Co. *

It's not really a fort, just a couple of little log cabins. But in 1854 Issac Roop, a pioneer, put up these buildings to protect himself from the Indians upon whose land he was squatting. It saw action in 1863, when a group of pioneers had a little battle (later dubbed the "Sagebrush War") over whether Nevada or California should "get" Susanville.

Weatherlow St., Susanville.

Camp Far West • 493 (1849–52) Yuba Co.

The camp here in the grassy foothills of the Central Sierra was in some ways typical and one way unusual of the many camps thrown up around central and northern California.

Typically, it consisted of only a few log barracks for a small detachment to "guard" a bunch of miners who were devastating the Nisenan people's land, and it lasted only three years.

Atypically, it was commanded by one Capt. Hannibal Day who was sensitive to the situation: "From all the information I can gather, the aggression was rather on the part of the whites toward the natives . . ." He apparently had no taste for his duty: ". . . So far as the mining population is concerned they are competent for their own protection . . ."

Writing with perceptive sarcasm, he proposed that the federal Indian agent advise the Nisenans as to "what will be their probable fate unless they discontinue their thieving and submit with a better grace to being shot down, although it may seem strange to them to be thus intruded upon by the whites . . . and they must vacate their hunting-grounds in favor of our gold diggers."[9]

Remnants: A few foundations, some tumbled gravestones. Property was once Johnson's Ranch (Mexican land grant of 1845), now churned by developers' machines.

From State Rte. 65 about 3 miles to a locked green iron gate with concrete foundations—S side of road. Walk a dirt road to the Huyu River's edge.

** **Sutter's Fort · 525** (built 1839) Sacramento Co.

One of the first persons to take advantage of the Mexican government's offer of land grants in central California was John Augustus Sutter, a Swiss ex-army captain. On his 50,000-acre grant called *New Helvetia*, he set up a small feudal empire, using local Indians as labor and as mercenaries to run the estate and to raid other Indian areas as necessary for supplies or to keep the peace.

Sutter's huge estate (Indian-built, of course) was nearly self-sufficient and was managed in a military manner (uniforms, canon blast at 6 AM, etc.). In addition to the adobe fort and travelers' hospice in what is now central Sacramento, he built outlying fortifications, especially one at his Hock Farm, eight miles south of Marysville on the Feather River. As happened to the Indian population of California, his estate was overrun and divided up by the forty-niners; ironically, in that it was upon *his* estate that gold was first found in 1848.

Remnants: Primarily, the large fort, with many of the original cannon, and reconstructed interiors.

L and 28th Streets, Sacramento. This is also the location of the State Indian Museum *(see p. 68)*.

Military Posts of West Central California

* **Benicia Arsenal and Barracks · 176, 177** (1851–present) Solano Co.

Though the Presidio of San Francisco was the "nerve center" for the military operations of the U.S. Army in northern California, it was the Benicia Arsenal from which supplies, munitions, men, and animals were dispatched. It was located on the north side of the San Francisco Bay and thus of more ready access to the field.

Situated from high on a treeless hill to the windswept tidewater's edge, this post provisioned almost all western California military expeditions against the natives, as well as Civil War and more modern operations. In 1859 an impressive stone fort with tall towers was erected to guard and oversee ship traffic in the Carquinez Straits. Other architecturally attractive structures were raised in the same decade, many of which survive.

On the eastern edge of Benicia, just below the Interstate 680 bridge across the Carquinez Straits.

Fort Ross · 5 (1812–1841) Sonoma Co. **

Russian fur-trading settlements in Alaska, mainly Sitka (founded in 1799), were in need of food obtainable only from warmer climes. Thus in 1812, a stockade and block-houses were erected by the Russian-American Company, a quasi-governmental business, something like the Hudson's Bay Company of Canada. The site is on a beautiful coastside terrace, with forests, fields, and orchards.

The Russians, in a unique gesture of territorial respect, pursued a policy of cooperation with the local Pomos with whom they seemed to have had no hostilities. A large Pomo village sprang up around the fort, as most of the labor was Indian. The Company traded with the Presidio in San Francisco, but the Mexican government became wary of Russian intentions and soon founded missions at San Rafael and Sonoma as a foil to Russian expansion.

The Russians retired in 1841, selling to Sutter (p. 164) supplies for *his* fort. (The deal included a cannon captured from Napoleon's troops outside Moscow in 1813.)

Remnants: A reconstructed stockade, church, original commandant's home, numerous relics of Russian, Spanish, and Pomo origin.

State Rte. 1 at the Fort Ross State Park. Camping sites nearby at Salt Point State Park.

Sonoma Barracks (Presidio de Sonoma) · 316 (1836–1851) Sonoma Co. *

It was Gen. Mariano Vallejo, whose baronial rancho was installed near here in Petaluma, who set up the first barracks at the tiny Pueblo of Sonoma, adjacent to the Misión Solano. His purpose was two-fold–nationally, to repel the Russian encroachment of settlers moving eastward from Fort Ross (see above) and personally, to guard and extend his fortunes, supported by Indian labor (see p. 17).

It was here that a group of Yankee settlers took over the town in 1846, raised the Bear flag, and declared themselves independent of Mexico. Indian fortunes were to change radically by this action, as Alta California passed into United States control three weeks later. The U.S. garrison abandoned the post in 1851, there being no more "Indian problem" in the area.

Remnants: Several barracks buildings, well-restored, on the Plaza in Sonoma.

Ft. Wright · (1858–75) Mendocino Co.
(See p. 75, Round Valley Reservation)

Post at Nome Lackee · 357 (1854–66) Tehama Co.

This was one of those desolate places that Army policy decided was suitable for an Indian Reservation. The Indians decided otherwise (see p. 75) and decamped.

Fort Bragg · 615 (1857–64) Mendocino Co. *

The fort here was only to keep the Indians of an ill-fated Mendocino Reservation "in check". As usual, the Army had made no provision for support of the people it had brought here. Both the reservation and the fort folded.

Remnant: A headquarters building on the grounds of the local lumber company, today a logging museum.

Fort Reading · 379 (1852–67) Shasta Co.

From this largest of forts in northern California essayed troops in all directions to quell the resistance of the Shastas, the Wintus, the Yanas, and the Pit River Achumawis. Named for one Pierson B. Reading, owner of the 26,000-acre Rancho Buena Ventura (established 1847). He was given some $25,000 for protection of the Wintus in a 35-square-mile reservation in 1852, but gold miners continued to assail the natives in spite of the Army's "protection". Eventually, the Indians who had survived periodic hunts, were force-marched to coastal reservations, removing the need for further occupation of the fort.

Six miles NE of Anderson.

Military Posts of Central California

Ft. Miller · 584 (1851–64) Fresno-Madera Cos.

The forty-niners of the central Sierra foothills were not too comfortable at first, owing to attacks of the Yokuts and Monaches. These natives were somewhat loathe to see their oaks torn out, their hunting grounds ripped up for the little yellow stones, and their grassy valleys taken over by pioneer settlers.

Consequently, the eastern Central Valley came to have its U.S. Army fort–this one, Ft. Miller, was established in 1851 on the San Joaquin River as it plunges out of the mountains a few miles north of Fresno. As became customary in most places, the fort was abandoned after the Civil War, the Indians having been totally subdued in less than seven years.

The Fort site is totally inundated by the waters of Lake Millerton, though an original log blockhouse of the post has been preserved in Roeding Park, Fresno, as a museum.

*** **Presidio of Monterey · 105** (1770)
(See p. 156.)

* **Presidio of San Francisco · 79** (1776)
(See also p. 158.)

The early Spanish *castillo* (fort) of San Joaquín was levelled in 1854 to accommodate construction of Ft. Winfield Scott (today Ft. Point), built in the style of Ft. Sumter, South Carolina. Activities at both the Spanish and U.S. forts were not primarily directed at Indians. Nevertheless, all U.S. Army operations against the indigenous peoples of California originated at this post.

[Note: Both the Spanish (no doubt with Indian labor) and the United States constructed numerous defensive fortifications about the San Francisco Bay: Ft. Mason (ex-Spanish Batería San José) 1863– ; Ft.

Baker (U.S., opposite Ft. Point on the Golden Gate); Alcatraz (Sp. and U.S.) 1859– ; Camp Reynolds (Angel Island, Sp. and U.S.); Camp Yerba Buena (Yerba Buena Island) 1867– ; numerous World War II batteries, now abandoned.]

Presidio of Santa Barbara · 636 (1786) *
(See p. 155.)

Hudson's Bay Company Headquarters · 819 (1841) San Francisco Co.
This quasi-military English-Canadian company placed a trading outpost of its huge western holdings here in the little year-old Mexican village of Yerba Buena. The post, in what was to become financial San Francisco, was set up for buying pelts and furs from trappers and Indians. The English were just one of the many countries interested in acquisition of California's native lands.
Montgomery St. at Commercial St., San Francisco.

[Note: **Camp Babbitt** (1862–66) in Visalia was a Civil War post only for the purpose of keeping Tulare Co. in the Union. A detachment at Yosemite Park (1890-1916) acted only in lieu of park rangers.]

Military Posts East of the Sierra Nevada and the Mojave Desert

Ft. Churchill · Nevada. (1860–69) **
Located only 40 miles from California, this largest of Nevada forts had considerable influence on the Paiutes and Washos at the eastern edge of California–the influence being their subjugation. These peoples had protested in violent fashion the kidnapping of their children and seizure of their lands.

Row upon row of crumbling adobe quarters somehow bring to mind the old Latin phrase: *sic semper tyrannis* ("Thus Always to Tyrants").
Take U.S. 50 east of Carson City to U.S. Alternate 95, 8 miles S of Silver Springs to Ft. Churchill State Park and Museum.

Ft. Independence · 349 (1862–77) Inyo Co. *
(See Ft. Independence Reservation, pp. 110, 121.)

• • •

Though the Spanish never succeeded in establishing a permanent post along the middle Colorado River, the push of immigrants into California in the 1850s made it necessary for the United States to establish a series of desert forts along the Government Road from Needles to Barstow. Mohaves and Paiutes were the peoples whose land was being trespassed upon and invaded.

Ft. Mojave was the first and largest, located near the present town of Needles, California. The others were strung out at well-spaced water holes along the parched track.

* **Ft. Mojave** • Arizona. (1859–90)

Originally a post for control of the local Mohaves and Paiutes, this fort on the California border became a part of the Union's southwestern defenses (though abandoned 1861–63 during the Civil War). From 1890 to 1935 the site was an Indian school. In 1942, the buildings were leveled, no doubt to the great satisfaction of the Mohaves, for whom the fort had been a repulsive symbol for nearly a century. Only sidewalks to nowhere and an abandoned cemetary remain.

Near Needles, on the north end of Ft. Mojave Reservation (p. 122), go 12 miles N on Arizona State Rte. 95 to Camp Mohave Rd., turn W to river levee road, then N for ½ mile to end of dike. Climb the cliff to fort site.

* **Ft. Piute** • (ca. 1867–68) San Bernardino Co.

This was the first post, some 22 miles west of Ft. Mojave, on the Old Government Road. The day I visited the silent, gray ruins the air was filled with a sudden, terrifying explosion, the thundercrack of a sonic boom in the midst of a rare desert sleet storm.

Two little hillocks above a gurgling stream bear the stone remnants of this little place. It is well that symbols of repression are in ruin, but is is also well that they remain. Here, now, are the only trees for miles, plenty of cactus, and a stock corral.

(Take water, have a high axle!) *Twelve plus miles S of Searchlight, NV on U.S. 95, ½ mile past the CalNevAz Casino, go just past a bridge over an arroyo, take well-graded road 3⅓ miles to power line road. Go left (S) 11⅓ miles to power poles 65E2 and 65W2 and two steel posts marking entrance. The road E to ruins is a very rocky 2 miles around Paiute Mountain (a cinder cone).*

Fort Piute, Ca., ruins in the desert, near Searchlight, Nev. The Paiutes lost many men guarding this, their one copious desert spring. (*dhe*)

Camp Rock Springs • (*ca.*1860–68) San Bernardino Co.

The ruins, next in line of forts are 30 miles from Valley Springs, but I have not visited them.

Camp Marl Springs • (*ca.*1860–68) San Bernardino Co.

These ruins, 18 miles west by washed-out Government Rd., from Cp. Rock Springs, are reported to be accessible.

Fort Soda • (*ca.*1860–68) San Bernardino Co. *

The fort is not exactly a ruin. As all the posts on the Government Road were, this is the site of springs; and the Indians, seeing their own water sources being expropriated, reacted accordingly with several raids on the redoubt.

The bubbling springs are rather salty, and empty onto a great, intermittently dry lake, rimmed in places by reeds, and surrounded by low, barren mountains. Once abandoned by the Army, in 1907 the Tonopah & Tidewater Railroad passed through for water. Then, in 1917, a chemical company in search of salts raised a few more buildings. Later, in 1944, one Mr. Spenger, a very religious man, appropriated the site, built hot mineral baths, planted palms and tamarack trees, and made it a desert resort, oriented toward religion.

Finally, the Bureau of Land Management took back the original government title. Since then it has been an environmental study center for various university groups, especially for the preservation of the Mojave chubb (a fish). One or two buildings preserve the foundations of the old fort walls.

About 55 miles E of Barstow, take the Zzyzx Springs Exit from I-15, go S about 3 miles to a locked gate. Walk ½ mile to the site.

[Note: **Camp Cady,** westernmost of the string of posts, has disappeared entirely into floodwaters in recent years.]

Ft. Yuma • **806** (1850–83) Imperial Co. **

Sailing up the Colorado River from the Gulf of California, the first high ground and the first rapid water is encountered at Yuma. The Spanish attempted to put a church/army post there in 1780, but a year later it was totally destroyed by the Colorado River Indian peoples. Not until 1850 was the strategically valuable area wrested from Quechan hands—this time by the U.S. Army.

Only a year passed before the outsiders were ousted once again—as the Army puts it: ". . . provisions at the post were exhausted." However, this time Indian control lasted only for a few months.

The government's original purpose for establishing the fort at this place was the protection of pioneer and forty-niner wagon trains along the southern route into California.

Today, a good museum has been made of the Quartermaster Depot building (1864) on the Arizona side of the bluffs. On the California side, the old officers' mess is a Quechan museum, and other former administrative buildings are used by agencies serving the Indians.

Top of the hill at the Ft. Yuma Reservation, California, and on the opposite bank in Yuma, Arizona.

An architect's rendition of what Fort Tejon must have looked like. Several buildings are restored or renovated. Ft. Tejon (on Interstate 5 at the "Grapevine") was the central marshalling place for roundups of the Kawaiisu, Tataviam, and Tehachapi peoples, who were eventually crushed and have nearly disappeared. (*St. Pk.*)

* **Ft. Tejon • 129** (1854–64) Kern Co.

In 1853, one of the first California Indian reservations was established near this site, 4,000 feet high in the Tehachapi Mountains. The fort itself was placed here in a pass to "protect the Indians", who had been rounded up from a number of neighboring peoples, most of whose cultures have disappeared entirely. The reservation was deserted by its 1,000 protectees by 1864, but not before it became a stop on the Butterfield stage line, and the site of the U.S. Army's first camel detachment. [Camels were introduced as a desert beast-of-burden experiment, which rapidly failed.]

One of the fort's former officers, one Lt. E.F. Beale, bought the defunct fort *and* the Indian reservation for his huge rancho. Several of the original buildings have been well-restored, and there is a local "early-days" fiesta every June.

The "Grapevine," on I-5 at Lebec, on the Los Angeles-Kern Co. line.

Drum Barracks • 169 (1861–66) Los Angeles Co.

As Camp Drum in 1861, it was headquarters and supply depot for many anti-Indian and Civil War defense activities in southern California. A two-story house remains at 1031 Cary Ave., Wilmington.

[Note: The **Ft. McArthur** fortifications at San Pedro and Palos Verdes in Los Angeles were not constructed until World War I.]

* **Castillo (Fort) Guijarros • 69** (1795) San Diego Co.

One of the first of the early Spanish forts, this one, like Castillo San Joaquín (now Ft. Point) in San Francisco, was not a presidio. They probably saw no anti-Indian activity, both being essentially national outposts. The U.S. Army's Fort Rosecrans (**62**), established in 1852, encompasses the Guijarros site.

San Diego-Point Loma area, near Ballast Point, off Cabrillo Memorial Dr. (State Rte. 209).

Presidio of San Diego • 59 (1769) San Diego Co. (See p. 153.) *

Ft. Stockton • 54 (1838–48) San Diego Co.
The original earthworks here were thrown up in 1838 by San Diego townspeople anticipating Mexican civil war. The site is near that of the original Presidio. Its present name was given in 1846 by the U.S. Army. As it was abandoned in 1848, it was not used in the Indian wars.

Appendix D
California Museums with Indian Artifacts

For anyone pursuing an interest in the history of the California Indians of a region, I strongly recommend a visit to a local museum, and, if possible, to one of the larger All-California museums. Specific directions and museum hours may be obtained locally by telephone.

[Caution: Several local museums with small budgets are sometimes open only for a few days a week or seasonally.]

Legend code for museum holdings

- a archaeology
- b basketry, beads
- c clothing, ceremonial attire
- l literature
- m military articles
- p photographs
- s stonework (arrow points, lance or spear points, grinding mortars)
- t textiles
- \+ other items (models, dioramas, boats, etc.)

Northwestern and Northeastern California

AUBURN Placer County Museum. *Maidu* (b, c, m, s)

BLAIRSDEN Plumas Eureka State Park. *Maidu* (b, l, s)

DORRIS Herman's House of Guns. *Karok, Yurok* (b, l, m, s)

DOWNIEVILLE Sierra Museum. *Maidu* (m, s)

EUREKA Clarke Memorial Museum. *Karok, Yurok, Hupa, Pomo* (a, b, c, l, p, s, +)

______ Fort Humboldt State Historical Park. (p, m)

FALL RIVER MILLS Ft. Crook Museum. *Achumawi, Atsugewi, Modoc* (b, l, p, s, +)

FORT BRAGG Georgia-Pacific Museum. *Northern Pomo* (b, m, p)

FORT JONES Fort Jones Museum. *Karok, other Klamath River peoples* (b, c, m, p, s, t, +)

HOOPA Hupa Reservation Museum. *Hupa* and *surrounding peoples* (a, b, c, p, s, +)

QUINCY Plumas County Museum. *Maidu* (b, c, l, m, p, s)

SHASTA Shasta Courthouse Museum. *Northeast California* (b, p, s)

TULELAKE Lava Beds National Monument. *Modoc, Klamath*, (a, b, l, m, p, s)

WEAVERVILLE Trinity County Historical Society–J.J. Jackson Memorial Museum. *Shasta, Chimariko, Wintu, Lassik, Wailaki, Yuki* (b, c, l, p, s, t)

YREKA Siskiyou County Museum. *Shasta, Karok, Modoc* (b, l, p, s)

West Central California

LAKEPORT Lake County Museum. *Pomo, Wappo, Lake Miwok* (a, b, c, l, p, s, t, +)

NOVATO Marin Miwok Museum. *Miwok, other California peoples* (a, b, l, p, s, +; June Festival)

PETALUMA Petaluma Adobe State Historic Park. *Miwok, Patwin, Wappo* (a, b, c, m, p, s, t, +)

The modern Sierra Mono Museum and Mono Tribal Center, North Fork, Madera Co. (*dhe,* 1979)

RED BLUFF Kelly-Griggs House Museum. *Yana-Yahi, Wintu, Maidu* (b, c, p, s)

______ Ide Adobe State Historic Park

REDDING Redding Museum and Art Center. *California* and *other U.S.* (a, b, c, l, p, s; Indian Heritage Day in November)

______ Shasta College Museum. *Wintu, others* (a, b, l, m, p, s)

SANTA ROSA Jesse Peter Memorial Museum. *Pomo, others* (a, b, c, s, t, +)

SONOMA Sonoma State Historic Park. *Wappo, Patwin*

WILLETS Mendocino County Museum. *Pomo, Yuki* (a, b, c, l, p, s)

Central California

BAKERSFIELD Kern County Museum. *Yokuts, others* (b, c, l, m, p, s, t, +)

BERKELEY Lowie Museum of Anthropology, University of California, Berkeley Campus. *All California, North America*

CARMEL San Carlos Mission. *Ohlone Costanoan, Esselen, Chumash* (a, b, m, s)

CARPINTERIA Carpinteria Valley Museum of History. *Chumash* (b, c, l, m, s, t, +)

COLUMBIA Columbia State Historic Park. *Miwok* (a)

FREMONT Coyote Hills Regional Park. *Ohlone Costanoan* (a, b, l, p, +)

FRESNO The Discovery Center. *Yokuts, other California, Plains* and *Southwestern peoples* (a, b, s, +)

______ Fresno City and County Historical Museum. *Yokuts* (b, c, l, m, p, s, t, +)

JACKSON Amador County Museum. *Sierra Miwok* (a, b, s)

JOLON San Antonio Mission. *Salinan* (a, b, s)

LAKE ISABELLA Kern River Valley Museum. *Tubatulabal, Kawaiisu, Koso Shoshone, Paiute* (a, b, l, p, s)

LODI San Joaquin County Historical Museum. *California, others* (b, c, l)

LOMPOC La Purissima Mission State Historic Park. *Chumash, other California* (b, l, m, p, s, +)

MADERA Madera County Historical Society.

MARIPOSA Mariposa County Historical Museum. *Miwok* (b, l, s, +)

MONTEREY Monterey State Historic Park. *Costanoan* (b, c, s, +)

______ Presidio of Monterey Army Museum. *Rumsen Costanoan* (a, m, p, s)

MORRO BAY Morro Bay State Park Museum of Natural History. *Chumash* (a, l, s)

NEW ALMADEN New Almaden Museum. *Costanoan, Yokuts* (b, l, p, s, t)

NORTH FORK Sierra Mono Museum. *Monache, Paiute, Yokuts* (b, l, p, s, +; Indian Fair in August)

PINE GROVE-JACKSON Chaw-Se Indian Grinding Rocks State Park. *Miwok* (a, b, c, l, p, s, +; Big Time in September)

PLACERVILLE El Dorado County Historical Museum. *Maidu, Miwok* (b, l, p, s)

PLEASANTON Amador-Livermore Valley Historical Society. *Ohlone, Costanoan* (a, b, l, p, s)

PORTERVILLE Porterville Museum. *Yokuts* (a, b, p, s)

SACRAMENTO State Indian Museum. *All-California* (a, b, c, l, p, s, t, +; California Indian Days in September)

SAN FRANCISCO California Historical Society. *Miwok, Costanoan* (l, p)

______ Presidio of San Francisco Army Museum. *Spanish* and *U.S. Military* (c, m, p, +)

______ California Academy of Sciences. *All-Indian* (a, b, c, p, s, t, +)

SAN JOSE San Jose Historical Museum. *Costanoan* (b, s)

SAN LUIS OBISPO San Luis Obispo Mission Museum. *Chumash* (a, b, p, s)

SAN MATEO San Mateo County History Center. *Costanoan, others* (a, b, l, m, p, s, +)

SAN MIGUEL San Miguel Mission. *Salinan, Chumash* (b, s, l)

SANTA BARBARA Santa Barbara Museum of Natural History. *California in general, others* (a, b, c, l, p, s, t, +)

SANTA CLARA de Saisset Art Gallery and Museum. *Costanoan, other California* (a, b, p, s, t, +)

SANTA CRUZ Santa Cruz City Museum. *Central California* (a, b, l, s, +)

SANTA MARIA Santa Maria Valley Historical Society. *Chumash* (b, l, s)

SANTA YNEZ Santa Ynez Valley Historical Museum. *Chumash* (a, b, c, l, p, s, +)

STOCKTON Holt-Atherton Pacific Center for Western Studies. *Northwestern California, Southwestern tribes, others* (b, c, l, m, p, s, t)

______ Pioneer Museum and Haggin Galleries. *Miwok, Washo, Pomo,* others (b, c, m, l, p, s, t, +)

VENTURA San Buenaventura Mission. *Chumash* (b, l, p, +)

______ Ventura County Historical Museum. *Chumash* (a, b, c, l, m, p, s)

VISALIA Tulare County Museum. *Yokuts* (b, c, p, s)

YOSEMITE NATIONAL PARK *Miwok, Paiute, Monache, Washo, Yokuts* (a, b, c, l, m, p, s, t, +)

Eastern and Southern California

BANNING Malki Museum. *Cahuilla, Luiseño, Gabrielino, Serrano, Ipai, Taipai, Chemehuevi, Chumash, Mohave, Yuman groups* (b, l, p, s, t, +; May celebration)

DEATH VALLEY NATIONAL MONUMENT *Shoshone* (b, l, m, s)

DESERT HOT SPRINGS Cabot's Old Indian Pueblo Museum. *Cahuilla, others* (b, c, l, m, p)

FORT TEJON Fort Tejon State Historic Park.

FORT YUMA Ft. Yuma Reservation Museum. *Quechan, other Colorado River peoples*

FULLERTON Museum Association of North Orange County. *Southwestern peoples* (a, b, s)

INDEPENDENCE Eastern California Museum. *Paiute, Shoshone, Washo* (a, b, c, l, m, p, s, t, +)

LONG BEACH Rancho Los Cerritos. *Gabrielino* (b, l, m, s)

LOS ANGELES California Historical Society. *Southern California and Southwestern peoples* (l, p)

______ Natural History Museum of Los Angeles County. *All-California and Southwestern peoples* (l, p)

______ Southwest Museum. *All-California, North America*

______ University of California Museum of Cultural History. *All-California, others* (a, b, c, l, p, s, t, +)

MISSION HILLS San Fernando Valley Historical Society–Andres Pico Adobe.

NEWBERRY PARK-THOUSAND OAKS Stagecoach Inn Museum. *Chumash* (a, b, l, p, s, +)

RANDSBURG Desert Museum. *Koso Shosone, Paiute, Mohave* (b, s; arrangements to visit Koso petroglyphs)

REDLANDS San Bernardino County Museum and San Gabriel Asistencia. *All-California, others (a, b, c, l, m, p, s, t,* +)

RIDGECREST-CHINA LAKE Maturango Museum. *(Koso* and *Panamint Shosone, Yokuts* (a, b, l, p, s)

RIVERSIDE Jurupa Mountains Cultural Center. *Cahuilla* (a, b, l, s, t)

______ Riverside Municipal Museum. *Serrano, Luiseño, Cahuilla, other California* (a, b, c, l, p, s, t, +)

SAN DIEGO San Diego Historical Society. *Kumeyaay, Gabrielino* (a, b, c, l, m, p, s, t, +)

——— San Diego Museum of Man. *All-California, others* (a, b, c, l, p, s, t, +)

SAN LUIS REY San Luis Rey Mission. *Luiseño* (b, m, s)

SANTA ANA Bowers Museum. *Southern California, other Southwestern peoples* (a, b, c, l, m, p, s, t, +)

SIMI VALLEY Simi Valley Historical Society. *Chumash, rancho* (s, l)

TWENTYNINE PALMS Joshua Tree National Monument. *Serrano, Cahuilla, Chemehuevi* (a, b, l, p, s)

YUCAIPA Mousley Museum of Natural History. *Serrano, Cahuilla, Luiseño, Mohave, other California, other U.S.* (a, b, c, s, t, +)

Appendix E
A Summary of Archaeological Sites

The reader will forgive me for not including the locations of many unprotected sites, for obvious reasons. However, included here is a good cross-section of accessible sites, listed north to south.

Lava Beds National Park Siskiyou Co.
Red and yellow pictographs (rock paintings) in a lava cave. Also petroglyphs at various sites (enquire of ranger).

Fort Jones Museum Siskiyou Co.
In front, rescued from a nearby highway project, a rock with rounded cup-like pits. A shaman would fill the cups with incense-water to cause rain, cover them to prevent rain. Underneath is a figure of an Atlas-type, holding up the rock.

Hoopa Valley Reservation Humboldt Co.
Ancient village sites restored.

Chaw-Se, Indian Grinding Rocks State Historic Park Amador Co.
Petroglyphs and grinding rocks (see pp. 91, 98).

Sunset at Chaw-Se, Indian Grinding Rocks State Park, Amador Co. (*dhe*)

Coyote Hills Regional Park Alameda Co.
A cross-section of a midden and reconstructed village (see p. 103).

Presidio of Monterey Museum Monterey Co.
A rain-rock similar to that at Fort Jones. These may also have had sexual significance, and are sometimes called "baby-rocks."

Kule Loklo Point Reyes National Seashore, Marin Co.
Village of Miwok design (see p. 84).

Yosemite National Park, Sequoia-Kings Canyon National Park
Several petroglyph sites (ask a ranger, and see the Visitor Center). Also typical ancient village, Sierra Miwok.

Chumash Painted Cave Santa Barbara Co.
Fantastic pictographs (see p. 104).

Tule River Reservation Tulare Co.
Painted Cave – Huge multicolored paintings of fantastic animals, guided tour. Also grinding rocks (see p. 101).

Maturango Museum (Ridgecrest) [(619) 446-6900] and **Desert Museum** (Randsburg)
Arrangements can be made to visit the Koso Shoshone petroglyphs, within the Naval weapons testing area.

Rock Maze San Bernardino Co.
Ancient furrowed field (see p. 123).

Giant Desert Intaglios Riverside Co.
Huge figures carved in desert pavement (see p. 124).

Providence Mountains State Park Intaglios San Bernardino Co.
Giant intaglios preserved (see p. 123).

Fish Traps Riverside Co.
Ancient fishing method on ancient Lake Cahuilla (see p. 136).

Hemet Maze Stone Riverside Co.
Small amazing carving (see p. 134).

Calico Early Man Site San Bernardino Co.
One of the earliest archaeological sites in the United States (see p. 139).

Corona Painted Rock • 190 and **Carved Rock • 187**
Pictograph and petroglyph of ancient Luiseño origin. Eight mi. S of Corona.

Anza-Borrego Desert State Park
Petroglyphs at Little Pass Primitive Campground.

Joshua Tree National Monument
Several fertility pictographs. See park interpretive center.

Dancehouses or Roundhouses may be seen at these locations:

Ahwahnee Village (Yosemite Park)
Big Valley Rancheria (PRIVATE)
Chaw-se Indian Grinding Rocks State Park
Colusa Rancheria
El-ém
Grindstone Creek Rancheria
Janesville (PRIVATE)
Laytonville Rancheria
Manchester Rancheria
Point Reyes National Seashore (demonstration only)
Stewarts Point Rancheria
Tuolumne Rancheria
Wassama Roundhouse (in the town of Ahwahnee)

With the exception of Chaw-Se and Point Reyes, *none* of these may be entered without permission.

• • •

The Archaeological Resources Protection Act of 1979, Public Law 96-95, 96th Congress, says:

"No person may excavate, remove, damage, or otherwise alter or deface any archaeological resource located on public lands or Indian lands unless such activity is pursuant to a permit . . ."

Further, the act prohibits the sale, exchange, purchase, transport (or offer of the foregoing) of any such resource, and provides penalties of up to $20,000 fine and 2 years imprisonment for violation of the act.

Appendix F
A Calendar of Indian Festivals, Dances, Powwows, & Events

Open to the general public. Most functions: NO CAMERAS OR ALCOHOL. Certain events are held on fixed dates, others are held only on approximate dates, which may vary. Please call first, or contact your local American Indian Center.

NOTE 1: Powwows are primarily intertribal dances, ceremonies, or festivals of Native American peoples from other states who reside in California, and who wish to maintain their tribal traditions, though many miles from home.

NOTE 2: The reason we see few ancient traditional dances in formerly missionized areas is that the early missions suppressed them. In their place, festivals and fiestas of Roman Catholic origin are presented.

NOTE 3: The author would appreciate knowing of any changes or additions to this calendar, since it will be reproduced and distributed separately.

Southern California Powwows

Monthly scheduled events:

1st Saturday of each month
Eagle Rock Recreation Center, Los Angeles
Sponsor: Little Big Horn Club

2nd Saturday of each month
Cecil B. DeMille Jr. High School, Long Beach, Los Angeles Co.
Sponsor: Many Trails Club: (213) 372-2026 or 372-1842

3rd Saturday of each month
Eagle Rock Recreation Center, Los Angeles
Sponsor: LACCIM (Los Angeles Co. Concerned Indian Movement) (818) 575-3512

4th Saturday of each month
Stanton Community Center, Stanton (nr. Anaheim), Orange Co.
Sponsor: Orange Co. Indian Center (Garden Grove): (714) 530-0221

Numerous powwows are offered throughout the year in Southern California at many locations on an unscheduled basis. Please see *Talking Leaf* or your local Indian Center for a month-by-month calendar.

Northern California Powwows

Almost monthly, time of month varies

D-Q University, Davis, Sacramento Co.
Sponsor: D-Q U.: (916) 758-1470

Various powwows are held during the year at many locations, especially around the San Francisco Bay Area, often at universities. Call your local American Indian Center for a current listing, or write the Intertribal Friendship House, 523 E. 14th St., Oakland, CA 94606, for their newsletter.

A Calendar of California Indian

Spring

February 21st & last weekend in February
Olvera St./Lincoln Park, Los Angeles
Cuauhtémoc Day (part of Ceremonial Week of *Cuauhtémoc En Aztlán*): Mexican Indian dances, entertainment. Xipe Totec, participant: (714) 774-9803

1st weekend in March
Ft. Yuma Reservation, Winterhaven, SE Imperial Co.
Powwow and BBQ. Sponsor: Native American Indian Organization of San Pascual School. (619) 572-0213

Weekend in March nearest Equinox (21st)
San Juan Bautista Mission, Hollister, San Benito Co.
Spring Powwow: dances, food, crafts. (408) 623-2379

Southside Park, Sacramento
Spring Fiesta: Mexican tribal dances, food. Sponsor: Danza Quetzalcoatl: (916) 739-1105

La Villa Park, Pasadena
Fiesta de Primavera: Mexican tribal dances, food. Sponsor: Xipe Totec: (714) 774-9803

Pre-Easter
Pala Reservation, N San Diego Co.
Holy Week services in Mission Chapel. (619) 742-3784

Mid-April
San Diego, beneath Coronado Bridge
Chicano Park Day: inter- (mostly Mexican) tribal dances, food, entertainment.

April or May
Stewart's Point Rancheria, W Sonoma Co.
Strawberry Festival: Pomo dances, others. (707) 785-2594

1st week in May
Pala Reservation, N San Diego Co.
Cupa Days: invited dances. (619) 742-3784

Weekend near May 5th
Martin Luther King Park, Berkeley
Cinco de Mayo: Invited Mexican dances, food, entertainment. Xitlalli, participant: (415) 821-1155

Mid-May, near May 11
Putah Creek banks, Univ. of California, Davis
Mexican Indian student gathering: tribal dances, food, entertainment.

Memorial Day Weekend
Morongo Reservation, Banning, Riverside Co.
Malki Museum Fiesta and Powwow: U.S. & Mexican tribal dances, food. (714) 849-7289

Summer

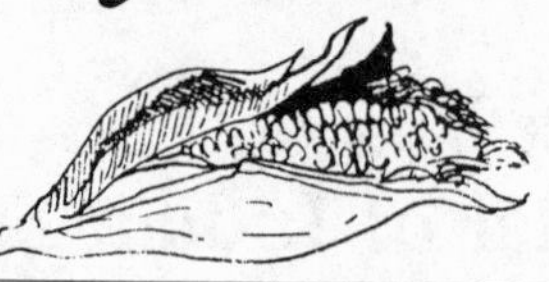

1st weekend in June
Ya-ka-ama, Healdsburg, Sonoma Co.
Spring Fair: dances, crafts, food, bingo, sports. (707) 887-1541

1st or 2nd Saturday in June
Miwok Park, Novato, Marin Co.
Indian Trade Festival. (415) 897-4064

1st Sunday in June
Pala Reservation, N San Diego Co.
Corpus Christi: religious festival. (619) 742-3784

Mid-June
Southside Park, Sacramento
Fiesta de Maiz (Corn Festival): Mexican tribal ceremonies and dances. Sponsor: Danza Quetzalcoatl: (916) 739-1105

3rd Week in June
San Diego Museum of Man, San Diego
Indian Fair Days: dancing, crafts. (619) 274-0313

3rd weekend in June
Visitors' Center, Yosemite National Park
Indian Day Big Time: Miwok dances, sweats, big dinner, handgames. Park information (209) 372-4461, or card to: J. Johnson, Yosemite N.P., CA 95389. (Admission fee to Park; Indians free; camping)

3rd weekend in June
Indian Hills Park, Tehachapi, Kern Co.,
Indian Hills Powwow: dances, food, camping (fee). (702) 642-6674

End of June
Stewart Indian Museum, Carson City, NV
Arts and Crafts Fair and Powwow: also games, dancing (702) 882-1808

San Gabriel Mission, Los Angeles
Gabrielino Powwow. (213) 283-4302

July 4th weekend
Hoopa Reservation, Humboldt Co.
Hoopa Rodeo, ceremonial dances. (916) 625-4691

1st week in July
Stewarts Point Rancheria, W Sonoma Co.
Tribal dances, July 4th BBQ. (707) 785-2594

Hopland Rancheria, Hopland, S. Mendocino Co.
Annual picnic: dances, food. (707) 744-1647

2nd Saturday in July
Kule Loklo, Point Reyes Natl. Seashore, Marin Co.
Native American Celebration (Miwok, Pomo, Wappo, others): dances, native foods, demonstrations. (415) 663-1092

1st weekend in August
Sierra Mono Museum, Northfork, Madera Co.
Indian Fair: dances, food, games, crafts, sports (209) 877-2115

Last Saturday in August
Dolores Park, San Francisco
Chicano Moratorium: sunrise and morning Indian dances, ceremonies, entertainment, food. Information: Armando Tavizon, Real Alternatives Program, 1950 Mission St., S.F.: (415) 621-1155

Festivals, Dances, Powwows, & Events

Summer

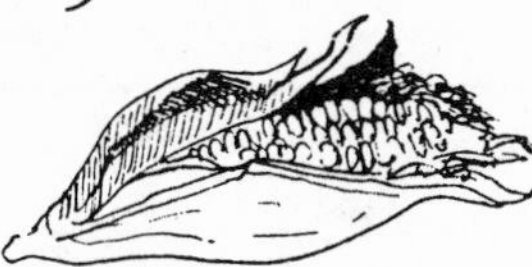

Late August or September
Hoopa Reservation, Humboldt Co.
White Deerskin and Jumping Dances. (916) 625-4211

September 3rd
San Gabriel Mission, Los Angeles
Gabrielino Festival. (213) 283-4302

Labor Day, 1st Monday in September
Bishop Reservation, N Inyo Co.
Labor Day Celebration: handgames, sports, picnic. Council office: (619) 873-3584

Saturday after Labor Day
Tuolumne Rancheria, Tuolumne, Tuolumne Co.
Acorn Festival: dances, food. (209) 928-4277

1st weekend after Labor Day
San Juan Bautista Mission, Hollister, San Benito Co.
Annual Indian Fair: crafts, juried art, exhibition dances. Reyna's Galleria: (408) 623-2379

2nd weekend in September
San Francisco
Annual American Indian Trade Fair and Exposition: dances of California, N. American, and Mexican tribes, crafts, food, handgames. Sponsor: Amer. Indian Center: (415) 552-1070

Weekend nearest September 15th
San Francisco
24th Street Fair: invited Mexican Indian dances, food, entertainment. Xitlalli, participant: (415) 821-1155

Mid-September
Ft. Mojave Reservation, Needles, E San Bernardino Co.
Powwow (not every year). (619) 326-4591

3rd Friday in September
Riverside, W Riverside Co.
Riverside Indian Days

3rd weekend in September
Sparks/Reno, NV
Sparks Indian Rodeo and Powwow: rodeo, dances, artifacts exhibit, food. (admission). (702) 356-2036 or 356-5402

3rd or 4th weekend in September
Chaw-Se Indian Grinding Rocks State Park, E of Jackson, Amador Co.
Big Time: dances, games, crafts, food. State Park: (209) 296-7488

4th weekend in September
California State Indian Museum, Sacramento
California Indian Days: dances, crafts, food. (916) 445-4209 or 324-0971

Colorado River Reservation, Parker, AZ
Combined Colorado River Tribes Fair and Indian Days: pageant, powwow, food, games, dances. (602) 669-9211

Ft. Yuma Reservation, SE Imperial Co.
Indian Days: powwow, food. (619) 572-0213

Fall and Winter

Mid-October
Hoopa Valley Extension Reservation, Humboldt Co.
Yurok dances. (916) 625-4275

Pala Reservation, N San Diego Co.
Children's Festival of St. Francis of Assisi. (619) 742-3784

October
El-em (Sulphur Bank) Rancheria, Clear Lake, Lake Co.
Big Head dance occasionally held. (707) 998-1666

Last weekend in October
Washoe Indian Community, Carson City, NV
La Ka Le'l Ba Powwow: dances, handgames, food, crafts, Indian games, tourney (admission). (702) 885-9759

November 1–2
Sacramento (location varies)
Dia de Los Muertos: vigil, prayers, Mexican ceremonial dances. Sponsor: Danza Quetzalcoatl: (916) 739-1105

Mission Neighborhood, San Francisco
Dia de Los Muertos: velación (late night). Sponsors: Xitlalli, Instituto Familiár de La Raza: (415) 586-0435

November 2nd
Campo Reservation, SE San Diego Co.
All Saints Day Festival: Mass for the Departed. (619) 478-5251

1st half of November
Palace of Fine Arts, San Francisco
American Indian Film Festival: films on Native American subjects, some crafts, food (admission). (415) 893-0326

1st week in November
Visitors' Center, Death Valley Natl. Park
49-er Days (benefit for Indian scholarship)

1st weekend in November (biennial, even years)
Redding Museum and Arts Center, Redding
Indian Heritage Days: dances honoring Wintu, Pit River peoples, food, demonstrations, oral tradition. (916) 225-4155

2nd week in November
Kernville, N Kern Co.
Kern Valley Indian Council Powwow. P.O. Box 168, Kernville, CA 93230

November 15th
Santa Ysabel Mission, central San Diego Co.
Feast Day at the Mission church

December 12th
San Diego (location varies)
Fiesta of Our Lady of Guadalupe. Sponsor: Danza Mexicayotl: (619) 428-1115

Loreto Church, Echo Park, Los Angeles
Fiesta of Our Lady of Guadalupe: ceremonies, dances, food. Xipe Totec, participant: (714) 774-9803

Mid-December
Sacramento (location varies)
Fiesta de Tonancin (Mother Earth Festival). Sponsor (with others) Danza Quetzalcoatl: (916) 739-1105

December 25th
Christmas services at all reservation churches.

Bibliography

1. Bauer, Helen, *California Rancho Days*. Doubleday and Co., Garden City, N.Y., 1953. One of those romanticized versions of early rancho days, but with a listing of extant buildings from that era.
2. California Department of Parks and Recreation, William P. Mott, Director, *California Historical Landmarks,* 1973 and later editions. Contains the wording of those bronze plaques around the state.
3. Camphouse, Majorie V., *Guidebook to the Missions of California*. Ward Ritchie Press, Pasadena, 1974.
4. Cook, Sherburne F., *The Conflict Between the California Indian and White Civilization*. University of California Press, Berkeley, 1976. The facts and figures of the California holocaust.
5. Forbes, Jack D., *Native Americans of California and Nevada*. Naturegraph Publishers, Happy Camp (CA), 1969. A sympathetic and wide-ranging history, strong on education and languages.
6. Frazer, Robert W., *Forts of the West*. University of Oklahoma Press, Normal, 1972.
7. Gillis, Mabel, *California* (American Guide Series). Hastings House, New York, 1939. An excellent WPA guidebook, out-of-print, but available at second-hand bookstores.
8. Grant, Campbell, *Rock Art of the American Indian*. Thomas Y. Crowell Co., New York, 1967.
9. Hart, Herbert, *Old Forts of the Far West*. Superior Publishing Co., Seattle, 1965.
10. Hart, Herbert, *Old Forts of the Northwest*. Bonanza Books, New York, 1963.
11. Hart, Herbert, *Old Forts of the Southwest*. Bonanza Books, New York, 1964.
12. Heizer, Robert F., and Clewlow, C. W., *Prehistoric Rock Art of California* (2 vols.). Ballena Press, Menlo Park, (CA), 1973.
13. Heizer, Robert F., and Whipple, M. A., *The California Indians, A Source Book*. University of California Press, Berkeley, 1971. A compilation of writings about the original California Indians.
14. Kroeber, Alfred L., "Handbook of the Indians of California," *Bureau of American Ethnology Bulletin* (78).
15. Kroeber, Theodora, *Ishi in Two Worlds*. University of California Press, Berkeley, 1971.
16. Margolin, Malcolm, *The Ohlone Way*. Heyday Books, Berkeley, 1978. Descriptions of the way of living of many coastal and riverine California cultures; these, however, are the Ohlone or Costanoans of the San Francisco Bay.
17. Margolin, Malcolm, *The Way We Lived*. Heyday Books, Berkeley, 1982. Required reading for anyone wanting to know the spirit of the California Indian people.

18. Sturtevant, William C., *Handbook of North American Indians,* (Vol. 8 [California] Robert F. Heizer, Editor; Vol. 10 [Southwest] Alfonso Ortiz, Editor). Smithsonian Institution, Washington, D.C.

Other Reading

Several other publishers have a special interest in specific tribes or aspects of California Indians. Their listings are too numerous to mention here; however, the reader may write for their catalogs:

Ballena Press, 833 Valparaiso, Menlo Park, CA 94025
Capra Press, Box 2068, Santa Barbara, CA 93120
Heyday Books, Box 9145, Berkeley, CA 94709
Malki Museum Press, Morongo Reservation, Banning, CA 92220
Naturegraph Publishers, 3543 Indian Creek Rd., Happy Camp, CA 96039
Stanford University Press, Stanford, CA 94305
University of California, Berkeley, Press, 2120 Berkeley Way, Berkeley, CA 94720
University of California, Los Angeles, American Indian Studies Center, 3220 Campbell Hall, Los Angeles, CA 90024
Westernlore Press, 11860 Pami Pl., Tucson, AZ 85704

Alphabetical Listing of Reservations and Rancherias

Military Posts (before 1900)

Missions and Asisténcias (by current designations)

Index